Hair

Susan J. Vincent

Hair

An Illustrated History

BLOOMSBURY VISUAL ARTS
LONDON · NEW YORK · OXFORD · NEW DELHI · SYDNEY

BLOOMSBURY VISUAL ARTS
Bloomsbury Publishing Plc
50 Bedford Square, London, WC1B 3DP, UK
1385 Broadway, New York, NY 10018, USA

**BLOOMSBURY, BLOOMSBURY VISUAL ARTS and the
Diana logo are trademarks of Bloomsbury Publishing Plc**

First published in China 2018

For legal purposes the Acknowledgements on p. 7 constitute an
extension of this copyright page.

Cover design: Adriana Brioso
Cover image © Cover image: *Pot Pourri*, 1897 (oil on canvas) by
Herbert James Draper (1864-1920), Private Collection. (© Paul
Fearn / Alamy Stock Photo)

A catalogue record for this book is available from the British Library.

ISBN: HB: 978-0-8578-5170-3
           PB: 978-0-8578-5171-0
           ePDF: 978-0-8578-5172-7
           eBook: 978-0-8578-5173-4

Typeset by Lachina
Printed and bound in China

To find out more about our authors and books visit
www.bloomsbury.com and sign up for our newsletters

Dedication
For Jill
A wonderful friend with
wonderful hair

Table of Contents

Acknowledgements

This book has had a long gestation. Portions of the work on early modern barbering and shaving from Chapters 2 and 3 have appeared in a different context in 'Men's Hair: Managing Appearances in the Long Eighteenth Century', in Hannah Grieg, Jane Hamlett and Leonie Hannan (eds), *Gender and Material Culture in Britain Since 1600* (London: Palgrave, 2016), 49–67. Likewise, a condensed version of early modern haircare from Chapter 1 and the discussion of early modern beards from Chapter 4 can be found in 'Beards and Curls: Hair at the Court of Charles I', in Abigail Newman and Lieneke Nijkamp (eds), *(Un)dressing Rubens: Fashion and Painting in Seventeenth-Century Antwerp* (New York: Harvey Miller, forthcoming). My thanks to Palgrave Macmillan and Harvey Miller respectively, for permission to reproduce this material.

The editorial staff at Bloomsbury Academic have been unfailingly supportive and astonishingly patient over this long process too, as other projects and all the crises and demands of ordinary life continued to delay the manuscript. My especial thanks go to Anna in the earlier stages, and Frances and Pari later on, who between them seemed never to lose faith and chivvied and inched it towards completion.

Huge thanks are due to my family, for both their endurance throughout this project and for providing me with wonderful snippets of hairy interest. My mother Barbara has an especial skill in finding thought-provoking examples and sending them my way. In answer to my emailed cries for help, my economist brother-in-law Andy has been a true champion, retrieving and explaining statistics to shed a light on even the most perplexing of questions. My particular gratitude goes, as always, to my husband Alan. His encouragement has been constant, his editing eagle-eyed, his interest apparently unfeigned, and the discussions of enormous help. I have also used him as a walking lexicon, and he has patiently borne with my peremptory demands for translations of obscure foreign-language sources. With love and thanks.

It also seems only fitting to acknowledge Stephen, my genius hairdresser – thought-provoking conversation and brilliant haircuts. What more could any client throughout the ages have wished for?

Introduction: Hair matters

Hair matters to us. As Sarah Cheang and Geraldine Biddle-Perry have written, 'All human bodies are created hairy.'[1] This biological bottom line, this hairy status, has been factored into every culture that has ever been. All the world's religions have tenets and teachings that concern it. Over the course of human history, rituals, rites of passage and transitions have been accompanied by its modification. It has been part of conceptualizations of physical acts and emotional states. It has accompanied us in our approaches to the divine. Anthropologically speaking, hair is some of the basic stuff with which we 'do' being human (Fig. 0.1).

Beneath these global and chronologically transcendent processes lie all the individual men and women whose collective activities and beliefs we designate as history. While there may be some who have been indifferent to the appearance and state of their hair, they would certainly be in the minority. Rather, most of us feel vividly the connection between our hair and our sense of self. Millions, when their hair begins to turn grey, for instance, dye it to a tint that they feel is truer to the more 'authentic' person within: the actual colour of their aging hair does not, in some way, correspond with their sense of who they are.[2] Likewise, an unplanned

FIGURE 0.1.
Hair: a part of being human.

FIGURE 0.2.
French president
François Hollande
meeting with
apprentice hairdressers
in 2015. Hollande is
sporting his €10,000
per month hairstyle.

loss of hair can force an abrupt crisis of identity, as the person whose reflection asserts one truth struggles to integrate this with an abiding self-image that is different. Chemotherapy is a clear case in point, with many undergoing treatment reporting that the shedding of their hair is harder to come to terms with than the fact of their illness. Even the universally understood phrase 'bad hair day' shows that all of us know what it feels like when our hair intractably refuses to align itself with how we feel it 'ought' to look.

Those who are wealthy enough and in the public eye can spend extraordinary amounts ensuring there is a congruity between how they want their hair to be and what it is in reality. Every Saturday, Marilyn Monroe would fly her colourist from San Diego to Los Angeles just to spend the day retouching her platinum blonde beauty.[3] And it's not just celebrities who make their living by their looks who devote time and cost to the enterprise of their hair. In a piece of reportage nicknamed 'Coiffuregate', it was revealed in 2016 that the then French president, François Hollande, paid his hairdresser nearly €10,000 a month. Especially given the close-cut simplicity of the president's well-receded hair, this is a very large sum (Fig. 0.2). A government spokesman, however, explained the reasonableness of the monthly bill, which also paid for the stylist's services on foreign trips: 'Everyone gets haircuts. This hairdresser had to abandon his salon and he's on tap 24 hours a day.'[4] There are no doubt few who would think this expense justified and even fewer who could afford it. However in a way the government spokesman was right: everyone *does* get haircuts, and like Hollande, everyone wants the actuality and the idea of their hair to match.

Perhaps because of this connection between our hair and our sense of self, we tend to view other people in the same light, forging a link between their hair and their personality. This is, of course, a well-worn trope in fiction, reaching its writerly extreme in nineteenth-century novels whose female characters in particular are explained through the appearance of their hair.[5] Jane Eyre's brown tresses are neat and unassuming, their wayward potential smoothed and disciplined; Blanche Ingram's are a showy raven-black, glossily curled and becoming; and the insane, bestial Bertha Rochester gibbers in her attic under 'a quantity of dark, grizzled hair, wild as a mane'.[6] The hair of these women is metonymic, with this small part of their person standing for the whole. In the film and visual media of today this technique is likewise fully exploited to communicate character and to forward the narrative.[7] And what goes for fiction goes also for real life, as, along with other visual cues, we use the information supplied by hair to inform our judgements about people we know and people we observe, whether or not these judgements turn out to be accurate.

Colour and character

The link between an individual's appearance and their personality is particularly freighted when it comes to hair colour. Associations between that and character are both long lived and remarkably consistent over time. Indeed, as we shall see, it might even be argued that these stereotypes are becoming *more* potent. As our knowledge of physiology and genetics has become increasingly accurate and our methods of dying hair more sophisticated, it seems that in some ways our rational grasp has become less secure and our prejudices more pronounced.

In previous centuries there was good reason for such stereotypes, for they were entirely consistent with contemporary medical theory and understandings of the physical world. According to early modern humoral theory inherited from classical thought, all matter – including the human body – was composed of four humours. A mixture of blood, phlegm, yellow bile (choler), and black bile (melancholy) gave rise to a person's inner state, or temperament, and these temperaments in turn influenced both appearance and personality.[8] For the physician, how a patient looked and behaved was therefore a diagnostic tool that could help him to see within, ascertain a patient's inner humoral state and provide appropriate treatments. In addition, the related science of physiognomy, also drawn from Greek and Roman thought, further reinforced the inalienable connection between the body and the mind by positing a correspondence between specific bodily features and specific psychological traits.[9] Once given the interpretive key, which included hair colour and texture, any observer could thus 'read' appearance to unlock the moral truth within (Fig. 0.3).[10] Given this overarching belief system, it was logical to conclude that character and hair colour were congruent and that a stereotype was an insightful truth.

These beliefs appear in countless texts from the sixteenth and seventeenth centuries, and span the genres from scientific treatises and self-help medicine to the cheap ballads

FIGURE 0.3.
An English manual of palmistry, 1648. It includes information on physiognomy and the four humours, and instruction on how to read faces, hair colour, and the size and colour of beards.

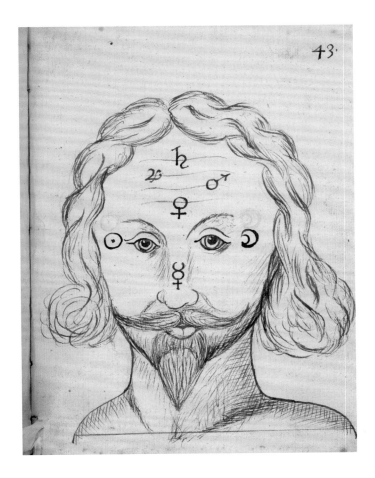

pinned in alehouses for singing and laughter. *The Shepherd's Calendar*, for example, was an influential and much read all-purpose compendium of knowledge, translated from French and reprinted throughout the sixteenth and seventeenth centuries.[11] In the 1570 edition, readers were told:

> They that haue red haire, byn [be] commonly yreful [ireful] and lacke wyt, and ben [be] of litle truth. Blacke haire, good visage, and good coloure sygnifyeth very loue of Iustyce [justice], Hard haire signifieth that the person loueth peace and concord, and is of good and subtill wit. A man that hath blacke haire and a red berde signifieth to be lecherous, disloyall a vaunter [i.e. boastful], and one ought not to trust in him. The yelowe haire and crispe [curled] signifieth man laughing, mery, lecherous, & deceitfull. Blacke hair and crispe signifieth melancoly, lechery, euil thought.[12]

For a more light-hearted take on the subject, *The English Fortune-Teller*, a ballad from the 1670s, offered advice on how to choose a wife:

> My skill in Physiognomy,
>   wherein I will shew you a light:
> By'th colour of hair on the head,
>   or else by the favor or face,
> You may know with whom for to wed;
>   and who you were best to imbrace.[13]

The song goes on to jest that the golden-haired will cuckold a husband, red-heads are dangerous, and brunettes witty but dissembling. This was not just a misogynist trope but a shared cultural joke, for there were also ballads narrating from the other side of the gender divide. Thus a more or less contemporary ballad *To Her Brown Beard* advised women as to the best husbands: whereas the sandy-haired are jealous, and the yellow and red apt to spend too freely in the alehouse, brown-haired men are true, kind and loving.[14]

In some form or other, this belief system lasted well into the eighteenth century and even beyond, with some books on medicine continuing to explain both humoral theory and its relation to hair colour.[15] Most particularly in the realm of popular knowledge, that demotic area where education meets entertainment, the 'truths' of appearance continued undiminished. In 1796 a ladies' almanac informed its readership of the meanings of hair, showing that its colour and texture were signs that pointed directly to moral qualities. The guidelines it laid out for decoding character thus included the rules that black smooth hair in both men and women denotes mildness, constancy and affection, whereas black curly hair indicates inebriety, a quarrelsome temper and a nature inclined to amorousness. In men, long red hair 'denotes cunning, artifice, and deceit', and in women, a glib tongue, vain nature and 'an impatient and fiery temper'.[16] While the material may have been included in much the same way that horoscopes are a standard part of periodicals today – to be read but not necessarily believed – the very fact of its inclusion points to some degree of continuing sympathy for the stereotypes of appearance.

As a consequence of pioneer geneticist Gregor Mendel's work, the nineteenth century saw the growing acceptance of heritability as the mechanism by which physical characteristics were produced and transmitted, and Darwin's model of natural selection tied this heritability to long-term success or failure in meeting challenges posed by the environment. However, the science of the period also explored other avenues that, instead of severing the old connections between appearance and essence, reinforced them. The study of phrenology was one such. Asserting both that the size and shape of different areas of the brain determined our intellectual and moral capacities, and that the skull was shaped over the organ it housed, phrenology

FIGURE 0.4.
(Facing page) Circulation leaflet for Professor Thomas Moore, Leeds phrenologist, c.1870. Professor Moore promises that his analysis of head shape will reveal a subject's inner character, and the diagram illustrates the different capacities he can bring to light by exploring the skull's bumps. These include combativeness, conjugal love, propensity to seek food (alimentiveness), and hope.

claimed that an accurate reading of the head's bumps and protuberances rendered personality an open book (Fig. 0.4). In tandem with this, physiognomy too was given new impetus in the nineteenth century.[17] Although practised on a rarefied level by specialists, these ideas were also part of a 'commonsense' hermeneutics on the ground by which ordinary people interpreted

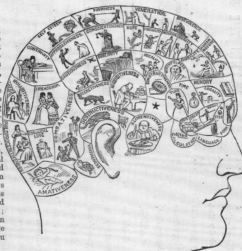

PROF. THOMAS MOORES,
PRACTICAL PHRENOLOGIST,
OF LEEDS,

Begs to inform the Lady and Gentleman of this residence that he is spending a short time in this town and neighbourhood before going to his summer quarters (Douglas, Isle of Man). Having completed his lecture tour for the season, he now proposes to spend a short time in visiting families, &c., to give Phrenological Examinations, Advice on the choice of Trades, Professions, Education, &c. Mr. Moores, in his Descriptions, points out what your physical and mental qualities are, and how you may best apply them to ensure success. He shows the excesses and deficiencies which characterise you, and how you may overcome them; putting within your possession a sure guide to self-knowledge and self-improvement. If you are a parent or guardian to children whom you are anxious to train aright, and put to the calling which will best agree with their health, and in which they have capacities to succeed, then try Phrenology, it has done it for thousands, and it can do it for them. Are you about to adopt some child in your family, and want to know what kind of a disposition it possesses? and whether it is likely to fulfil the desires which lead you to take it? Mr. Moores can tell you, and guard you against making a wrong choice. Have you servants whose characters are a puzzle to you? or, are you just going to engage one, and want an impartial character of them? Mr. M. will describe their characters with unerring accuracy.

MR. MOORES' experience as a Practical Phrenologist is a very wide one. His practice in Public and Private have been well tested, and his abilities well acknowledged both by the Press and the Public. The following may be given from hundreds who have borne equal testimony:—

"The Phrenological Examination I have undergone by MR. T. MOORES is very correct, it gives me every confidence in his abilities as an examiner."

-H. BONE, Wesleyan Minister.

"MR. MOORES closes his Lectures with Public Examinations of persons chosen from the audience. They are *very* good, and give great satisfaction."—*Bacup Times.*

THE FOLLOWING IS FROM A WELL-KNOWN SOLICITOR.

"MR. MOORES has examined three of my family, and the startling descriptions convince me of his thorough knowledge of Phrenology."

and categorized their social world. Together, phrenology and physiognomy coloured ideas of race, criminality, deviance and superiority. The application to hair is obvious: the appearance of a person's hair was an index to his or her character, an idea that surfaces repeatedly in the literature of the Victorian era.

Despite its persistence over the centuries, however, the science of appearances was inexact. The tints and shades of hair were numerous and might be expected to infinitely parse the broad significations of meaning allotted to them. In addition, no doubt for every person who seemed to fulfil the rule, there were as many who acted as exceptions. One thing that is remarkably consistent, though, is a voiced attitude to red hair. Although shades could come in and out of fashionable sight – on the surface as it were of the ongoing cultural discourse – there is an underlying thread in every age that articulates a position with regards to this particular colour. As may have become apparent from some of the quotes above, commentary on red hair is almost universally opprobrious and is found across the centuries and across the genres. For instance, a midwifery manual from 1612 advising as to how to choose a wetnurse, warned that 'especially she should not haue red haire'. There is even a reiterative marginal note to drive the point home: 'A red hair'd Nurse discommended.'[18] In 1680 a London physician, advertising the diseases that he could cure, included amongst the list of complaints (agues to worms, pains to piles) the information that he could change the colour of red hair, thus tacitly claiming it was a disfigurement at best, at worst an illness.[19] Perhaps he prescribed hair dye – as we shall see in the next chapter, there were many recipes and products available – or maybe the use of a lead comb to darken it. Perhaps clients came to him to avoid teasing, for even name-calling has an ancient pedigree when it comes to this shade. As early as 1662 there is mention as a well-known fact of the 'Jeer, as in England among the Vulgar, to call a Red hair'd Person Carrots'. That the author, the compiler of an Italian–English grammar and dictionary, is using this piece of knowledge to explain another saying, indicates that it was indeed familiar and already well established by the Restoration.[20] Given that the orange-coloured carrot was only introduced to England earlier that century (having been developed as a strain by the Dutch), the uptake of both the carrot variety and the nickname must have been very rapid. Hawked on street corners and sung in alehouses around thirty years later, the rollicking 1690 *Ballad of an Amorous Coachman* declares:

> To Jenney they wisht me, indeed she was fair
> But a pox on her Carrots, I lik'd not red hair,
> Her skin I did lov, but her hair I did hate,
> I ne'r in my Life coud love Carrot-pate.[21]

The opprobrium continued through the succeeding centuries (Fig. 0.5) and is of course commonplace even today. Most redheads report teasing and many bullying, which for some

FIGURE 0.5.
An eighteenth-century advertisement for Princes Dye, suitable for both men and women. It is said to be especially efficacious against the disfigurement of grey or carroty hair.

GREY or CARROTY WHISKERS are a great disfigurement to Gentlemen. Ladies or Gentlemen making trial will be convinced of the utility of PRINCE's DYE, being so improved that no doubt now remains of making Grey or Carroty Hair dark or black immediately. Oberve, there has been many attempts to prepare articles for a similar purpose, but found to be only impositions. Any Gentleman having Carroty or Grey Whiskers, calling on Mr. P. will be convinced of the efficacy of the Russian Dye in a few minutes.

does lasting psychological damage and leaves them with a profound sense of difference and discrimination.[22] And we all know about this teasing, for ginger jibes are heard everywhere: in 2011 even Labour's then deputy leader and, ironically, former equalities minister Harriet Harman, called a fellow MP a 'ginger rodent' – something for which, after an outcry, she subsequently apologized.[23] As to the bullying, in some cases in the UK it has escalated to unprovoked and violent hate crime, directed at individuals and entire families, apparently for the sole reason of their red hair.[24] In response to such prejudice there is now a growing move towards affirmative action, with redheads worldwide joining together in Ginger Pride marches and events (Fig. 0.6). The first in Britain was held in 2013 during the Edinburgh Festival, but they are spreading, with events currently planned around the globe.[25]

FIGURE 0.6.
Participants at the 2013 Ginger Pride Walk in Edinburgh.

FIGURE 0.7.
Peroxide blonde Jean
Harlow, 1933.

In the twenty-first century we have no excuse for judging a person's value and acceptability by their external appearance. In earlier periods structures of knowledge were based on a perceived relationship between the physical and the moral world, but we have a different story. Rather than proceeding from 'gross humours', 'ill blood' and a choleric nature, we know that red hair is passed on by certain recessive genes. There are very few redheads in the world – global estimates put it at just one per cent – although the proportion is much higher in some countries, like those in the British Isles.[26] Being recessive, there are also many more of us who carry redheaded DNA, but it has been masked by the genetic coding of more dominant hair colours. And in the rarity of red hair lies the reason for continuing modern prejudice and stereotyping: it is the story of the exclusion and difference of a minority.

A related but different course has been tracked particularly over the last century by attitudes to blonde hair. Like red, the genes for blonde hair are recessive, and globally speaking pale shades are uncommon, with estimates of just two per cent: in terms of hair colour, the world is overwhelmingly dark.[27] In certain areas though, like northern Europe and North America, the proportion is much higher and has exercised a marked cultural fascination. Its most poisonous manifestation has been the Aryan myth, where under the Nazis a belief in the superiority of blonde hair particularly in tandem with blue eyes, was linked to forced breeding programmes on the one hand, and on the other to genocide.[28] But there are other forms of cultural imperialism that have spread the belief in blonde superiority by stealth. Starting in the

FIGURE 0.8.
The young Margarita
Cansino's career
began performing
Spanish numbers in
a dancing duo with
her father. Here she is
aged around twelve, in
a photo that appeared
in *The American
Magazine* in 1942.

1930s, the Hollywood machine has produced blonde screen goddesses galore and a string of film titles that have elevated hair colour to a state of being. Kicking off with *Platinum Blonde* in 1931, starring Jean Harlow (Fig. 0.7), and finishing with *Gentlemen Prefer Blondes* in 1953, starring Marilyn Monroe, there were seventeen movies featuring 'blonde' in the title – nearly one a year.[29] As for the women whose blonde locks became so iconic, hair dye achieved what nature could not. The most striking instance of this cultural agenda is not the makeover of Monroe's light brown to bleach blonde, but the transformation of the Spanish American Margarita Cansino to blonde bombshell Rita Hayworth, with a name change, hair dye, and electrolysis to raise her hairline (Figs 0.8 and 0.9).

This particular version of beauty has had a global impact, via media, advertising and personal-care products.[30] It also created Barbie (Fig. 0.10), the doll that socialized generations of girls into aspiring to her looks, an aspiration that seems to have stayed with them as they grew. Today, for middle-aged women blonde is now the new black, with millions believing that tints and highlights from the yellow range are more flattering and younger-looking than the colour produced by nature as their own hair's pigment recedes. According to some estimates, in the west nearly one in three white women have their hair dyed a shade of blonde.[31]

Clearly, the potency of blonde and red in different ways shows the extent to which we still link the appearance of hair with a range of personal characteristics and stereotypes.[32] Despite our knowledge that it is through the mutual interaction of genetics and environment that our unique selves are produced, en masse we persist in treating hair as a direct sign pointing to personality. Obviously we do this with other aspects of appearance too: with body shape, size and complexion, and of course with dress. These are the visual cues by which we read those around us and by which we also read ourselves. However, hair holds a special place amongst these signifiers, being neither quite one nor the other. It is biological, but it is worn. It is certainly part of our dressed appearance yet it is also a body part, though malleable in a

FIGURE 0.9.
(Above) The apotheosis of Margarita Cansino: blonde bombshell Rita Hayworth, pictured here with Orson Welles in *The Lady From Shanghai*, 1947.

FIGURE 0.10.
(Facing page) Barbie, in a hair outfit by fashion designer Jean-Charles de Castelbajac created for a 2009 exhibition celebrating the doll's fiftieth birthday. Castelbajac's wearable hair has encapsulated a key part of Barbie's appearance and message

way that the rest of our body is not. It can even be cut off to assume a life independent of us. It is to this separate existence that we now turn.

Subject/object

While intimately connected with our individual identities and a part of our collective, human experience, hair is not confined by this ontological role. For all its importance to subjectivity, it has a curious tendency to become objectified. Hair is part of us, unique to our individual selves; it shares its precise genetic information with nothing and no one else in this world. Yet it is also a thing that can be cut off, can exist separately and with far greater longevity, and can take on vastly different meanings. The way this of-the-person-but-not-the-person state leads to hair functioning as a sentimental keepsake needs no explanation. We are all familiar with the idea of it as a personal token, and a lock from a baby's first cut is a common memento. A quick trawl through the internet reveals advice for different and decorative ways of keeping this, as well as a market for jewellery like lockets and pendants in which hair can be enclosed.

This practice has a long tradition. In 1617, for instance, Lady Anne Clifford noted in her diary that she had sent her sister-in-law 'a lock of the Child's hair', that child being Anne's daughter Margaret, then a toddler.[33] Some seventeenth-century portraits show sitters wearing hair bracelets or necklaces woven from treasured strands, and personalized mourning jewellery also became popular in the second half of the century. Such items incorporated some of the deceased's hair, usually set under crystal or glass for permanence and beauty, with the addition of gems and precious settings.[34] It was probably a token like this – 'a Hair-Ring, with a Cipher in the middle, and a Diamond on each side' – that was advertised in September 1701 as having been lost and for which the owner offered a guinea reward.[35] There is also plenty of written evidence on the use of hair to materialize relationships, with texts of all sorts revealing people requesting and conferring locks of hair, to be kept either as love tokens in life or for remembrance in death. The most famous instance of hair taken as a token has to be Alexander Pope's mock heroic poem, 'The Rape of the Lock', written originally in 1712.[36] The poem is a comically inflated account of what happens when a curl of hair is snipped without permission from the heroine Belle as she is bending her head over her coffee cup at afternoon tea. The perpetrator, in love with her and unable to stop himself, plans to have the hair made into a ring, which for Belle adds insult to injury (Canto IV, lines 113–16):

> And shall this prize, the inestimable prize,
> Exposed through crystal to the gazing eyes,
> And heightened by the diamond's circling rays,
> On that rapacious hand for ever blaze?

The poem is based on an actual event, when Arabella Fermor, the real-life protagonist, broke off her engagement to Lord Robert Petre when he cut off a lock of her hair. A mutual friend, concerned at the estrangement between the two families, urged Pope to write the poem to bring about some kind of reconciliation. 'The Rape of the Lock' was Pope's attempt to, in his words, 'make a jest of it, and laugh them together again'. While the poem became a literary classic it failed to persuade Arabella, and the marriage did not take place.

For an example of hair being used in post-mortem remembrance, we are lucky enough to have a letter written by Sir Kenelm Digby (1603–55) in 1633, just two and a half weeks after the death of his wife, Venetia. It is addressed to their young children, and its homely detail reveals the emotional significance of some locks of Venetia's that he has kept, showing how they acted as a prompt to memory and functioned to keep her present even in her absence. Incidentally, the letter is also illuminating in other ways, shining a light on early modern beliefs about the correspondence between hair type, character and constitution, and on the intense physical stress suffered by Venetia during labour that caused her hair to shed (today still recognized as a cause of temporary alopecia). It also reveals four-hundred-year-old routines of styling hair with curling irons, and the annoyance of this long-dead woman when her full, fine and soft hair refused to take the curl she had painstakingly put in. This section of Sir Kenelm Digby's letter is so remarkable that it is worth quoting in full:

> Her hair was tending to browne, yet shining with a strange naturall luster and brightnesse; It was by many degrees softer then the softest that euer I saw, which hath often brought into my consideration that the rules of Physiognomy many times fall out to be true; for they direct to iudge [judge] of the mildenesse and gentlenesse of ones disposition by the softnesse and finenesse of their haire. Nothing can be imagined subtiler than hers was; I haue often had a handful of it in my hand and haue scarce perceiued I touched any thing: she had much and thicke vpon her head; and it was very longe before she shedde most of it lying in of one of you, but it was so soft & fine that when it was made vp it seemed to possesse no roome. This which euery bodie else admired it for, hath oftentimes made her much displeased with it, for it was so gentle and soft that it would not continue curled one quarter of an houre; the very moisture of the ayre would vndoe it, it being incident onely to harsh and strong haire to keep long the impressions of a hott iron. This is the onely beauty remayning of her that death had no power ouer; before she was embalmed and putt into her cere clothes [i.e. grave clothes, winding-sheet], I made it be cutt off, and shall keepe it whiles I liue as a holy relike of her, and as a part of her beauty that I am confident no woman in the world can parallele.[37]

It was the nineteenth century, though, that saw both the cult of hair and its transformation into wearable tokens and decorative work reach its zenith.[38] Hair became the common currency of sentimental exchange, reaching not just to lovers and close family but also to friends and esteemed connections. The most outré example of this widespread practice must be Lady Caroline Lamb's bestowal on Byron, at the end of their public and torrid adultery, of cuttings from her pubic hair.[39] Sometimes gifts of hair were stored away carefully, like the 'long lock of black hair' belonging to his fiancée that Frederick Hale keeps in his pocket book, in Elizabeth Gaskell's novel of 1855, *North and South*.[40] However, both men and women also had them crafted into jewellery and trinkets to wear (Fig. 0.11). This is vividly captured in the description from 1888 of the Hon. Harriet Phipps, one of Queen Victoria's ladies-in-waiting, who was bedecked in these reminders and remains of her family: 'She wore dozens of bangles which rattled as she walked. . . . Attached to these were many minute lockets containing the hair of her relatives past and present.'[41] Even adored pets might be remembered this way. The British Museum, for instance, has in its collection a gold brooch adorned with a tiny crystal portrait of a white Pomeranian dog (Fig. 0.12). An inner compartment holds a curl of white hair and on the back the inscription reads 'FAITHFUL AND TRUE', with Muff's name, and date, place and age of death.[42]

Perusal of the British Library archives in this light creates an extraordinary sense of the holdings being a repository, not just of textual remains, but also of human. Folded into envelopes, pinned to papers, and contained within pocket books, numerous hanks, locks and strands of human hair have found a final resting place in its vaults and basements. Much of it was cut from the heads of people named but now unknown, whose family papers one way

FIGURE 0.11.
Victorian hair jewellery and mourning adornment containing locks from the deceased. The largest brooch also uses hair to depict a sentimental scene, showing a tomb, lake and weeping willow.

or another came into the library's possession. But there are also a large number of items that memorialize the famous: a lock of Beethoven's, cut at his death in 1827 and sewn to paper; some hair from Charlotte Brontë, taken after she died in 1855; Dickens's hair, along with a note written by his sister-in-law certifying its authenticity. Nelson's in a wooden box, Goethe's in an envelope, and a whole collection of locks harvested from the Hanoverian royals (Fig. 0.13). There is even some hair of Simón Bolívar's, the revolutionary leader who helped forge a South America independent of Spanish rule.[43]

These extraordinary remains stored in the British Library remind us that it is not only loved ones who can be memorialized in this way. Hair can also become a relic of the famous. Most common in the medieval period's cult of saints, whose inventory of sacred body parts and fluids naturally included this most conveniently detachable of bits, the veneration of hair can also be actuated by the original bearer's secular fame. This variation on objectification is not only still with us, but probably growing in potency, as with money we pay homage to our modern, secular icons: celebrities. Thus, five months after his death in 2016, a lock of David Bowie's hair was sold at auction for $18,750. He is far from alone in having his hair become a commodified collectable, as locks from Che Guevara to Justin Bieber, John Kennedy to John Lennon are bought and sold, often through the internet (Fig. 0.14). While huge prices can be

FIGURE 0.13.
A lock of hair from the collection of the Science Museum, London, purporting to come from George III. It was bought at auction in 1927, folded in the paper documenting its origins.

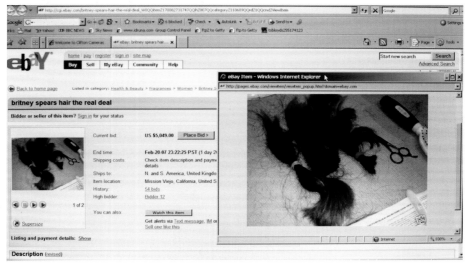

FIGURE 0.14.
Ebay auction of Britney Spears's hair, 2007.

paid for a tiny snip or a few threads, so far the overall record sum stands at $115,000 for some strands from the head of Elvis Presley.[44]

In all of these uses of hair, its objectification is securely based in its relationship to subjectivity. It is not just any old hair that was set under crystal or sold for a large sum, but locks belonging to a *particular* person. Hence the importance of provenance and those authenticating notes in the British Library archives that assert the truth of the hair's identity. But there are many other ways in which hair has been adapted into art or craft forms that do not depend for meaning on the source of the harvest, and that sever the very relationship with subjectivity that the crafting of individual locks seeks to preserve. In the nineteenth century, hair was used as a substance in its own right to create artefacts of wonder (Fig. 0.15). In the

FIGURE 0.15.
A cap woven entirely from human hair, c.1850.

Great Exhibition of 1851 there were two locations given over to the display of such items of crafted human hair, and the thousands of visitors were amazed by the 'earrings, bracelets, brooches, rings, purses, hair worked in any possible way – in all kinds of coils and curves, in imitation of feathers and flowers, in scrolls or bouquets . . . and a basket, about eighteen inches square filled with flowers and fruit'.[45] Hair-work appeared at International Exhibitions thereafter: the 1855 Exposition of Paris even featured a portrait of Queen Victoria, full length and full size, made solely of hair.[46]

However, the form that hair-as-object most often took was as a supplement to another's body. Hiding in plain sight, harvested hair was re-crafted into wigs, additions, hair pieces and postiches, items hugely important in the fashions and bodily practices of the eighteenth and nineteenth centuries (Fig. 0.16). This transformation was not without irony. The original hair was processed and manufactured, divested of its personal nature to become an anonymous commodity ready for sale. Once bought and worn by its new owner, however, it was invested with a new identity; mimicking the wearer's 'real' hair it became implicated in a new subjectivity (Fig. 0.17).

But all this hair-work begs some questions: where did the raw material come from and how was it supplied? In Britain, the hair trade rose to prominence in the eighteenth century, with wig-wearing expanding the market massively, creating the opportunities for enterprising individuals to carve out a living by sourcing and supplying the natural product. Those involved in the trade spread across the social and financial spectrum, ranging from lowly hair buyers at the bottom, who wandered the country purchasing hair where

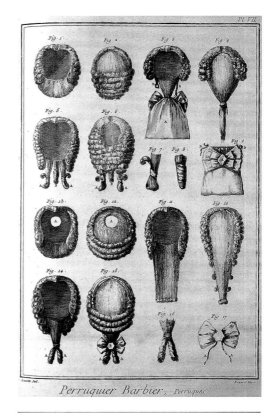

Perruquier Barbier, Perruques

Paris. Tresseuse de cheveux.

FIGURE 0.16.
(Top) A page from Diderot's *Encyclopédie* illustrating different kinds of wigs, 1762.

FIGURE 0.17.
(Bottom) An early nineteenth-century engraving showing a woman holding a simple hair piece, ringlets attached to a ribbon.

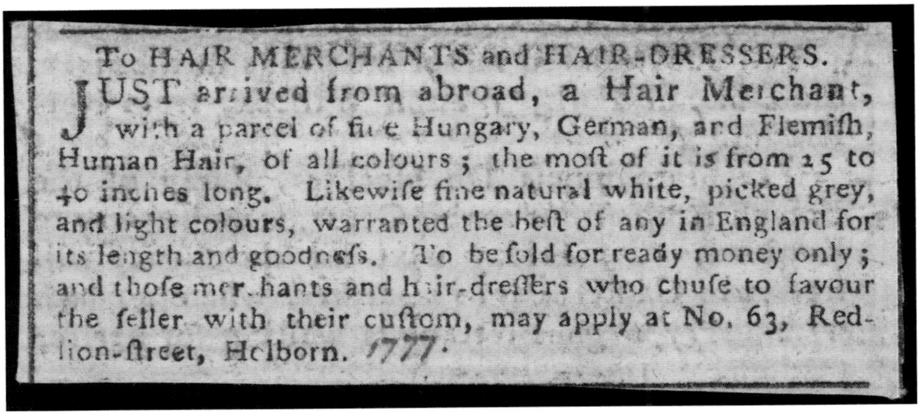

FIGURE 0.18.
Newspaper
advertisement notifying
hair merchants and
hairdressers of a newly
imported stock of
human hair, 1777.

> **To HAIR MERCHANTS and HAIR-DRESSERS.**
> JUST arrived from abroad, a Hair Merchant, with a parcel of fine Hungary, German, and Flemish, Human Hair, of all colours; the most of it is from 15 to 40 inches long. Likewise fine natural white, picked grey, and light colours, warranted the best of any in England for its length and goodness. To be sold for ready money only; and those merchants and hair-dressers who chuse to favour the seller with their custom, may apply at No. 63, Red-lion-street, Holborn. *1777.*

and how they could, to the merchants at the top who bought their goods. Merchants also imported hair, and, according to the 1747 description provided by the consumer guide *The London tradesman*, generally sorted and processed it, ready for supply to the wig-makers (Fig. 0.18). Merchants' wares could be extensive, with considerable capital held in goods. In 1744, Thomas Jeffreys advertised that he was leaving the business and auctioning off his stock. This included 'a great Variety of all Sorts of Human Hair in the Sweat [process of curling], and Ready Curl'd'. Jeffreys also had horse, goat and mohair for sale (used in lower-grade items), plus different styles of finished wigs, and 'every Kind of Goods and Implements made Use of by Periwig-Makers'.[47] Hair merchants at the top of the trade could do very well indeed, like the 'eminent' Mr Banyon, who in 1738 married the wealthy Miss Tomlin of Northampton and her £5000 fortune.[48] It was also a trading concern that was to a certain extent open to women, such the widowed Elizabeth Ure, who in 1774 took over the business from her late husband.[49] At the other end of the spectrum were the humble itinerants who trudged from town to town in search of girls and women willing or forced by circumstances to sell their hair, whether because of poverty or perhaps ill health (fever was often treated by cutting off a patient's hair). Sometimes – it was feared – hair was sold after death.[50] Before, and overlapping with, the emergence of the designated hair buyer, some packmen and pedlars also bought hair: it turns up fairly commonly in later seventeenth- and early eighteenth-century inventories of their goods.[51] Life on this bottom rung of the trade could be hard and uncertain, as we can see by the report of a hair buyer who worked the area around Gloucester, found dead in a ditch one November morning.[52]

The low start-up costs and the high demand for hair must have meant that there were plenty of men willing to take a chance on the trade. However, it also provided a cover for less legitimate purposes. In the eighteenth century a peripatetic life was viewed suspiciously: householders stayed in one place, and only those without work and property roamed about –

vagrants, absconding servants and apprentices, those on the windy side of the law. The role of hair buyer, though, seems to have offered a handy disguise or excuse for travelling. Perhaps it was a way of allaying questions, and maybe offered opportunity for both chance pilfering and planned burglary. Thus we find that eighteenth-century advertisements alerting the public to escaped criminals not infrequently warn that they may be masquerading as hair buyers. Such a one was John Urlin, who broke out of gaol on the first day of February in 1716. His full description is given and the information that he 'hath pretended to be a Hair Buyer'. The reward for his capture was set at two guineas plus reasonable expenses.[53]

Driving the trade at all levels was the amount that could be fetched by good-quality hair. The trader who lost a quantity of imported Flanders hair in 1715 decided to advertise for its return. The hair weighed around 20 lbs, for which he calculated it was worth his while to offer a £20 reward 'and no Questions asked' – a sum equivalent to nearly £3000 today.[54] If this outlay left him still able to make a profit on the hair, then it clearly shows the value of the commodity. Such valuable and highly portable merchandise, however, could make a hair buyer vulnerable to theft and mugging, like the hair merchant in 1725 who was attacked on a dark December evening in Lincoln's Inn Fields by two footpads. He was robbed of 'fine humane Hair' of 'great Value'.[55] The sums involved also offered the temptations of swindles and cheating, as seen by the career of the unnamed Edinburgh hair merchant who was imprisoned in 1729 for regularly defrauding wig-makers by selling them wool mixed with horsehair, but passing it off as human.[56]

While the nineteenth century saw the abandonment of wigs for men, the use of additional hair for elaborate and fashionable female coiffures increased (Fig. 0.19). By the latter part of the century these became known by the generic term 'postiches' and included an array of readymade arrangements, including chignons, plaits and fringes, set on a foundation which was secured into the lady's own hair. The fashion continued to grow into the early years of the twentieth century: the French hairdresser Emile Long, writing his monthly column for the English trade periodical *Hairdressers' Weekly Journal*, in 1918 estimated that up to 80 per cent of French women wore some kind of postiche. In keeping with the steady democratization of fashion over the period, whereby mass production and bulk retailing saw ever greater numbers participating in modish styles, most of these women would be buying postiches cheaply from department stores and drapers. At the top end, though, postiches from elite hairdressers cost up to 500 francs, a sum that, according to Long, was the equivalent of £20 (around £870 today).[57]

Clearly, all this hair had to come from somewhere. Sometimes women collected their own, gathering the shed hair from combs and brushes: a 'hair tidy' might sit on her dressing table for the purpose, a bag or container with a hole at the top for putting in the loose hair (Fig. 0.20). Most hair, however, was commercially traded. In 1863 the first volume

FIGURE 0.19.
Illustration from fashion
periodical *Le Bon Ton*
depicting different
postiches and how they
can be incorporated
into hairstyles, April
1865.

of the *Hairdresser's Journal* discussed the false hair business, describing how collectors visited hairdressers, buying remnants and brushings. Some sources were more problematic though, and women were known to sell their hair in ill health, desperation or greed. There were particular concerns at the ethics of harvesting hair from prisons whose female inmates had been forcibly shaved, a practice many recognized as degrading to the victim and morally indefensible.[58]

Because of the high value of hair and difficulties of domestic supply, enterprising buyers cast around for other sources. Georgiana Sitwell, born in 1824, as a girl had very fair hair which fell in curls below her waist. She later recounted that when she was twelve a Brighton hairdresser offered £20 for it, for 'it was the exact colour required for old ladies' fronts'.[59] There

a

b

are indications that some were less scrupulous in their business dealings, with the occasional theft of living hair being reported. In America, a young Boston woman was coming down some steps when she felt someone pull at her hair. When she got home she found that her braid had been cut through with a knife, but because it was pinned to her head the thief had been unable to detach it. Ten years later, in 1889, a spate of hair thefts were recorded in Pennsylvania, with each teenage victim being held by her assailant while another cut off her hair.[60] In Britain, a letter to *The Times* of January 1870 suggests there was similar, albeit occasional, opportunism at work on this side of the Atlantic. The writer sought 'to warn ladies against the scoundrels (male and female) who are now infesting the thoroughfares and omnibuses of London and stealing hair'. A friend of the writer's had suffered in this way: in the

FIGURE 0.21.
A Hindu woman having her head shaved at the Thiruthani Murugan Temple in Thiruttani, India. The hair will be donated to the temple, processed and sold into the global market.

midst of a crowded street she had 'the whole of her hair' cut off and her bonnet string severed, without being aware anything was amiss until her return home.[61] While it is initially hard to credit, hairstyles and millinery of the time – the hat or bonnet perched on top of the head, combined with a chignon at the back of the neck that was sometimes left to hang down loose – makes this version of light-fingered pick-pocketing more understandable.[62]

Many of the features and concerns of the historical hair trade are still apparent today. Although many wigs and extensions are now synthetic, human hair makes the best-quality and most expensive items, and is therefore still in demand as a product. The domestic supply, once tapped by itinerant hair buyers and pedlars, has dried up, and imported wares now account for the majority. Worldwide, most of this comes from Asia, a region whose women typically grow their hair long, and for financial or cultural reasons may be willing to sell it.[63] Much of the trade is well regulated, like that stemming from various Hindu temples in India. At these, for ritual reasons, every day thousands have their heads shaved and their hair donated to the temple (Fig. 0.21). This is collected, cleaned, sorted and graded at processing factories, and then auctioned into the global fashion market. However, there are also private agents all over Asia working at ground level in the trade, like the hair buyers of eighteenth-century England, who roam the country collecting from individuals. Women save the hair that is shed while combing and washing, and in this first step in the supply chain sell it on to these itinerant pedlars. Once again though, the profits to be made from this human commodity mean that in this unregulated trade some are made vulnerable. There are suggestions that sometimes women have their hair removed forcibly, or are coerced into selling by relatives. There is, incidentally, no intrinsic reason why it is women's hair that makes up most of the trade, other than the fact that theirs is longer. Pigtails cut from Chinese men as part of the huge cultural transformation that occurred with the founding of the Chinese Republic in 1912 were also sold, and still today short hair has commodity use in Asia, where it is crafted into items like rope. Person and not-person, real and fake, both subject and object, dead but growing: hair is protean, wondrous stuff.

A hairy genealogy

Biologically unavoidable, sartorially inescapable, deeply implicated in both individual lives and broader cultural practices, the subject of hair is vast. It also therefore interacts with many different discourses and concepts within a given society, whether to do with gender and sexuality, age, ethnicity, religion, access to power, political challenge, constructions of the 'other', or the health and hygiene of the body. There is much, therefore, that this book does not cover. What it does do is put hair at the centre of the discussion to examine in a historical frame the key ways that it has been managed over the last five hundred years, and how these can help illuminate broader social developments and cultural processes.

The first chapter explores the practice of haircare and its associated material culture, probing the fine line between allowable therapeutics in tending to the body and those disallowed practices of pampering and remaking. Preparations for haircare, hand written as recipes in personal collections and published in early printed books, were initially home produced. In the eighteenth century readymade products reached the market, proliferating in the nineteenth century to eventually form a global industry that touts itself with the cachet of named celebrity hairdressers. Despite these vast market changes and the transformation of fashions, looking closely at haircare products reveals that the problems and desired outcomes of hair's appearance have been broadly consistent across time. The one exception in this continuity of grooming interventions and hairdressing tools is ideas about what constitutes cleanliness, ideas that turn out to be inextricably linked with the availability of material resources.

After the 'how' of haircare, the second chapter focuses on the 'who'. This is important: a good job bolsters the confidence and self-esteem of the person being attended to, a poor job undermines it. And while mistakes are not irreparable, they can take months to be erased. Looking at the historical record we find this concern is a constant in a trade that has developed and changed, and whose skill set has encompassed many ostensibly different jobs. After considering the role of family members, servants, and varied haircare professionals, the discussion turns to examine the nature of the relationship that exists in the activity of hairdressing. Its intimacy has fostered social pleasures, invited confidences, and facilitated sexual encounters. It has also constructed enduring stereotypes of its practitioners as garrulous, libidinous and gay.

'The art of being hairless' explores the long-term efforts that have been put into depilation. It opens by considering non-consensual acts of hair removal, invariably experienced as traumatic assaults on identity, before considering the shaving of male facial hair. As a performance of masculinity, this has been bound up with ideas of social fitness, politeness, hygiene, and social networks of shared experience. The creation of a 'natural' hairless femininity is the subject of the chapter's last section. Closely tied to fashions in dress, depilation has followed the rise and rise of clothing's margins, the tide of disclosure matched by the removal of the body's newly exposed hair.

The last three chapters present a series of case studies. 'The practice of being hairy' examines three points when facial hair was fundamental to a particular construction of manliness: the Tudor and Stuart period; the nineteenth century, whose Beard Movement self-consciously crafted mid-Victorian manhood; and the counter-culture of the twentieth century. The last section listens to the quiet voice of the bearded woman, a persistent presence at the edge of the cultural conversation despite all the efforts to tame the wayward hairiness of the feminine.

The final chapters investigate the potency of hair length as a sign of opposition to the political or social status quo. The starting point is the 'roundheads and cavaliers' identification from the English Civil War, which like a historical sporting fixture pits the uncouth parliamentarian pudding-basin cuts against flowing royalist tresses. After scrutinizing the origins and truth of this enduring image, the chapter turns to its second case study, the republican crop of the 1790s. Informed by revolutions abroad, reformist agitation at home, and the furore over the infamous hair powder tax, this new short style became embroiled in the politics of appearance. Chapter 6, 'Social challenge: The long and the short of it', examines the politicization of style in the twentieth century, focussing first on the long hair of the youth and hippie movements. The book closes with the Bobbed Hair Controversy of the 1920s, which articulated a global anxiety about modernity and the role of women within the emerging world order.

What we do now with hair and how we think about it is particular to our own time, place and culture. It also, however, has a very long past, and looking at this past can shed light on our current customs and beliefs. We have a hairy genealogy, and I hope this book helps illuminate our place in it.

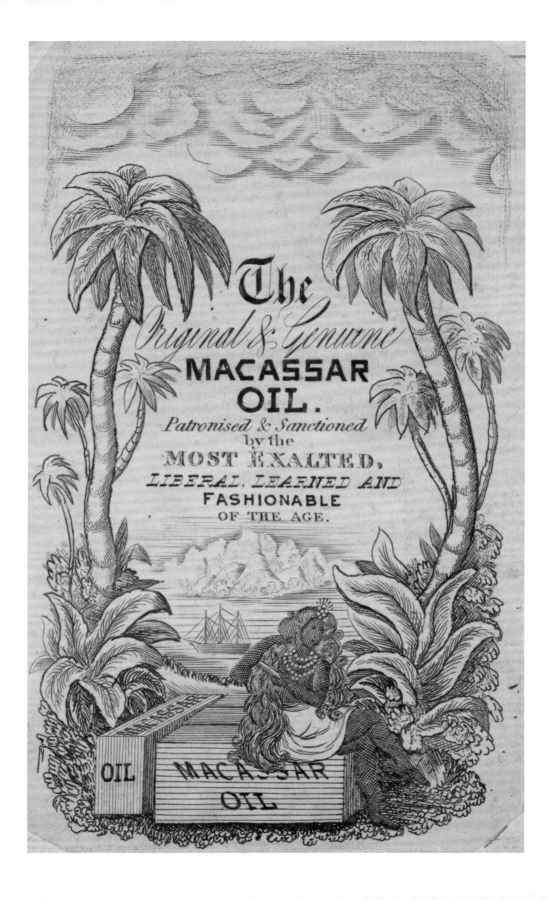

Chapter 1
Care for your hair

Problems and solutions

Collected among the household receipts of Lady Ann Fanshawe (1625–80) is a special recipe she obtained during a period spent living in Madrid (Fig. 1.1). While her husband Sir Richard, England's Spanish ambassador, was engaged with diplomatic affairs, Ann was occupied with a round of reciprocal visiting and gift-giving with the ladies of the court. It is perhaps from one of these that this recipe comes. Signed by Lady Ann and dated 8 December 1664, it is called The Queen's Oil and it is a preparation to make hair grow (Fig. 1.2). Ann Fanshawe admired many aspects of Spanish culture, including the looks and cleanliness of the Spanish women. 'Their hair', she was later to write, is 'most delicate'.[1] We must imagine, then, that these observations constituted a strong recommendation for the recipe's desirability. Three hundred and fifty years later, however, Lady Ann's nostrum seems merely to illustrate the gulf that separates us from early modern practices. It is for this reason that it forms such a suitable starting point for this discussion of haircare.

Take the best olive oil, Lady Fanshawe wrote, and put it in a glass bottle. To this add four live lizards, two ounces of flies, four ounces of white wine and the same of honey.[2] The whole is to be shaken and then stood in the hottest sun for fifteen days. The quality of heat was important, for Lady Ann notes at the end that the summer months of June, July and August are the best for making the oil. Following the slow putrefaction, the contents of the bottle are put in a skillet, brought to the boil and strained through a cloth. Then two ounces each of benjamin and storax are added (both fragrant gum resins), the mixture is heated until they melt and the whole is strained again. Kept in an airtight bottle to preserve it, a small amount of this oil is to be nightly rubbed into the roots of the hair and then a cap or coife placed immediately on the head.

This formula for Queen's Oil is typical of countless hair preparations whose properties and virtues were carefully noted by their recipe's compiler, along with the ingredients and the necessary instructions for their making and successful use. They are found amongst receipt books, collections of handwritten recipes usually concerning a broad range of cookery, medical, cosmetic and household matters. In Lady Ann's receipt book, for instance, Queen's Oil sits between an abortifacient ('red powder good for miscarryings') and a medicine for a cough in the lungs. The genre appeared in the sixteenth century and lasted through to the nineteenth, by which time printed advice and the availability of manufactured products had largely superseded this manuscript tradition. Most often compiled by women, these collections were frequently handed on to others in the family who would in turn annotate and add to the contents, resulting in a multi-authored working text. Inside the olive morocco cover of Lady Ann's receipt book, for instance, is an inscription written by her eldest surviving daughter, Katherine, recording the book as a gift passed to her from her mother on 23 March

FIGURE 1.1.
Portrait of Lady Ann
Fanshawe.

FIGURE 1.2.
Ann Fanshawe's receipt
book, showing the
recipe for 'Queens
oyle' on the left.

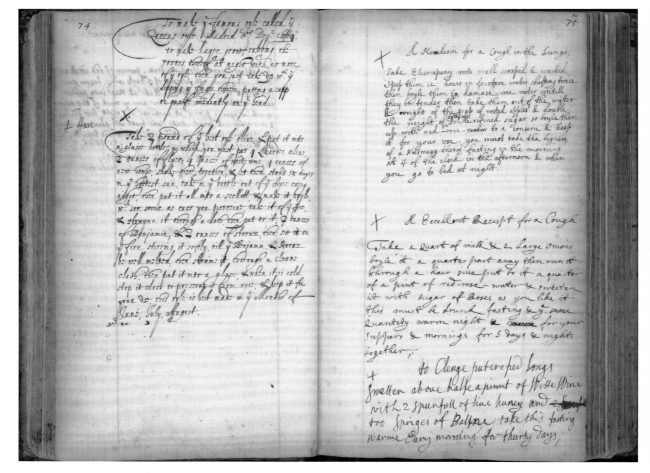

1678, and within its pages are a number of different hands, including Ann's and Katherine's own and that of Joseph Averie, apparently Ann's amanuensis.

This manuscript receipt genre existed alongside a growing number of printed texts. Unlike those compiled for private use, these latter collections were most often authored by men. There was, however, a fluid interchange between and among the two, and it is possible to find identical recipes circulating into and out of print and manuscript forms. For example, the recipe to promote beard growth that appears in *The widowes treasure*, a collection published in 1586 whose title appeals to women's knowledge and practice, also appears in a Latinized form in a medical text printed three years later, which might suggest the intended readership to be masculine and possibly professional.[3] Across a much greater time span, the same cures for 'falling' or thinning hair that employ the ashes of hyssop roots, frogs and goat dung, feature in both a manual of physic published in 1582 and *The Accomplish'd lady's delight*, an immensely popular advice text attributed to Hannah Woolley that ran to many editions from the 1670s through to the eighteenth century.[4] To see the influence between printed and manuscript texts we can turn to *The Queens closet* of 1655, which seems to have been the source text for a recipe for pomatum recorded in the Boyle Family receipt book, compiled *c.*1675–*c.*1710. While the manuscript version attributes the receipt to 'Lady Shannon' – illustrating both how a recipe's provenance was often noted for future reference and that recipes were frequently passed among friends and relatives – it seems most likely that Lady Shannon had the formula from the printed text, or that they both shared another, earlier source. To make a good pomatum, both recipes advise, first cause a puppy to be killed (the Boyle/Shannon version specifies using a spaniel) so that the blood does not settle into the fat. A long process of rendering and refining eventually results in fine, white cakes of pomatum that will last two or three years.[5]

Perhaps most intriguing of all are renditions of the same recipe in different manuscript sources, though whether the copying occurred between these texts or a third, unknown printed or manuscript source is unclear. A notable example is a receipt to make hair grow that is recorded in an anonymous collection of the mid-seventeenth century, and again in a compilation attributed primarily to Elizabeth Okeover dating *c.*1675–*c.*1725. Requiring new yellow wax and powdered red brick, the versions are identical. They even share the same textual lacuna, where it seems the copyists had trouble with a particular word, and both finish with the same endorsement that this oil 'worketh wonders' on those that shed hair of either their head or beard.[6]

This repetition and interchange of recipes speaks to a consistency of practice regarding haircare, both in the making of preparations and in the purposes they served. It also reveals that the same products were administered by women within the home and by male medical professionals. Finally, the receipt genre indicates that in this context haircare sat outside

FIGURE 1.3.
Nineteenth-century advertisement for macassar oil. So much a part of Victorian culture was macassar oil that it appears in both Byron's *Don Juan* (1819–24; canto 1, stanza 17) and Lewis Carroll's *Through the Looking Glass* (1871; in the White Knight's poem 'Haddocks' Eyes'). Bearing clear colonialist assumptions, the advertisement here plays with desire for the exotic.

the cultural tradition that identified cosmetics and beauty aids as morally flawed. Instead, drawing on an even older praxis stemming from the ancient world, the maintenance of hair was situated within a larger domain of health care. Tending to the body's surface was a legitimate and necessary part of therapeutics.[7] The recipes were not especially difficult to make,[8] though often labour intensive and time-consuming, particularly when it came to turning unsavoury raw ingredients – the lizards and flies of Ann Fanshawe's hair oil or the spaniel's fat of Lady Shannon's pomatum – into a processed cosmetic. Aside from fats and oils, and the (for us) unexpected ingredients like powdered bees or animal excrement, recipes most often utilized herbs and other plants, and perfuming agents like rosewater and resins.

Towards the end of the seventeenth century, haircare preparations began to be available for purchase, readymade. An early example is furnished by an anonymous and enterprising woman who advertised in the *Athenian Gazette* in May 1693, claiming that she had for sale a water that would colour the hair a very good brown or black, which would neither come off with sweat nor washing.[9] By the second half of the eighteenth century hair preparations were being sold in increasing quantities, particularly pomatums and powder, which at the time were the standard products for nourishing, styling and cleansing.[10] Finally, in the Victorian period the insistence on both head and facial hair made advertisements ubiquitous and products like brilliantine and macassar oil into bywords (Fig. 1.3).

Most of these early haircare products were qualitatively no different from the preparations that could be made in the home. As can be seen from eighteenth-century manufacturing formula books[11] and nineteenth- and early twentieth-century pharmaceutical manuals, they drew on the same recipe tradition, but were produced in bulk and packaged for sale. Buying them readymade just saved time and labour. The same key ingredients therefore recur frequently, and demonstrate a remarkable longevity of use. Bear's grease, for one, was prized for its capacity to nourish and restore hair. It is occasionally employed in both manuscript and printed hair-growth formulas of the sixteenth and seventeenth centuries, and by the eighteenth, probably as a result of increased availability, was featuring

FIGURE 1.4.
Labels for bear's grease, a desirable product for hair from the sixteenth to the late nineteenth centuries.

in the most desirable of manufactured pomatums and was also sold neat in little ceramic pots whose lids were decorated with bears (Fig. 1.4). In the words of an advertisement of 1770, 'the active, volatile, and penetrating Properties this Substance possesses over that of other Animals, gives it that specific, and efficacious Quality of increasing, strengthening, and preserving the Hair'.[12] Towards the end of the century hairdresser Alexander Ross devoted a whole treatise to further explaining the virtues of this wonder product, and as the nineteenth century progressed the popularity of bear's grease continued unabated. *The Druggist's General Receipt Book* of 1850, a trade manual aimed at the burgeoning number of chemists and pharmacists who were rapidly reconfiguring the Victorian health sector, included it in recipes for nourishing pomatums and as a preparation for the cure of baldness.[13] Although later in the century the supremacy of bear's grease came to be ousted by other products, as the Victorian era drew to an end it could still be obtained by the old-fashioned for the sum of around one shilling.[14] A similar pattern emerges with cantharides, or Spanish Fly, present from sixteenth-century receipts for restoring hair growth, through to tonic preparations in the twentieth century. Likewise orpiment, a compound that could cause arsenical poisoning if applied to broken skin, was used as a depilatory from at the least the sixteenth century to around 1930.[15]

Available initially from private sellers – like the woman who advertised her hair dye in the *Athenian Gazette* in 1693 – as the eighteenth century progressed, haircare products were increasingly stocked by hairdressers, barbers, wig-makers and perfumers, the four overlapping professions that had come to dominate the tending and grooming of hair. Druggists and apothecaries, too, would either make up their own recipes or nostrums brought to them for that purpose by customers. However, as the importance of the Victorian pharmacy grew, so too did its market share of hair preparations, in keeping, incidentally, with the positioning of hair within the remit of health care. Indeed, a significant number of global companies that today dominate the contemporary market date from this period. Proctor & Gamble, the health-care giant that manufactures a large number of the hair products on our shelves, was born in the United States in 1837, with the partnership of soap-maker James Gamble and William Proctor a candle-maker. Unilever, that other vast conglomerate, began life in England around fifty years later, with founder William Hesketh Lever also selling soap. Relative latecomers Schwarzkopf and L'Oréal appeared in 1903 and 1907 respectively. The former was started by a German retail chemist of the same name, who created a shampoo powder; the latter originated with the development of a safe synthetic hair dye by French chemist Eugène Schueller, working from his home laboratory.[16]

Let us return for a moment though to consider Ann Fanshawe and what it was she hoped her receipt for Queen's Oil would achieve. It is, in her words, designed 'to make hayre grow'; but what of other recipes and other products? What was it that those who invested the time and resources in their making or the money in their purchase wanted these substances to achieve, and what can such preparations tell us about the conceptualization of problem hair and the appearances which constituted the ideal? For a start, Lady Fanshawe was far from alone in wanting something to boost and improve hair growth: perhaps the majority of recipes are directed to achieving this for either facial or head hair. Related to these are the preparations to prevent or restore hair loss, a condition generally known as 'falling' hair or, then as now, baldness and alopecia. While insufficient hair was a problem, so too was superfluity, and there are plenty of depilatory recipes and products aimed at removing unwanted hair growing in unwanted places. While we can legitimately doubt the efficacy of hair restorers, the effectiveness of at least some depilatories, which frequently employed quicklime and orpiment either singly or in combination, is not in question. One receipt manual of 1660 that gives instructions for applying an ointment of equal quantities of arsenic and lime, adds what seems to be the rather magnificently understated rider, 'and see that it burn not'.[17] Other texts suggested taking palliative steps: 'As for the use of the foregoing medicines, you are to foment the place with warme water a little before you apply them; a quarter of an hour after wash with hot water, and when the haire is taken away anoint the place with some cooling oile.'[18]

Between them, receipts for hair growth and hair removal account for most of the preparations, certainly of the manuscript genre. There are also a small number of solutions designed to curl hair, either by their application alone or when used as a fixative in combination with mechanical techniques for inducing curl. The manuscript collection belonging to Bridget Hyde includes an example of the former, a preparation of benjamin, storax, wine and dew to be sponged on the hair, and the Boyle Family receipt book contains a very similar recipe with the instructions to 'wet your hair when you Curl it up'.[19] The mechanical (as opposed to chemical) techniques for producing curls included the use of curling irons, or crisping pins as they were sometimes called, which had been known since antiquity.[20] Likewise Thomas Jeamson in his beauty manual *Artificiall embellishments* noted that, 'Some to make their haire curle wind it up going to bed upon a hot Tabacco pipe or iron.'[21] And rolling hair in curl papers or rags was certainly practised from the eighteenth century, and very likely long before. This was the method apparently favoured by Byron (1788–1824), who as a student in Cambridge was allegedly discovered by a friend one morning with his hair *en papillote*, or folded into papers. Said his friend, Scrope Davies, 'it was my conviction that your hair curled naturally'. 'Yes,' replied Byron carelessly, 'naturally every night'.[22]

Although undoubtedly at different periods curls were considered attractive and fashionable, how can we explain the relatively small number of recipes for curling solutions? In part it seems likely that the availability of other, probably more effective techniques meant that until the twentieth-century development of the 'permanent', chemical curling products were relatively under-represented in haircare preparations.[23] Another factor may well be that curling the hair was a practice less securely grounded in health and more obviously related to the unnecessarily cosmetic. Nudged out of the medical realm and into the fashionable, therefore, artificial curling could be construed as worldly and vain.

In addition to curling solutions, restorers and depilatories, printed recipe collections feature a large number of preparations to colour hair, and such dyes were also commonly available for sale – note that the advertisement in the *Athenian Gazette* of 1693 was for a water that was guaranteed to permanently dye the hair a very good brown or black. Like depilatories these products could be hazardous for the user, and some recipes stipulated that care should be taken to avoid contact with the skin. According to eighteenth-century hairdresser David Ritchie, such substances not only damaged the hair – leaving it brittle, in poor condition and subject to breakage – but, absorbed through the pores, were injurious to the brain. William Moore, a hairdresser practising in Bath at around the same time, also attested to the toxic effects of these products, citing the example of one of his clients. Against his advice this lady had purchased and used a particular hair dye: her temples blistered as well as her fingers, her hair crumbled at the touch, and she was ill for two months.[24] While the ingredients of some dyes were harmless – like honey, fig leaves and green walnut rinds – preparations also commonly included lead, aquafortis and oil of vitriol, the two latter known to us as nitric and sulphuric acid. It is therefore neither surprising that many manufactured dyes and depilatories reassured their prospective users of the product's safety, nor that the L'Oréal empire was built on the foundations of a harmless synthetic hair colourant. Despite this, in 1931 the training manual by Gilbert Foan, *The Art and Craft of Hairdressing*, still saw the need to incorporate a section entitled 'Hair Dye Poisoning', which discussed the toxicity of certain dyes, the legal position for hairdressers and the advisability of professional insurance. It also recommended the use of patch tests to check an individual's susceptibility to chemical risk.[25] Although today patch tests are a legal requirement, the paraphenylenediamine (PPD) chemicals of which Foan was warning are still in use and causing extreme allergic reactions in a small, but growing, percentage of the population. In some cases, for both home users and salon clients, the dyes have been fatal.[26]

There are three further noteworthy points about hair dyes, whether in recipe or manufactured form: first, both men and women were considered to be potential users; second, both head and facial hair could be subject to colour change; and third, they testify to the enduring unpopularity of grey and (as discussed in the Introduction) red. As a medical advice book from 1664 put it: 'Some old men desire to be black or the like, and to seem young. And young men if they have any grey Hairs in Head or Beard, as often is seen, they desire to have them like the rest, or to make red hairs black.' The text goes on to suggest different recipes and methods for hair colouring, but also warns against home-dyeing disasters:

> In blacking of hair, you must note that these Medicines are so to be ordered that they completely make black, least the same happen to them that use them as did to an old Man, not long since, who marrying a young Wench, desirous to make his grey hairs black, to please his Spouse with a sophisticated Youth: made his hair of his Head, Beard and Eye brows green, to the great Laughter of the Beholders.[27]

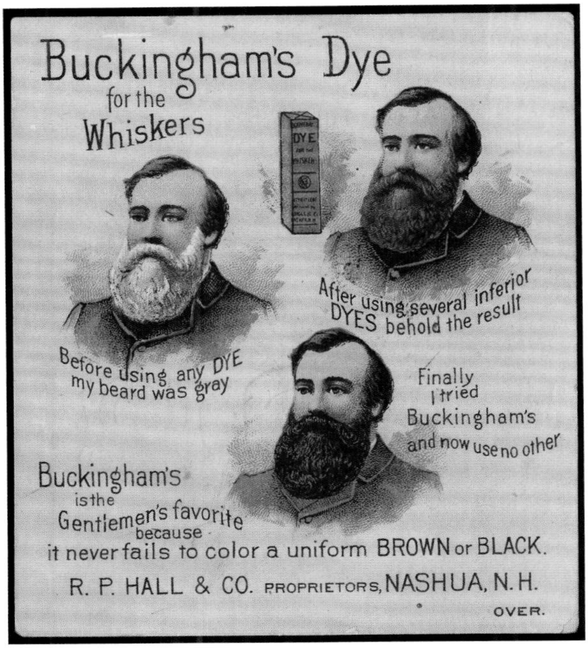

FIGURE 1.5.
Advertisement for Buckingham's Dye, c.1870–c.1900.

Advertising ephemera from the nineteenth century, which sold increasing numbers of things to increasing numbers of people, also attest to the fact that hair colour was regarded as a concern appropriate to both sexes (Fig. 1.5), and personal testimony supports further the idea that at least some men coloured their hair. Among them was Prince Pückler-Muskau (1785–1871), an impoverished German aristocrat seeking to repair his fortunes by making an advantageous second marriage. From 1826 he spent a number of years in England looking for a rich wife to answer the purpose, which naturally required him to look his best. One of his letters describes something of what this entailed:

> The operation of dyeing my hair has fared so badly, the devil knows why, that this evening I had to begin all over again . . . But the reign of the devil cannot last forever, and if care has turned my hair white before its time, art must make it black once more, and so care will turn to joy.[28]

Pückler-Muskau was forty-one at the time; a portrait dated 1837, when he must have been in his early fifties, still shows him with a head of black hair, with whiskers to match (Fig. 1.6).

So far the 'how' of haircare as revealed by recipes and early products may not be familiar, but the 'why' shows itself to have changed very little. Considering again Lady Fanshawe's recipe for Queen's Oil, stewing four live lizards and some flies in a jar of olive oil reveals an unbridgeable gulf in daily practice. Focusing, however, on what Lady Ann wanted the product to achieve – in this case hair growth – shows there to have been a continuity over hundreds of years in what constituted the problems and the promise of hair. Then as now, people wanted their hair to be thick and full; they attempted to cure baldness and hair loss; they styled it, changed its colour and removed it from growing in unwanted places. This consistency of desired outcome stretches from the recipe tradition through the era of early manufactured products and continues to drive the global haircare market today.

The tools of haircare show a similar continuity; indeed many of them date back to antiquity. The basic item, and perhaps the oldest, was the comb. Made of wood (generally box wood, which has a fine grain and resists water), horn, bone or for the finest examples ivory or tortoiseshell, the comb was a multipurpose tool used to clean, groom and style.[29] The famous painting of Lady Elizabeth Vernon gives us a rare glimpse of its use at a dressing table four hundred years ago: note that her comb is inscribed with the words *menez moi doucement*, or handle me gently (Fig. 1.7). Jacobean dialogues written around the same time

FIGURE 1.6.
Portrait of Prince Pückler-Muskau. His impoverished finances led him and his wife to concoct a plan whereby their divorce freed him to come to England to seek a rich spouse, whose money he planned to plough into his estates and also support wife number one. In the end the plan failed, but his published letters documenting his travels became a best seller and repaired his fortunes.

give another rendition of this daily dressing practice. First the lady has her head rubbed with a linen cloth to clean it, then another combing cloth is placed around her shoulders to protect her clothes – in exactly the same way hairdressers' gowns are used today – and finally she is combed. Reading the dialogue between the lady and her waiting woman feels a little like eavesdropping:

I praye you Jolye rubbe well my head, for it is very full of dandrife, are not my combes in the case? Where is my Iuorye [ivory] combe? Combe mee with the boxen [i.e. box wood] combe: giue me first my combing cloth, otherwise you will fill me full of haires, the haires will fall vpon my cloathes, Combe backe-ward, O God! You combe too harde, you scratch me, you pull out my hayres, can you not vntangle them softly with your handes before you put the combe to it?[30]

Scissors, razors, curling tongs, tweezers, pins and a mirror complete the list of the most common implements used for grooming head and hair. Aside from the curling irons, these tools were available even to the poorer sort, and most rural dwellers would have sourced them from an itinerant pedlar, or perhaps at a local market or fair. Stock inventories of these sellers indicate their typical wares. Richard Riddings of Bury in Lancashire, whose inventory was taken in 1680, had in stock twenty-four combs made of horn valued at 17d. per dozen, twelve of white bone at 8d. per dozen, and at the top of his range, ten combs of ivory worth 2d. each. In addition he was carrying twelve comb cases (for keeping combs safe, these were usually made of fabric rather like jewellery wraps) and three pairs of scissors. Likewise, in 1642 William Mackerrell of Newcastle was selling tweezers, scissors, combs, comb cases and beard brushes, and in 1730 in Norfolk John Mackie was peddling combs, looking glasses and shavers (presumably razors).[31] In the larger urban settings haberdashers would also have supplied such goods, and from the eighteenth century they were increasingly available from the tradesmen associated with haircare: hairdressers, barbers, wig-makers and perfumers. These tools changed very little over the centuries, and only mechanized production of the Victorian era and, from the late 1860s, the development of plastics made a significant difference to availability and price.[32]

There was, however, one significant development. Although clothes brushes, beard brushes and brushes to clean combs were in use earlier, the hairbrush was an item that only became common from the late eighteenth century. In the Victorian era it became a key component in the armoury of hygiene and personal care. Men and women were enjoined to the discipline of daily brushing to cleanse and stimulate their scalps and impart a gloss to their hair. But although conscientious brushing was required of both sexes, the practice

was gendered in particular ways. Hair-brushing for men conjured a brisk neatness. The brushes themselves usually had no handles, an absence that rendered them so masculine that they became known as military hairbrushes. These typically came in pairs and might in fact be wielded together, brushing either side of a parting (Fig. 1.8). By contrast, advertisements pictured women with a superabundance of Rapunzel-like locks and a long-handled brush: a visual shorthand for idealized Victorian femininity (Fig. 1.9). Hair-brushing in this context was about the luxury of controlled excess: the brush rhythmically bringing order to abundance with the paradigmatic 'one hundred brush strokes' every night, a semi-eroticized and disciplining task.[33]

So keen were Victorians on the benefits of brushing, that they combined it with that other exciting technology, electricity. In the 1880s the Pall Mall Electric Association produced Dr Scott's Electric Hair Brush. In advertisements jammed full of endorsements, these were claimed to not only prevent hair from thinning, cure dandruff, stop greyness and make the hair grow long and glossy, but also soothe the brain and in five minutes cure neuralgia and headaches (Fig. 1.10). Bold declarations indeed, especially given that there was nothing at all electrical about the brush aside from its name (rather, the handle contained magnetized iron rods). Undeterred, the company also produced an electric comb. A genuine invention was the rotary hairbrush, first patented in 1862 and used by barbers and hairdressers as a modern therapeutic technique. Each rolling-pin shaped brush was connected to a belt, which in turn was driven by a rotating shaft suspended at the ceiling. The operative held the brush handles on either side and applied the device to the customer's hair (Fig. 1.11). Originally a mechanical invention powered in a variety of ways, electrification occurred from 1904; the system remained common until after the First World War.[34]

Electricity was incorporated into haircare in other ways, too. Electrolysis for hair removal was introduced from around the 1880s, though was used medically rather than by the hairdressing professions or in the domestic setting.[35] The first machines for producing permanent waves began to appear in the early 1900s. For many years these were both massively cumbersome and massively time-consuming, and involved the client being

"Mama, shall I have beautiful long hair like you when I grow up?"
"Certainly, my dear, if you use **'Edwards' Harlene'**."

FIGURE 1.12.
(Facing page)
An early permanent-
wave machine being
demonstrated at the
Hairdressing Fair in
London, 1928.

attached to the tentacles of what looked like a giant octopus and then being plugged into the mains for hours (Fig. 1.12). The enforced immobility could be more than merely tedious. As an apprentice hairdresser in the war years, Vidal Sassoon recounted that each cubicle held the warning notice: 'Madam, during an air raid, you are permed at your own risk.' With her hair wrapped around the machine's rods a client was unable to move, and so when an air raid siren sounded she was reassured – 'Excuse me, madam. I'm going down to the shelter. I promise I'll be back' – and while the staff went to the basement she stayed trapped in her chair. As an apprentice it was Sassoon's job to turn the off the electricity to the perming machine. One day he forgot and a client's hair was all burnt off, but at least she escaped the bombs.[36] Hairdryers also date from the late nineteenth century. Initially air was heated by gas burners; then around 1900 electric fans were added to blow the hot air. After this an electrical element was used as well, and with time the hand-held blow-dryer was developed.

Aside from this incorporation of electricity, when we consider both the aims and technology of haircare we are engaging with a long-standing tradition that in many respects has changed little in hundreds, if not thousands, of years. There is, however, one area in which a paradigm shift has occurred: in our understandings of cleanliness and hygiene.

Keeping it clean

Neither recipes nor early manufactured products were concerned with preparations whose function was to cleanse as we would understand this. In keeping with contemporary ideas about the hygiene of the rest of the body, immersion in water was considered to be neither the way to become clean, nor the way to stay healthy. Bathing and temperature fluctuations carried risks and were undertaken only rarely. John Evelyn (1620–1706), for instance, noted in his diary that he had begun to wash his hair annually, once a year using warm water and a decoction of sweet herbs, followed by a cold spring-water rinse.[37] As French doctor Jean Liebault warned: 'When it is a question of cleansing the hair of the head, washing should only be employed with the greatest caution.'[38] Instead, the fundamental cleanser was the comb: combing hair removed tangles and dirt, and spread the scalp's natural oils. As surgeon William Bullein described in his guidelines to health published in 1558, the slovenliness of those who 'verie few times combe their heads' is seen by the 'floxes, nittes, grease, feathers, straw, and such like, which hangeth in their haires'.[39]

As Bullein's words remind us, combing also helped to combat parasites (Fig. 1.13). Grooming to remove lice and nits is a practice grounded in our extreme evolutionary past, a biological necessity that we share with every other land mammal.[40] Our species may have come down from the trees and out of the caves, but our little living cargo of parasites has come with us (Fig. 1.14). Today we still employ nit combs as a tool in their removal, and also – as in Bullein's day – further facilitate the process with a variety of lotions and applications.

FIGURE 1.13.
(Facing page) *A Mother Combing the Hair of her Child (Hunting for Lice),* c.1652–3.

FIGURE 1.14.
(Right) Male human head louse, *Pediculus humanus capitis.*

Typically, early modern recipes employed both greasy and acidic substances, like lard and vinegar. As grease would immobilize the adult lice and acid would loosen the egg (nit) from the hair shaft, it is likely that in conjunction with combing this was a more or less effective treatment. The removal of scurf and dandruff was another hygienic and cosmetic concern, and again printed recipes and medical texts offered advice and various ointments and waters for accomplishing it. Sometimes writers included a diagnostic guide, likening the appearance of dandruff to small flakes of bran.[41] Thought to be the result of internal humoral imbalance – a distemper – elevated to the head, medical opinion accepted it was not dangerous but still 'causeth some kind of deformity and much trouble'.[42] As with lice, the condition has remained commonplace, although modern research has identified the aetiology of severe forms as fungal.[43]

Cleanliness was primarily located, therefore, in the removal of extraneous matter, such as dirt, tangles, scurf and lice. Even as late as 1845, in stating the importance of 'particular cleanliness' with respect to the hair, an etiquette guide advised that this was to be achieved by brushing and combing every morning and evening, 'or the dust will accumulate upon the long hair of ladies'.[44] Clean hair would have looked smooth, glossy with the hair's natural oils and with added products. Perhaps it also smelt not unpleasantly musky.

The use of water as a habitual cleanser, perhaps with the addition of soap, probably started to develop around the beginning of the nineteenth century.[45] The approximate frequency of this washing might be gleaned from advice contained in a gentleman's self-improvement book from 1830. *The Whole Art of Dress,* aimed at an aspirational but financially cautious readership, gives direction as to how to dress and look well on a budget. The chief attributes of hair, the excellence of which can make up for an 'indifferent' countenance, are curl, strength and gloss. It should be trimmed once a month, the author recommends, and likewise washed once a fortnight in the summer, and once a month in the winter. Clearly, we are seeing in operation here a very different belief structure from that which identified washing as potentially injurious, but equally it is a regime still considerably removed from the norms of the twenty-first century.

The word 'shampoo' made its appearance in the eighteenth century, and like so many British cultural borrowings originates from India. It derives from the Hindi *champo*, meaning to press or knead, and was initially used to describe a body massage. From the mid-nineteenth century this coalesced around the specific act of massaging the scalp with a cleanser, most usually a combination of soap and water, and from here 'shampoo' took on the noun form referring to the preparation itself.[46] Initially shampoos came in various types (Fig. 1.15), the most common being liquids that required water to lather and clean the hair. However, there were other solutions that were massaged onto the scalp and sponged or towelled off without water, a practice rather confusingly known as 'dry' shampooing. Another variant were powders

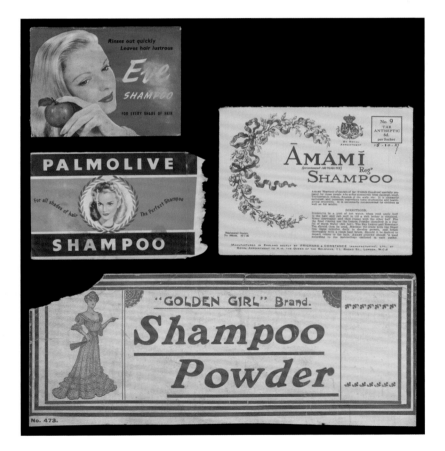

FIGURE 1.15.
Early shampoo labels.

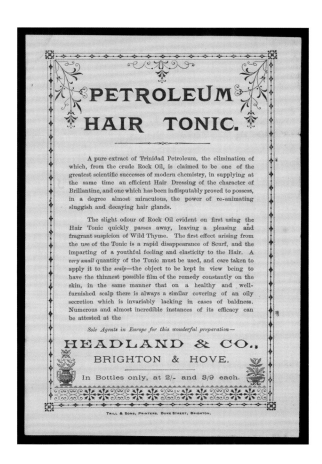

that acted as liquid shampoos when the user added water, but there were also powders that were used in their dry form, worked into the hair to absorb grease and then combed out, a technique dating to the seventeenth century. Finally came the cream shampoos, which by the 1950s had come to dominate the market as they continue so to do.[47]

The 'dry' shampoo liquids were based on solvents like petroleum (Fig. 1.16) or carbon tetrachloride, and it takes only a little familiarity with basic chemistry to work out that their use carried considerable risk. The petroleum-based variety, which spread from Paris to London in the 1890s, was highly flammable and under the right conditions could combust spontaneously. Add this volatility to the presence of the open flames used to heat curling tongs or early hairdryers, and what emerges is a health and safety scenario of nightmarish proportions. Although the instances of injury in fact seem to have been exceptionally rare, in a few well-publicized cases the results were fatal. One such hit the news in the July of 1897, and concerned the death of thirty-year-old Fanny Samuelson. On a visit to London from her home in Yorkshire, Mrs Samuelson entered the premises of hairdressers Emile and Co.

around midday on 26 June and asked to have her hair cleaned with a petroleum wash. The hairdresser checked first to see that the gas stoves were all out, and then proceeded to apply the lotion. Suddenly an explosion occurred and he and Mrs Samuelson were engulfed in flames. The fire was put out, but not before Fanny sustained such burns, principally to the head, that she subsequently died. Like every cautionary tale this one includes a moral. In Fanny's own words as spoken to her friend who was present: 'Never have your hair done with petroleum.' The coroner's inquest into the accident was adjourned several times while further expert evidence was sought, and the case prompted the London County Council to become involved, though it was not until over a decade later that a parliamentary committee recommended that the use of petroleum as a hair wash be made illegal.[48]

Actually, the dangers of petroleum hair wash were very slight, as nothing compared to the risks of using petrol in lamps, a practice that in the months around Fanny Samuelson's accident caused thirty-six deaths at hairdressers.[49] But somehow this failed to make the same impact as a single case of 'explosive hairwash'. One of the reasons for this was the social status of the victim. The status of the hairdressing establishments was also significant: West End salons with French coiffeurs. Petroleum hair wash held a fashionable lure, and other known accidents had occurred at Monte Carlo and Paris. This perhaps explains why Fanny Samuelson, despite being told her hair did not need the treatment, insisted. It may also explain why the small number of salons that continued to offer petroleum washes reported that following Fanny's death there was a greatly increased number of requests for the treatment.

The alternative dry shampoo was the highly toxic compound carbon tetrachloride. Just as it was known that petrol was flammable, so there was some understanding of the potency of this substance and ideally the solution was applied where there was good ventilation. Nevertheless, despite the precautions of an open window and an electric fan, in July 1909 a fatality occurred in the hairdressing department at Harrod's.[50] In many ways it echoed the case of Mrs Samuelson twelve years earlier: a prestige establishment, a high-status victim – in this instance twenty-nine-year-old Helenora Catherine Horn-Elphinstone Dalrymple – and lots of publicity. Having had the process explained to her, including the warning that the fumes may make her feel faint, Miss Dalrymple made an appointment for a dry shampoo. Within a couple of minutes of the solution being applied she said she felt unwell and then collapsed. Resuscitation was attempted, but she died almost immediately. Again, it must be stressed that this fatality was an extremely unusual occurrence. At the inquest and subsequent trial for manslaughter of the salon manager and the shampooing assistant, it was revealed that Harrod's had been using carbon tetrachloride for six years and twenty to thirty thousand customers had been treated, with no more serious consequences than a few cases of faintness. In the words of the public prosecutor, Harrod's 'had been most remarkably lucky' – as, not to mention, had the twenty to thirty thousand clients. Although both medical experts and the

Guild of Hairdressers advised against it, carbon tetrachloride continued to be used into the 1930s.[51]

An advantage of dry shampooing – whether by a hazardous solvent or a harmless powder – was that it did not need water, a commodity that, along with bathrooms, was not universally available in British houses in ample and heated quantities until the second half of the twentieth century. When trying to establish the frequency of hair-washing, therefore, it is important to remember that the practice was heavily dependent on class, cultural norms and the availability of resources. This is illustrated by promotional literature for Harlene's Cremex shampoo powder, an Edwardian product sold in sachets, six per box, for the cost of one shilling. Applied with water and worked to a lather, Cremex, according to the company's advertising, was designed especially for use in the home. An illustration pictures a man, woman and youth in various stages of shampooing, leaning over basins with hot and cold taps (Fig. 1.17). The text explains:

> Really Beautiful Hair is cleansed Hair. And to be thoroughly cleansed the hair must be regularly shampooed with a safe, scientifically prepared tonic shampoo powder, which will give it that shimmering halo-like radiance which evokes the admiration of everyone.[52]

The broadly contemporaneous nature of this advertisement with the news coverage of shampoo-related deaths makes the stress on safety and health especially pertinent. Its emphasis on lightness and shimmer as defining characteristics of clean hair shows also a significant departure from earlier norms. The suggested timetable of cleansing with Cremex

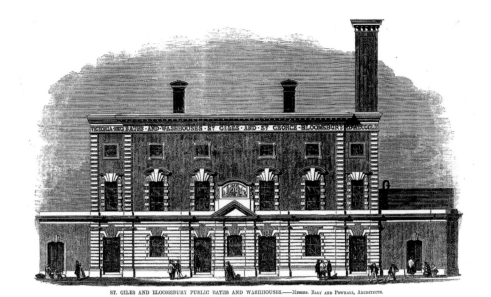

ST. GILES AND BLOOMSBURY PUBLIC BATHS AND WASHHOUSES.——Messrs. Baly and Pownall, Architects.

is further indicative of changed practices: for those who live in the country, shampoo once a week; twice a week for those who live in the town.

Against this evidence of advertising ephemera, however, must be placed the state of minimal plumbing that was the reality for perhaps the majority of the population. So widespread were insanitary conditions in nineteenth-century Britain – the period that gave rise to the phrase 'the great unwashed' – that the public baths movement was established as a response (Fig. 1.18).[53] The unhygienic conditions that the baths movement was designed to address was no Dickensian spectre confined to the slums of Victorian Britain, but one that haunted public health well into the twentieth century. Vidal Sassoon, born in 1928, visited the public baths once a week, later writing feelingly of being brought up in the East End with 'no bathrooms, no internal toilets – just cold running water in tiny kitchens'. It wasn't until the late 1940s that he moved into a house with a bathroom and hot water on tap.[54] Perhaps unsurprisingly given the scarcity of resources and the state of housing in much of Europe immediately after the war, outside America 'shampoo consumption was not widespread'.[55] In 1949 British women were reported as washing their hair 'on average between once a week and once a fortnight'.[56]

Throughout the twentieth century, the interconnected relationship between cultural attitudes and material conditions continued to determine varying hygiene regimes around the world.[57] In recent decades, however, both changing expectations of cleanliness and the expansion of the Western beauty industry into Asian and African economies means that the challenges of the future are likely to concern issues of resource use and sustainability – of how we will find the water, the energy and the processes of waste-management for more than seven billion people across the planet to cleanse, condition, dry and style their hair.

We began this chapter with Ann Fanshawe steeping lizards and flies in a jar of olive oil. Although the journey, by way of bear's grease and poisons, has covered some alien territory, with the notable exception of cleanliness the basic landscape has proved remarkably familiar. Certainly at the surface level of fashion hair styles have altered massively over the centuries, but the underlying reasons for, and ways of, caring for hair changed little. In the next chapter we turn to those people who were responsible for this cultural domain – the servants, barbers and hairdressers of the past – and to the intimacy that flourished with the grooming and tending of hair.

A Hint to y̆ Husbands, or the Dresser, properly Dressed.

London, Printed for R. Sayer & J. Bennett, N°. 53 Fleet Street, as the Act directs 14 Augˢᵗ. 1777.

Chapter 2

From servant
to stylist

The people

If, on 5 October 1662, we had been able to spy on Samuel Pepys (1633–1703) and his wife, we would have found them in bed, having an argument. They had been enjoying a Sunday lie-in, only somehow the subject of Sarah came up, their maid. Pepys (Fig. 3.4) thought she was as good a servant as any they had had, but Elizabeth wanted to get rid of her because she wanted 'one that could dress a head well'.[1] This conjugal squabble later recorded in brief by Pepys in his diary reveals the simple truth that historically most hairdressing was a domestic occupation. The majority of people simply looked after their own hair, with assistance from family members, and those further up the social scale like Samuel and Elizabeth Pepys also had the help of servants (Fig. 2.1). In Pepys's house there were no hard and fast distinctions about how this was done. We know that Elizabeth had assistance from her maid, and that he had his hair combed and cut by his wife, by the household maids, and also by Elizabeth's sister-in-law and her brother.[2] This fluidity is entirely characteristic of the tending of hair, it being an activity that could be invested with different levels of emotional significance, and that could occur equally within a contractual, professional relationship or as part of the interaction of equals.

For those who did have servants to dress their hair proficiency was important, and the maid in question could lose or keep a job on the strength of it.[3] A servant's reputation could travel even beyond the household: as Fanny Boscawen (1719–1805) wrote to her cousin, 'I know Lady Falmouth's maid dresses hair in perfection.'[4] It was not just maids whose skill was valued, but man servants too. As Isabella Beeton's 1861 book of household management stated, hairdressing was the most important part of the duties of a lady's maid, but a valet also needed to be 'a good hairdresser', able to groom and cut to advantage both the hair on the head and the face.[5] The memoirs of John MacDonald (b. 1741) breathe extraordinary life into this plain statement of household management. A servant in the eighteenth century, MacDonald's reminiscences provide a rare bottom-up glimpse into the experience of domestic service. Over the course of thirty-three years MacDonald was employed by twenty-seven different masters, in varying capacities from groom to body servant, and in countries from Scotland to India. His skill in dressing hair helped considerably when finding a position and opened opportunities of both a remunerative and sexual nature. MacDonald's abilities with razor, powder, pomatum and pins were put to the service of not only his master and sometimes mistress, but also members of other establishments, including children. Moreover, he took good care to keep these transferable skills honed, at one point boarding with a hairdresser for a number of months in order to up his game.[6]

The desirability of hairdressing as a skill for servants can also be discerned through the less subjective evidence of newspaper advertisements. In advertising for situations wanted and vacant, the ability to manage hair figures prominently. The numbers of such advertisements

FIGURE 2.1.
(Facing page) A lady sits while a maid dresses her hair.

grow rapidly in the last decades of the eighteenth century, the expansion of the newspaper industry intersecting with both increased levels of literacy and more complicated fashions in hair. Often they specify a skill in dressing hair 'in the present taste', demonstrating a concern for fashionability and a desire to be up to date. They show both men and women seeking employment, and in turn being sought. Thus, in the columns of the *Morning Herald* of 4 January 1781, a woman of about thirty states that she 'can dress hair' and wants a place as a lady's maid, while a single gentleman seeks a servant of whom it is 'indispensible to dress hair and shave well'.[7] While female servants offer hairdressing as a skill exclusively to female employers, it is not unusual for male servants, in the manner of John MacDonald, to be able to attend to both their masters and mistresses, as in the case of the steady man of about thirty-eight who sought a place, and could 'dress Ladies or Gentleman's hair in the present taste, and shave well'.[8] It was not just body servants for whom hairdressing skills increased employability, but for men and women seeking or being sought for a surprising variety of positions: one gentleman looked to employ an experienced groom who could not only shoe horses, but 'will be expected to understand a little of hair-dressing'; a woman wanting a place as an assistant teacher at a boarding school flagged her ability in French, in needlework, and in dressing hair.[9]

As a lure to prospective employers some enterprising individuals like John MacDonald took lessons from professionals, for although the trimming and tending of hair occurred primarily in the home, independent hairdressers did exist. As early as the sixteenth century tire-women specialized in women's hair, cutting, curling, colouring and styling. Blanche Swansted, for example, was tire-woman to Anne of Denmark, wife of James I. After Anne's death in 1619 Blanche petitioned James for a pension, stating that because of her attendance on the late queen she had lost her former customers and her livelihood.[10] Samuel Pepys tells us that the tire-woman to Charles II's queen, Catherine of Braganza, was a Frenchwoman called Mrs Gotiers (Gaultier).[11] In 1747 R. Campbell, in his account of London trades, described the tire-woman as 'Prime Minister' to a woman's beautifying – a topical allusion to the relatively recent creation of that political office. The tire-woman 'arms the Sex with these dangerous Weapons, nice Curls, and enchanting Ringlets: She cuts their Hair into all Shapes, suitable to the Fashion'. This trade, so Campbell advised, is 'abundantly profitable'.[12]

However, by the time Campbell was writing the term 'tire-woman' would probably have seemed increasingly old-fashioned. A new breed was developing called hair-cutters or hairdressers, and these were primarily men. Throughout the course of the eighteenth century the numbers of these professionals grew exponentially: at George II's coronation in 1727 it was reported that in London there were only two hairdressers; in 1795 contemporary estimates put the number in Britain at fifty thousand.[13] They tended the hair of men and women, sold perfume and haircare products (Fig. 2.2), and, in an age memorable for its

FIGURE 2.2.
Early nineteenth-century hairdressing trade card. The hairdresser makes home visits, offering his services to ladies and gentlemen, families and schools. The display cabinet to the right illustrates the wares he sells, including combs and brushes, and products like hair dye, macassar oil, bear's grease and soap.

FIGURE 2.3.
Newspaper advertisement from 1778 for a Mr Paintie, a ladies' hairdresser who has opened an academy to teach the art of dressing a lady's hair.

wig-wearing, also dressed perukes and styled with hair pieces. Some offered lessons, others opened formal teaching academies (Fig. 2.3), still others raised the stakes by entering the publishing world, writing treatises and manuals on hair and its dressing. It was a boom century for the hair trade. A few of these hairdressers reached something akin to celebrity status. While Queen Catherine had a tire-woman, one hundred years later Queen Charlotte, wife to George III, was waited on by a hairdresser called Suardy; in 1619 Blanche Swansted had had to petition the king for a small pension to enable her to live, but by 1788 Suardy was demanding £200 for attending on Charlotte for just one summer.[14] This was a massive sum by anyone's standards, equivalent today to over £22,000.[15] The queen, it turned out, would not agree to this expense, arranging only to employ him at that rate as and when required, on a

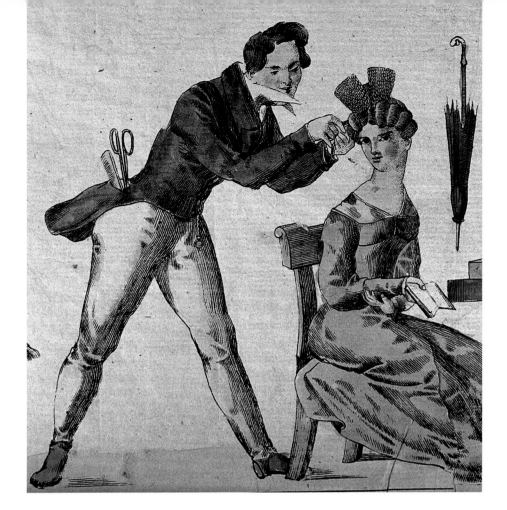

FIGURE 2.4.
An early nineteenth-century male hairdresser attending a woman. Comb and scissors, the tools of his trade, are to hand in his coat pocket. The high points of his starched shirt, the seals hanging from his waist, and his fitted pantaloons, fixed with a strap beneath the instep, show him to be a modish fellow who pursues the latest fashions.

pro rata basis. Whether or not she consented to the full-time contract is in a sense immaterial, however, for this incident serves to illustrate the extraordinarily rapid establishment of a trade, the professional eclipse of women by male hairdressers, the acceptance of the paradigm whereby men groomed female clients, and the notion of the hairdresser as a style genius who could dictate terms to the most powerful (Fig. 2.4).

According to Mrs Papendiek (1765–1840), one of Queen Charlotte's waiting women, at that time hairdressers' services were accessed in one of two ways. Most ladies in elite circles, she explains, employed a hairdresser either on a quarterly contract for daily hairdressing, as in Suardy's proposed terms to the queen, or for particular one-off occasions, as in the queen's response to Suardy.[16] For special events, Mrs Papendiek herself used the services of a Mr Kead. Between the words of her memoirs, we can glimpse what must have been a close professional relationship between the two of them. She trusts him completely, calling him 'the cavalier of the day' and relying on his 'inimitable dressing' to make her look her best for concerts, for the christening of her eldest child and for a portrait-sitting to the famous artist

Johan Zoffany. And as with any trusted hairdresser, the inferior skills of another grated with Mrs Papendiek, so that when she sometimes had to make do with the attendance of a certain Mr Theilcke, she thought herself 'not so becomingly finished', even complaining that 'bad was made worse'.[17] Queen Charlotte fared similarly when replacing the extortionate Suardy with another hairdresser, Mr Duncan. Despite the personal recommendations of some of her ladies-in-waiting, Duncan, she said, had 'no taste', and lacking Suardy's creativity 'was no hand at arranging anything beyond the common art of hairdressing'.[18]

Although they were tradespeople with shops or premises, tire-women and hairdressers also visited clients in their own homes. For genteel women this would have been the most usual way of gaining access to professional hairdressing services. In urban areas such visits were quite easily made. Rural clients were also visited at home, although the hairdresser might take the opportunity to see several at the same time – which was how, although living around eight miles from town, Nancy, the niece of the Norfolk parson James Woodforde (1740–1803), came to be invited to the home of the local squire to spend the day 'and to have her Hair dressed by one Brown, the best Ladies-Frisseur in Norwich'.[19] Novelist Fanny Burney (1752–1840) on one occasion reported that, not having the services of a maid, she ordered a hairdresser from Oxford, five miles away, for six o'clock the following morning. To her satisfaction he arrived punctually, and then worked for two hours on dressing her hair.[20] Some hairdressers went even further afield. In 1780 when Richard Cumberland (1732–1811) visited Spain to negotiate British trade deals, he took with him for the convenience of his wife and daughters 'a London hair-dresser of the name of Legge'.[21]

The performance of women's hairdressing within the private domestic space continued through into the Edwardian period. Cecil Beaton (photographer and designer, 1904–80) as a very young child remembered the special-occasion visits to his mother of a man with a brown leather bag whose heated curling tongs helped create her elaborate coiffures.[22] This was the last gasp of the tradition however, for the early decades of the twentieth century witnessed another revolution in the hair trade. Women's increasingly public lives, their new bobbed styles and the development of new technologies like the permanent-wave machine meant that very quickly the normal way for women to access professional hairdressing became through a visit to the salon. To meet this demand the number of hairdressers boomed. Unlike earlier expansions of the trade, this time the workforce was almost exclusively female, as it remains today. In twenty-first-century Britain, 88 per cent of the people working in hairdressing and barbering are women, as are 79 per cent of salon owners.[23] The emphatically feminized nature of the industry, however, hides a profound inequality: almost every one of the famous stylists – whose names sell product lines and whose influence has shaped an aesthetic – are men.[24]

Barbers

Hairdressers and servants account for only part of the trade. As Samuel Pepys noted in his diary, while he had his hair cut and combed by the members of his family and household, he also both shaved himself and used the services of a barber. Historically these professionals belonged to the guild of barber-surgeons, licensed to perform minor surgery as well as shaving, grooming and cutting hair. In practice though, individuals probably specialized in either one or the other domain well before the formal dissolution of the combined guild in 1745.[25] By Pepys's time, barbers had adapted to new trends in fashion and had ventured into the wig trade as well: he thus visited the barber for shaving and haircuts, but also bought wigs from him as well as from specialist wig-makers, and had his purchased wigs cleaned and mended by the barber too (Fig. 2.5).

Barbering at the top end of the market was a luxurious business. Sums paid to reimburse the kings' barbers for outlay on linen and such things as razors, combs and soap indicate a level of lavish indulgence. In 1636–7 Thomas Davies, barber to Charles I, was given £91 for a year's barbing linen and £60 for six month's consumables, a total sum equivalent to over £21,000 today.[26] At the bottom of the range things were very different: the barber's allowance paid to sailors in Charles I's navy was just 2d. per month.[27]

Barbers plied their trade in a range of settings. The poorest, itinerant workers serviced rural populations who were out of reach of, or unable to afford, a local barber's shop. Barbers were also associated with inns, perhaps as convenient meeting places for local clients, but also in order to cater for travellers whose coaches used inns as staging posts and depots. Pepys reports being trimmed (i.e. shaved) at the Swan and also sending for his barber to meet him there to view an ordered wig; while visiting Huntington he was shaved at the Crown, and in Bristol by 'a very handsome fellow' at the Horse Shoe in Vine Street. In addition he mentions a number of different barbershop locations around London, and also once being shaved 'in the street'.[28] One hundred years later Norfolk parson James Woodforde's diaries tell a comparable story. Woodforde shaves himself *and* goes to a barber, also using the latter for the supply and dressing of his wigs. He visits barbers locally, further afield in Norwich, and on his periodic travels to Oxford, Bath and London. On these occasions he sometimes goes to a shop, or is shaved at the inn where he is staying. For occasional barbering services Woodforde paid up front, otherwise generally by the quarter or half year in arrears, as was standard.

Like hairdressers, barbers also visited their clients in person. Pepys was frequently trimmed at home, either in the morning, at night, or during the day – he didn't seem to have a preference – and very often on a Sunday. Once the barber stayed so late that he was locked inside, and Samuel had to call up a servant to let the barber out.[29] We get a sense from this of barbers being permanently on call, expected to travel to important or remunerative clients at almost any time of the day, just like Enoch Ellor, a barber from Manchester, who in 1664 was summoned between midnight and one in the morning to the house of John Leeds to there shave a stranger.[30] The hours of work were evidently a source of long-term tension, with repeated attempts on the part of guilds, local authorities and central government to prevent Sunday barbering and enforce Sabbath closure of barbershops.[31] Even the Sunday Closing Act of 1930 designed to finally extinguish the practice made exceptions for clients attended in their homes or in a hotel.[32]

One of the reasons that enforcement proved so difficult was the popularity of the barbershop as a place of resort (Fig. 2.6). According to the memoirs of Salford barber Richard Wright Proctor (1816–81), who was apprenticed in 1826 at the age of nine, for the ordinary working man the barbershop on a Sunday provided a 'welcome haven' from the other six days of toil. There, for a time, 'they forgot their individual cares' in the 'all-engrossing' discussion and sharing of news.

> Many of these newssmongers resided at a distance of from one to two miles, yet they seldom failed to make their appearance duly as Sunday morning came. So early did they rattle at our door, in summer, that David [Proctor's master] frequently thought it useless to go to bed, and passed the interval between closing and opening in setting his razors, smoking his pipe, and conning the newspaper.[33]

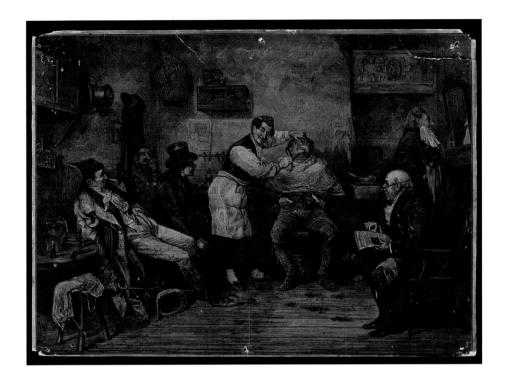

Providing not only the pleasures of grooming, barbershops were convivial gathering places full of gossip, news and entertainment. Customers might talk, read, smoke or listen to music, the latter being another long-term association with the barber's trade.[34] Through Pepys's diaries we can see these generalized observations brought to life in the particularity of individual experience, whether he was drinking ale with the barber, browsing a copy of verses belonging to another customer, or having his hair cut while listening to the barber's boy playing the violin.[35] We can also get a glimpse of the kinds of talk that might while away a shave or a haircut – gossip about the personalities and marital status of the actors of the day, or news of a mysterious illness that had left some local tradesmen mad or dead.[36]

The barbershop is usually thought of as a quintessentially masculine space. It is an identity still articulated in barbering establishments today, apparent in nearly everything from the name above the door to the pile of motoring and men's magazines on the coffee table (Fig. 2.7). While this overt masculinization is not open to debate, there is evidence it was less absolute than has been assumed.

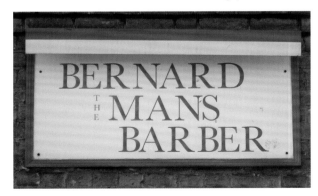

In 1786 James Woodforde visited London with his niece Nancy (1757–1830). Together they walked 'to one Smiths in Surry Street, Strand, a Barber'. Nancy 'had her Hair full dressed', and Woodforde 'was shaved and had my Wig Dressed there'. For the shaving and dressing he paid the barber 1s. 6d.[37] It is inconceivable that Woodforde, a respectable country parson, would have taken Nancy anywhere that might have compromised her standing or reputation, or have in this regard ventured outside the norms of his social position. Nancy's visit is given pictorial, albeit caricatured form, in a print published just eight years earlier (Fig. 2.8). In this a village barber whose primary client base is male (the wigs hanging from the wall are men's) is dressing the hair of a lumpish local woman. As he pins in the extravagantly excessive hair pieces, his assistant, another woman, holds a mirror so the customer can see.

FIGURE 2.8.
The Village Barber, 1778. A barber in a grotesquely large wig is dressing the hair of a woman, attaching an outsize cushion over which he will arrange hair, both hers and the hair piece she holds. A female assistant stands with a mirror and is able to hand the barber hair pins from the table and the sausage-shaped rolls for padding out coiffures. Men's wigs hang from the wall behind.

THE VILLAGE BARBER.

If women as clients in the barbershop have been overlooked by history, the third figure in this print hints at a further erasure, that of female barbers. In the seventeenth century there was a small but persistent number of such practitioners, with girls and women apprenticed to the trade, and some widows continuing a husband's business after his death (Fig. 2.9).[38] Likewise Maria Cohen, the daughter of a merchant, was apprenticed in 1702, and her case and others suggest that over the eighteenth century barbering become an increasingly respectable occupation for women (Figs 2.5 and 2.11).[39] From 1815 we have a description from personal experience, as the artist and antiquary John Thomas Smith (1766–1833) made a point of trying out a female barber. He wrote that while she shaved him her husband, a strapping Guardsman, sat smoking his pipe, indicating that this was a two-income household with the wife practising her trade in her own right.[40] Smith's tone, curious but accepting, also suggests that while women barbers were rare, they were also allowable – unusual, in other words, but not unthinkable. This is confirmed by later evidence. Mrs Crawford was a female barber in Northumberland for around sixty years. She began working as a girl, c.1876, and was still shaving customers in 1936. From around 1901, a Mrs Howe assisted her husband in shaving the inmates of the Bourne Workhouse in Lincolnshire, working with him for at least a decade (Fig. 2.10). The Norths in County Durham were another family that kept barbering as a household trade, with great-grandfather, grandfather and father, Jim North, all becoming barbers. Each of Jim's four sons and four daughters trained with their father, and all eventually started barbering on their own. The last, Cissie, closed her barbershop in 1951.[41]

All this serves to further underline the fluid and adaptable nature of hairdressing practice. Rather than being the province of just one occupation or specialized trade, it was a skill set shared by servants, tire-women, hairdressers and cutters, barbers and, to a certain extent, wig-makers as well. The divisions between these trades were permeable too, with servants training with hairdressers, and hairdressers and barbers tending hair, making and servicing wigs and extensions, and selling perfume and haircare products. The geographical location of hairdressing activity was similarly adaptable, ranging from shop and salon, to an itinerant's tent or roadside stall, to an inn or a chamber in a private home.

FIGURE 2.9.
La Belle Estvuiste (The Beautiful Groomer), second half of the seventeenth century. Translated, the text reads: 'This barberess has so many attractions, / Putting her art into practice, / This fellow, although a rustic, / Says that he would never tire of them.' Commentary and images suggesting it is pleasurable to be shaved by a female – whether because she is dextrous and gentle or for more lewd reasons – recur often.

FIGURE 2.10.
Mrs Howe, a female
barber, shaving at the
Bourne Workhouse,
Lincolnshire, 1911.

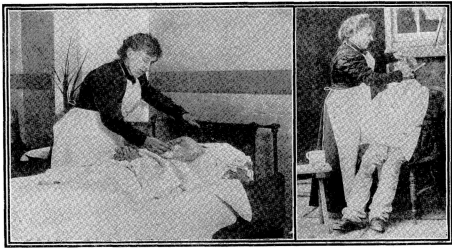

WOMAN BARBER SHAVES INMATES OF A LINCOLNSHIRE WORKHOUSE.

Owing to the illness of the hairdresser who holds the contract for shaving the inmates of the Bourne Workhouse, the work is now being done by Mrs. Howe, his
wife. Mrs Howe is no novice. She has assisted her husband off and on for ten
years, and is a most skilful shaver. Above, she is seen shaving two aged inmates.
Note the business-like way in which she holds the razor.—(*Daily Mirror* photographs.)

Once Pepys noted being shaved in his kitchen.[42] The relationship of gender to haircare
was similarly fluid. Some male servants tended the women in the household, and male
hairdressers catered for both a male and female clientele. Barbers could on occasion dress the
hair of women, and women sometimes wielded the razor to shave men. The one constant for
all these people was the process of grooming, an activity that was close, physical and intimate.
As we shall see, this intimacy had profound consequences.

The relationship

According to Benjamin Franklin (1706–90), being able to shave himself meant he was never
subjected to 'the dirty fingers or bad Breath of a slovenly Barber'.[43] His words conjure the
physical proximity and level of touch between a hairdresser and client – in Franklin's case
being unable to turn away as the barber breathed into his face, with grubby fingers stretching
and feeling around Franklin's mouth, nose and cheeks as the razor travelled the contours of
his skin. This little vignette invites us to consider the physicality of hairdressing, the way its
intimacy helped shaped attitudes towards its practitioners, and the profound consequences
of such intimacy for the relationship between client and professional.

Benjamin Franklin was far from alone in his distaste, with the same concerns appearing in contemporary letters and diaries, and being articulated in pictorial form (Fig. 2.11). The impact of the practitioner's cleanliness within hairdressing remains as pertinent today as it was in the eighteenth century, as anyone who has 'had a smelly, sweaty armpit over their face while supposedly enjoying a relaxing cleanse and condition' will know.[44] For this reason,

the national standards that framework the present-day training of hairdressers and barbers are explicit about personal hygiene: daily showers, deodorant, brushed teeth, clean and manicured hands and moisturised skin, it is made clear, are the means by which to keep away sweat, germs and halitosis.[45] However, proximity is a two-way street, and the bad breath, body odour or skin conditions of clients have also to be endured by their hairdressers.

While proximity to such bodily declarations is unpleasant, the physical nature of hairdressing is experienced in more serious ways. Occupational demands are embodied by practitioners in varicose veins, same-place cuts that are persistently re-opened, and painful skin conditions[46] – according to UK occupational health statistics, 70 per cent of hairdressers suffer from dermatitis at some point in their career.[47] Furthermore, the bodily proximity to clients reflects in the statistically significant association between hairdressing and barbering as an occupation and death from infectious disease.[48]

This corporeal nature of hairdressing, the stylist's examination and grooming of the client and their mutual awareness of each other's physicality, helps explain why historically hairdressing was a locus for advice and health interventions. (It also further underlines the sense in which looking after hair was seen as a therapeutic rather than solely cosmetic practice, as discussed in Chapter 1.) More affordable than doctors and with the added pleasures of a sociable atmosphere, early modern barbers were the first stop for the hygiene demands of teeth, nails, ears and skin, and, it has been suggested, for sexual advice.[49] Whether or not there is an unbroken historical continuity in this it is hard to tell. Certainly the identification of infections and diseases of the skin and hair, and referral of clients to relevant medical specialists, now forms a standard part of the hairdressers' training curriculum.[50] And in the twentieth century before condoms became widely available, the barber's role in supplying 'something for the weekend' was legendary.[51] The early modern position of the barbershop as quasi-health centre is also mirrored by recent public health programmes in both the United States and UK. These have used barbershops and hair salons as trusted venues from which to access a selected demographic, both to disseminate health information and launch interventions in such areas as cancer, cardiovascular disease and HIV illness (Fig. 2.12). In some cases, barbers have been trained as health advocates.[52]

Such programmes are grounded in the trust that exists between a hairdresser and client. On the one hand this trust is exercised every time we put our physical appearance in

FIGURE 2.12.
HIV/AIDS awareness poster in a barbershop in Hyderabad, India.

another's hands. At a more basic level, it allows a client to be confident, despite the scissors cutting near their eyes or the open razor passing over their throat (Fig. 2.13). It is only when something goes wrong that the vulnerability of the person in the chair is revealed. For example, the renowned fashion partnership between Vidal Sassoon and Mary Quant began when Sassoon cut more than her hair (Fig. 2.14): 'I was dancing around the chair as was my custom, scissors in one hand, comb in the other, when I inadvertently nipped her ear with the scissors. Blood started to flow.'[53] A recent description of the hairdressing trade written by another celebrity stylist explains:

FIGURE 2.13.
A traditional wet shave with an open razor.

FIGURE 2.14.
Fashion luminaries: Vidal Sassoon cutting Mary Quant's hair, 1960s.

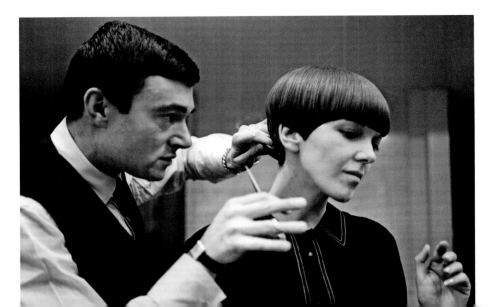

You see, for some bizarre medical reason, if you cut someone's ear, and I don't know why, maybe it's because it's made up of tissue and not muscle, or perhaps all bloody eight pints are stored there, it never, ever seems to stop bleeding.

Having himself cut someone's ear, he describes the blood-soaked plasters, the wadding of tissues and the client's spattered shirt. 'It is like Lady Macbeth', he says.[54] More seriously, Paul Bremmer, the diplomat who led the provisional government of Iraq following the US invasion in 2003, was assessed by US security as being the most threatened American official anywhere in the world. A threat taken particularly seriously was the suggestion that an Iraqi barber had been hired to kill him when he got a haircut.[55] Given the reality of a client's vulnerability, the only wonder is that the cultural imaginary does not team with scissor-wielding maniacs, and that the murderous Sweeney Todd brandishes his cut-throat razor alone (Fig. 2.15).[56]

Instead, the trust and intimacy of hairdressing has been more often associated with a lowering of the normal barriers of reserve. This is nicely illuminated by the early twentieth-century diaries of society matron Lady Cynthia Asquith (1887–1960; Fig. 2.16), who in them refers to intimate talking sessions with women friends as 'hair-combing'. They talked secrets, feelings, gossip and sometimes sex: 'We ended up with a fairly obscene hair-combing arising from discussion of Dr Stopes' *Married Love*, a book Diana is quite missionary about. Didn't go to bed until past two.'[57] Asquith's name for these sessions neatly conjures the emotional quality that often accompanies the tending of hair. It is a physically close and soothing activity in which rhythms and touch encourage relaxation, and the temporarily exclusive and trusting relationship between client and stylist lowers normal barriers of reserve. This intimacy leads many clients to confide in their hairdressers, disclosing information and conversing in a way that is unusual in a business relationship.[58] As Vidal Sassoon claimed: 'I've cut the hair and listened to the secrets of some of the most beautiful women in the world.' In the simple words of another stylist, 'clients tell their hairdressers everything'.[59] For some clients the hairdressing service includes not only being listened to, but advised. A subject interviewed within a project investigating intimacy in service relationships explained it as: 'kind of like a feedback, about your problems and say "well why don't you do this?" They are like an advice thing while they are doing your hair.'[60] In these cases the hairdresser may see him or herself as therapist, counsellor or life coach. It is little

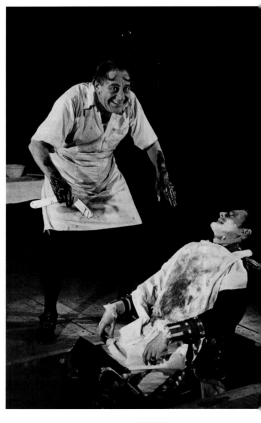

FIGURE 2.15.
Fictional barber Sweeney Todd, a creation of the nineteenth century. He killed his clients, tipping their bodies into the cellar with his rigged barber's chair, where they were disposed of in meat pies.

wonder therefore that established clients exhibit high levels of loyalty to their chosen stylist.[61]

The paradigm of hairdresser or barber as confidant or collector of secrets is very old, but so too is their character as a garrulous gossip. They may be seen as a vessel for secrets, but invariably the vessel proves a leaky one. Here's a joke:

> A man goes to get his hair cut by a talkative barber.
> 'How would you like your hair done?' asks the barber.
> 'In silence,' replies the man.[62]

The joke is a Roman one. And here it is repeated nearly 1,500 years later, around 1825:

> The two *Barbers* I have mentioned, invariably put the general question of, how will you have your hair cut? I would recommend gentlemen to answer – *without saying a word* – this will at least preserve their *ears* from annoyance.[63]

FIGURE 2.16.
Lady Cynthia Asquith, 1912.

Likewise, the hairdresser's reputation as a gossip is as old as the profession. In 1787, for instance, the writer Elizabeth Steele complained that

> This kind of gentry [hairdressers], having access to the ladies, frequently hear things in one house, which they carry to another. Ladies are too apt to converse with these fellows, and ask questions; and, for every piece of intelligence they communicate, they are rewarded with news in return; so, that many women are as much diverted with their slander, as embellished by their art.[64]

Such a characterization may be stereotypical, but it is one with which hairdressers may self-identify. Uncannily echoing Elizabeth Steele, a twenty-first-century stylist has written, 'most hairdressers are extremely nosy and more than a little gossipy'. He continues: 'Every funny tale, every amusing ditty, every uncovered indiscretion, every deep-rooted insecurity you've confided is probably recounted to their colleagues in the staff room while their chair is still warm from your visit'[65] (Fig. 2.17).

At times, private gossip merges with public affairs. In such instances we see hairdressing as a site for the voicing of political and religious opinion. This is illustrated in the print 'Intelligence on the Change of Ministry', where we see the eager talk generated by the news being read out by one of the barber's waiting clients (Fig. 2.18). Sometimes such comment could be construed as a threat to authority and order, and thus we find an unexpected window onto this social space of the barbershop provided by official records of seditious talk. Thus in 1710 we have the deposition of Edward Griffin, barber of Holborn, who gave evidence that while shaving a customer in his shop, a local pastry cook came in to be likewise shaved. And 'there passed some discourse' between Griffith's client and the pastry cook relating to Dr Sacheverell (bap. 1674–1724), a controversial clergyman whose fiery preaching against

FIGURE 2.17.
Gossiping at the salon, New York, 1949.

FIGURE 2.18.

Intelligence on the Change of the Ministry, c.1782. Here the barbershop is a venue for ordinary people to discuss political news, hot off the press. As the text beneath the image explains, Snip the tailor has just come in bearing the paper with its news of a political resignation. The barber, more interested in the talk than in shaving, slices the face of the customer in the chair, who vows never to come back.

Catholics and non-conformists led to his trial before Parliament for sedition and incitement to violence. It was this conversation that led Griffin to inform the authorities, reporting the pastry cook's support of Sacheverell and opposition to the royal family.[66]

While the barbershop was a public space in which to air opinion, by tending to clients in their homes barbers and hairdressers might be witness to private news or happenings (Fig. 2.19). Enoch Ellor, the Manchester barber called out after midnight mentioned above, alerted the authorities that twenty people had been gathered at the house where he was summoned, relayed as many names as he knew, and recounted what he could remember of their suspicious talk. He described the daggers in their pockets and what seemed to be hand grenades lying on the table. There was also a bag on the table, and when Ellor put his hand on it, was warned to take care. He was not told what was in the bag, but the barber observed it to be soft and white like powder, and when he held his candle closer to inspect it, was again told to be careful.[67]

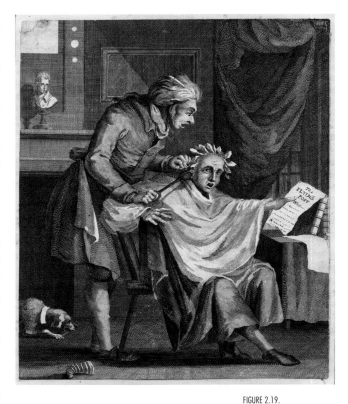

FIGURE 2.19.
The Barber Politician, c.1771. Distracted by reading the client's newspaper, by mistake a barber on a home visit applies his heated curling irons to the man's ear. The paper, The Flying Post, was a strongly partisan Whig publication. In the foreground, in front of the hairdresser's foot, is a bellows used for puffing hair powder.

Lest we think that the overlap between hairdressing, politicized gossip and the edginess of authority was found only in early modernity, consider the much more recent case from the FBI files. In June 1951 Mrs Baxter, an FBI employee, visited a salon. In the course of conversation, the hairdresser and the beautician began gossiping about the FBI director, J. Edgar Hoover – 'that S–O–B', they called him. They said it was common knowledge that he took bribes, and they had also heard Hoover 'was a sissy, liked men, and was "queer"'. Mrs Baxter reprimanded them, saying that such talk was untrue and it played into the hands of the Communists. She then left, and informed on them. Two FBI agents were duly despatched to the salon to question, confront and bully the 'gossiping rumormongers', leaving them in no doubt that such statements 'would not be countenanced'.[68] This glimpse of the political paranoia of the McCarthy era is also a striking insight into the continuity of talk in the spaces devoted to the grooming and tending of hair.

The intimacy and conviviality of tending hair has lead, therefore, to the identification of barbers and hairdressers as the insecure repository of spilt secrets. They are seen as behaving with a kind of social promiscuity. The physical and emotional closeness of tending hair leads also, however, to a more explicit sexualization. Hair is sensuous; touching the face, head and neck creates a frisson. Quite simply, hairdressing can have sexual overtones. For Samuel Pepys (Fig. 3.4) this was certainly the case, and his diary records the pleasures he received, and took, when the maid servant combed his hair. Initially these seem to have been sensuous encounters in which Pepys, sometimes for up to an hour, enjoyed only the physical gratification of grooming.[69] Gradually his passive enjoyment became more actively sexual and his prose became more secretive, as he hedged his meaning in the private code reserved for his erotic experiences: 'and all the while Deb did comb my hair I did tocar her with my mano para mi great pleasure [I did touch her with my hand for my great pleasure]'.[70] Finally Elizabeth catches him at it:

> and after supper, to have my head combed by Deb, which occasioned the greatest sorrow to me that ever I knew in this world; for my wife, coming up suddenly, did find me imbracing the girl con my hand sub su coats [with my hand under her petticoats]; and endeed, I was with my main [my hand] in her cuny.[71]

For eighteenth-century servant John Macdonald, mentioned above, hairdressing became the locus for either real, or imputed, sexual activity, particularly because tending their hair gave him privileged access to women in their private chambers – a demonstration of what Don Herzog has called 'the tense economies of anonymity, body space, and sexuality'.[72] Because of this, some at the time felt that 'Ladies are certainly injudicious in employing so many *male* friseurs about their persons. The custom is indelicate'.[73] A similar idea is captured in a number of contemporary prints. In 'A Hint to [the] Husbands, or, The Dresser, properly Dressed' from 1776 (Fig. 2.20), the older husband bursts in on his wife while she is having her elaborate hair arranged. The wronged spouse raises his whip to the hairdresser, a young man in an exaggerated Macaroni-style wig. Behind the husband, an amused maid raises her fingers to form cuckold's horns, while on the wall at the back hangs a portrait in which the female sitter is slipping her hand through the placket of her skirts, reaching for her genitals. The wife, in undress, holds in her hand a long, and probably phallic, hairpin. The inference is clear. This characterization of the libidinous hairdresser is one that that remains a familiar part of the profession today: 'What better job for any young, healthy male with a voracious appetite for totty than to get intimate with twelve women a day? It's definitely one of the major advantages of choosing hairdressing as a career.'[74]

It is interesting that barbers stand here as non-participants. Despite their role as purveyors of condoms or advice and their intimate physical engagement with their clients, they themselves remain asexual. Barbers also preside over a nexus that is markedly (though

FIGURE 2.20.
*A Hint to [the]
Husbands, or, The
Dresser, properly
Dressed, 1777.*

A Hint to ÿ Huſbands, or the Dreſſer, properly Dreſſed.

London, Printed for R. Sayer & J. Bennett, Nᵒ 53 Fleet Street, as the Act directs 14 Augᵗ 1777.

not exclusively) homosocial, but not homosexual. By contrast, the figure of the male hairdresser has a different trajectory. He is, as we have seen, constructed as sexually active – a potential or actual threat to a woman's virtue and her husband's conjugal honour. He is also, however, perceived as effeminate, an ineffectual male (Fig. 2.21). This different cultural treatment of the hairdresser and barber stands despite the permeability of their trades, and the fact that to a marked degree they share the same skill set. No doubt the conjoined emasculation and sexualization of the hairdresser owes itself to the degree to which he deals with a female clientele, his pretensions to a social status higher than the barber's, and his overt engagement with fashion, both in his self-presentation and in the creation of modish hair styles for his clients.

The two opposing ideas about the hairdresser – effeminate and womanizing, heterosexually active and homosexual – have frequently been held simultaneously. Thus writer Mary Hays (1759–1843), in her argument for women's rights from the close of the eighteenth century, wondered that women of the higher ranks who might be supposed

FIGURE 2.21.
Monsieur le Frizuer,
1771. This image
presents a French,
or Frenchified,
hairdresser. In his
hand he grasps some
curling irons, and from
his pocket descends
a hair piece. His
finicking presentation
– patches, rapier,
patterned breeches,
striped stockings
and a large clubbed
wig – all speak to his
effeminacy.

MON.^R LE FRIZUER.

to have more delicacy, should 'admit without scruple – men hair-dressers'. Yet at the same time, she labels such hairdressers as 'she-he gentry'.[75] This simultaneous promulgation of the homosexual characterization, and its vehement denial in the form of heterosexual promiscuity, has continued unabated. Hairdresser Raymond (1911–92), whose television appearances and mannered self-presentation made him a celebrity in the 1950s, deliberately cultivated a camp persona. Known as Mr Teasy-Weasy (after his trademark styling of 'teasy-weasy' curls), he looked 'incredibly *soigné*', with tailored suits, silk handkerchiefs, faux French accent and long cigarettes (Fig. 2.22). Yet he had 'an infamous way with women'. He was 'the original "Italian stallion" and the ladies queued for him to attend them'.[76] Likewise, Vidal Sassoon talked of the ambivalent sexualization within his own salon in similar terms. Holding a staff meeting once to address the 'overactive libidos' of his stylists, he suggested that it was not ethical to seduce a married client. To which one of them replied: 'Nobody cares.

FIGURE 2.22.
(Facing page)
Raymond Bessone, Mr
Teasy-Weasy, in 1954.

They think we're all homosexuals anyway.[77] And then there's the very term 'crimper'. Used self-referentially by stylists regardless of their sexuality, it originates in Polari, the gay male language of the twentieth century.[78] From this specialist lexicon 'crimper' has colonized the salon, and its overtones of effeminacy have been incorporated, either with or without irony, into the professional personae of many of its referents.

From the smells and germs of unwanted proximity, to the sensuous pleasures of grooming and the social pleasures of conversation, the experiences afforded by haircare have proved historically durable. There is a longevity to hairdresser and barber stereotypes that sees barbers positioned as the no-frills 'manly' hair professional and the male hairdresser as the effete and sexualized one. In tandem with this runs a corresponding continuity in the client–stylist relationship and, above all, an overwhelming persistence in the intimacy of tending hair.

BEGIN EARLY   SHAVE YOURSELF

Gillette Safety Razor
NO STROPPING NO HONING

Chapter 3

The art of being hairless

Non-consensual acts

The first act of the Victorian penal system was to examine the bodies of the newly convicted and then crop their hair. The coerced removal dramatically stamped the prisoner as the property of the prison and fundamentally undermined his or her autonomous sense of self, violently rewriting a new identity. A flex in the muscle of institutional power, this gratuitous barbering was bitterly resented, especially by the female prisoners. 'Oh yes,' said a warder at Millbank to the nineteenth-century journalist and social reformer Henry Mayhew, 'they'd sooner lose their lives than their hair!'[1]

Enforced hair loss is deeply traumatic, and is experienced as an assault on the self that fractures an individual's identity. Its use as an instrument of humiliation and control has thus been common. The most systematically inhuman instance was in the Nazi concentration camps, where on a vast scale prisoners' hair was not only shorn from their heads, but was then sold into the textile and furnishing industries for thread, rope, felt and stuffing. Auschwitz houses nearly two tons of it still, a portion of that found when the Russians liberated the camp in 1945 (Fig. 3.1).[2] A survivor wrote of the experience:

> The haircut has a startling effect on every woman's appearance. Individuals become a mass of bodies. Height, stoutness, or slimness: there is no distinguishing factor – it is the absence of hair which transformed individual women into like bodies. Age and other personal differences melt away. Facial expressions disappear. Instead a blank, senseless stare emerges on a thousand faces of one naked, unappealing body. In a matter of minutes

FIGURE 3.1.
Tons of hair still remains at Auschwitz, shorn from the murdered victims of the gas chambers.

even the physical aspect of our numbers seems reduced – there is less of a substance to our dimensions. We become a monolithic mass. Inconsequential.[3]

Closer to home and closer in time, from 1922 until 1996 the Catholic Church in Ireland operated Magdalene Laundries. These were institutions that received girls and women sent by the courts, by government services or by their families, and in which they were imprisoned and forced to work unpaid, sometimes for years. One of the physical and psychological abuses perpetrated at the Laundries was the cutting of victims' hair.[4] Again and again survivor testimonies recall this. The violent assimilation to the identity of Magdalene inmate was experienced not only as a reception ritual, but was used throughout the term of imprisonment to punish, the scissors wielded in what can only be described as sadism on the part of those through whom the institutional power was enacted. Mary Merritt was kept in a Magdalene Laundry in Dublin working unpaid for fourteen years. Once she escaped. Returned by the police, the nuns put her in a windowless punishment cell and 'cut my hair to the bone'.[5]

The cutting of Mary's hair – and the hair of numberless other men and women in positions of vulnerability – was entirely gratuitous, its only purpose being to punish and control, to shame and disempower. Its effectiveness in achieving these ends is a direct correlation of hair's importance. Sociologist Anthony Synnott has written that hair is 'a powerful symbol of the self'.[6] It is, however, much more than that. It does not just stand for the self; hair is *part* of the self, and although it regrows when cut, its loss is traumatic. Like any other facial feature, head hair is a fundamental part of how we *personally* look, and of who we feel ourselves to be. No wonder its loss and removal against our volition can trigger profound distress and a dramatic dislocation of identity. Note that hair removal that is consensual is frequently practised as a discipline in institutions to which new members are incorporated with especially strong ties – the tonsure of the religious for instance, or the buzz cut of the US Marines (Fig. 3.2). Simultaneously severing strands of hair and previous attachments, a novitiate's past identity is cut away and in its place is fostered submission, homogeneity and obedience to the dominant values.

When this form of subjugation is practised against women, there are

FIGURE 3.2.
One Marine giving a haircut to another in the troop barbershop on the USS Bataan, 2009.

often sexual overtones, some even terming such acts as a substitute for rape.[7] Certainly, hair is highly sexualized and is deeply involved in understandings of gender, most especially – in the length and abundance of head hair – with the dominant paradigm of femininity. The non-consensual loss of hair is nevertheless still experienced negatively by men, including in physiological contexts where its disappearance is both gradual and natural. One review in the *British Medical Journal* has found that androgenetic alopecia, or male-pattern baldness, is for most men an 'unwanted and stressful event', diminishing the sufferer's satisfaction with his body image and being associated by him with both aging and lowered levels of physical and sexual attractiveness. The author suggests that any medical interventions should be complemented by measures to enhance self-esteem.[8] The existence of hand-written and early printed recipes for alopecia treatments dating back hundreds of years (see Chapter 1) suggests that our society has a long history of experiencing even expected processes of hair loss as traumatic. Despite male-pattern baldness being the genetic inheritance of significant numbers of men (of four times greater likelihood in white men than black, experienced by fifty per cent of Caucasian males by the age of fifty),[9] it is a natural process that ironically seems to usher in an unnatural, or less authentic, self. As an event, or a series of tiny multiple events, the unwilling shedding of hair thus demands an individual readjust his or her identity.

Such a challenge is faced in a different way by those in ill health – that state of departure from the 'real' us – the effects of which can sometimes be seen in the thinning and lankness of hair. For those with cancer, it is ironically the treatment that does the harm. In chemotherapy, the body's processes are hijacked by chemicals that are toxic not only to cancers but to all rapidly dividing cells, including hair follicles (Fig. 3.3). The resulting loss, where hair can come out in handfuls or lie shed on the pillow in the morning, is reported by many to be

FIGURE 3.3.
Young woman receiving chemotherapy.

as difficult to come to terms with as the surgical operations that have cut away other of the body's parts. When faced with this inevitability, many act pre-emptively, wresting a brief victory by getting in first. As one woman wrote, 'I had my head shaved at the salon after I'd learned that the first chemo would cause it to fall out by the fistfuls.'[10] Another, finding clumps of her hair had fallen overnight, 'went downstairs with a can of shaving foam, sat on a stool, and asked her husband to shave her head'.[11]

But most consensual hair removal is of a less dramatic nature. Behind the closed door of the bathroom, in the barber's chair or the treatment rooms of a beauty salon, regular practices of grooming maintain self-image rather than abruptly realign it. Depilation in these cases involves a complex negotiation between personal preference, social norms and material conditions, although the outcome of such negotiations seems so 'natural' it is rarely examined. In the rest of the chapter we will turn to the history of this removal of face and body hair, looking first at men and then women.

Smooth men

On 17 September 1666, Samuel Pepys (Fig. 3.4) recorded what seems to have been relief at being able to get rid of his stubble: 'Up betimes, and shaved myself after a week's growth; but Lord how ugly I was yesterday and how fine today.'[12] Pepys's simple diary mention reminds us of the significance of shaving, both as an occurrence that makes a difference to

FIGURE 3.4.
Samuel Pepys, 1666.

an individual, and also in its cumulative importance, whereby it contributes to the normative understandings of how a man ought to look and behave. In contrast to the sixteenth and earlier seventeenth century, when beards were the accepted sign of mature masculinity, by the time Pepys was writing in the 1660s, to have a cleanly shaven chin was the manly norm.[13] This clean-shaven look has proved a persistent ideal, interrupted only by those Victorian years from the mid-nineteenth century, in which facial hair was such a striking presence. For most of the last three hundred years therefore, to quote scholar Dene October, the 'repetition of the shaving ritual makes it an important site for the cultural production of masculinity'.[14]

Although removing facial hair has been such a significant part of the masculine appearance, historically the difficulties surrounding this practice have meant that it presented an ongoing and never fully resolvable problem. To start with Pepys, we thus find mention in his diary of the trouble he found in dealing with his stubble. Initially he used the services of a barber, but then in May 1662 began to use a pumice stone to scour off his whiskers. This he found 'very easy, speedy and cleanly', an assessment that suggests he was making a comparative judgement and that his experiences of barbering were at times difficult, slow and messy. He resolved to continue to pumice.[15] This method of depilation by abrasion is an ancient one, used by the Greeks and Romans and still recommended by the 1956 edition of *Pharmaceutical Formulas*, the then-standard professional handbook for chemists and druggists.[16] A description of the technique comes from a nineteenth-century manual on hair removal, written by a surgeon and skin specialist, who advises oiling the skin first to soften it, then, using small pieces of pumice, stretching the skin slightly and with 'a light hand' working in a to-and-fro movement against the direction of the hairs' growth. He warns, though, that care should be taken to stop as soon as the hairs have been ground short enough, and that on the delicate skin around the mouth, pumice 'is apt to cause rawness'.[17]

Pepys did not have a manual from which to learn; instead, he was taught to use pumice on his facial hair by an older acquaintance, Mr Marsh, Storekeeper of the Ordnance, with whom he was in contact in a professional capacity. Naval administrator Pepys was in Portsmouth on Admiralty business when Marsh showed him what to do: it seems likely that Pepys was looking for a barber, or they were chatting about the difficulties of getting a good shave. That Pepys was impressed with the pumice method is clear, and he must have resolved to try it himself. He was so struck with the ease and speed of self-pumicing that on impulse he cut off his moustache, 'only that I may with my pumice-stone do my whole face, as I now do my chin, and so save time – which I find a very easy way and gentile'.[18] Despite such good beginnings, the pumice turned out not to be the answer after all. Perhaps he used the stone too heavily, or found that it did indeed aggravate the sensitive skin around his mouth as the nineteenth-century manual warned it might. For whatever reason, after four months Pepys was again getting himself shaved, though he seems to have been happy to pumice 'where I cannot conveniently have a barber'.[19]

Sixteen months later however, in January 1664, Pepys experimented again. This time he stopped using a barber and instead began to shave himself. 'This morning I begun a practice which I find, by the ease I do it with, that I shall continue, it saving me money and time – that is, to Trimme myself with a Razer – which pleases me mightily.'[20] Pepys described the advantages of his new method of depilation with the same ideas of ease, convenience and time, and with the added consideration of cost. However, the drawbacks quickly became apparent, and within days he wrote that he had twice cut himself, which he blamed on the bluntness of the razor.[21] This reminds us that shaving required a set of additional skills and further equipment. First the razor needed to be kept sharp, both by regularly using a strop (a strip of leather against which the razor was smoothed to sharpen its edge) and occasionally having its edge honed or reground.[22] It also needed soap, a shaving brush, linen (that in turn needed to be regularly laundered), a mirror and hot water. Hot water meant that, summer and winter, the water not only had to be fetched, but that it was necessary to build, light and tend a fire to heat it. Shaving was a practice, then, in which equipment needed to be actively maintained and the supporting material resources replenished. Less than two years later Pepys was back to regularly using a barber.

James Woodforde (1740–1803), a country parson whose diaries were written during the second half of the eighteenth century, like Pepys both shaved himself and used the services of a professional. He noted buying new razors and the purchase of items like soap, shaving brushes and shaving powder, and a hone (a whetstone used for sharpening). Although from time to time he recorded having his old razors sharpened and reset by a razor grinder or cutler, in between he used a strop. In a memorandum diary entry of March 1769 – a note to self – he wrote: 'as I was going to shave myself this morning as usual on Sundays, my Razor broke in my Hand as I was setting it on the Strap without any violence'. He added, and this is the point of the memorandum, 'May it be always a warning to me not to shave on the Lord's Day or do any other work to profane it pro futuro [for the future].'[23] Here Woodforde was referring to the enduring prohibition on Sunday shaving, subject of repeated civic, guild and parish regulations, though probably more honoured in the breach than the observance. As a clergyman, it is not surprising that he felt he ought to be dutiful in this regard. For our purposes, the significant aspect of the prohibition and Woodforde's uneasy conscience is that shaving was indeed considered work: it required time and effort. Grooming the male body was labour.

The sense that we get of Pepys and Woodforde making the best of an inconvenient chore is echoed in comments made by writer and cleric Jonathan Swift (1667–1745; Fig. 3.5) in the 1710s. On what he called his 'shaving days', Swift repeatedly made reference to how much time this activity demanded and that he had to consciously build it into his morning schedule or risk missing later appointments.[24] Also like Pepys he was familiar with the problem of a poor cutting edge. 'The Razors will be a great Treasure to me', he wrote in acknowledgement to his friend Charles Ford. He added that, 'for want of good ones I pass one hour in eight and fourty [*sic*] very miserably'.[25] This simple comment suggests a number of things. First, it shows his shaving days to have been alternate; second, it indicates the sort of time the task consumed; third, it reinforces the point that male grooming could be incorporated into the pattern of friendships, with the exchange of objects, advice and anecdote. Similarly, James Woodforde also participated in an informal exchange economy with his peers when a student at Oxford University. On one occasion he swapped the lace from his hat for 'a very neat Razor'.[26]

FIGURE 3.5.
Jonathan Swift,
1709–10.

At this point it is helpful to consider the razor as an object. The better blades produced in Woodforde's time led, Alun Withey has suggested, to a rise in self-shaving. It is an increase that we can see reflected in the development of new forms of furniture in the mid-to-late eighteenth century, shaving tables and dressing stands that feature adjustable mirrors and insets for a basin or bowl.[27] Withey further proposes that in the second half of the eighteenth century, razors were explicitly linked to masculinity through discourses of technological advance, and that newly crafted blades became aesthetically desirable to men as personal belongings. The example in Figure 3.6 is a fine illustration of this. With steel blades and ivory handles, the seven matching razors fit in their specially crafted box. The blades all bear the maker's name and place of manufacture (Samuel Last, London), and each is also engraved on the edge with a different day of the week. As a Victorian commentator in *The Englishman's Magazine* put it, 'A razor is surely the emblem of manhood.'[28] This is an enduring sentiment, which after the advent of safety and electric razors has only developed nuance. In *Have His Carcase* (1932), a Lord Peter Wimsey detective story by Dorothy Sayers, the cut-throat razor – the murder weapon – signifies a world of elite and traditional masculinity. The way

FIGURE 3.6.
A set of seven matching razors, nineteenth century.

the blade is treated, furthermore, indicates individual character, and there is a sense that the arcane mysteries of barbering are open only to true gentlemen: by their razors shall ye know them. More recently, the renaissance of the traditional close shave has garnered a different appeal, to a younger, fashion-conscious metrosexual masculinity (Fig. 3.7).

But to return to the eighteenth century, as well as being masculine, shaving was a 'polite' practice: it 'was socially, culturally and fashionably imperative'.[29] It is clear that for all three of our diary writers, being groomed was a significant part of their self-presentation, a pre-condition for social readiness. To take Woodforde's case first, although he made only infrequent mentions of actually shaving himself, it is telling that he specifically noted doing so before the bishop's visitations and when preaching in Oxford before the Vice Chancellor. Reading these entries, one has the feeling that he was consciously preparing and putting his best ecclesiastical foot forward. Likewise, he noted shaving before a day's outing to see the royal family.[30] Conversely, if unshaven in the company of visitors Woodforde felt ill-kempt and ill at ease. If these visitors included the Squire's wife, Woodforde refused the social interaction altogether: 'Mrs. Custance with 3. of her children and Mrs. Collier called here this morning & stayed some time – The Captain [Woodforde's nephew] and self purposely took a walk out of the way, not being shaved or properly dressed.'[31]

FIGURE 3.7.
The new desirability of the traditional shave: straight razor, shaving bowl and badger brush on a wet slate.

If obliged by circumstances to miss being shaved, Pepys and Swift felt similarly uncomfortable and inadequate. 'Mr. secretary St. John sent for me this morning so early that I was forced to go without shaving', complained Swift, 'which put me quite out of method: I called at Mr. Ford's, and desired him to lend me a shaving, and so made shift to get into order again.'[32] For Pepys, a morning spent working from home was an opportunity to avoid the bother of shaving and instead settle straight to business. However, he found that without being properly groomed he felt unfocused and unprepared; his professional persona eluded him. In his words:

Up betimes, and down to chamber, without trimming [shaving] myself or putting on clean linen, thinking only to keep to my chamber to do business today; but when I came there, I find that without being shaved I am not fully awake nor ready to settle to business, and so was fain to go up again and dress myself; which I did, and so down to my chamber and fell roundly to business.[33]

Despite the social significance of being groomed, however, daily shaving was rare. As we have seen, it was a bodily discipline that required an investment of time and resources, and also fortitude in the face of discomfort and wounds. Pepys, Swift and Woodforde all shaved two to three times per week, and despite the ample eighteenth-century portrait evidence depicting full wigs and smooth chins, in reality stubble must have been a common sight.

The alternative to self-shaving was to use the services of a professional barber, the most common option at the time. Domestic and professional shaving were not mutually exclusive however, and a man might combine these grooming practices as Pepys did. For James Woodforde the decision of whether to shave himself or use a barber seems to have been based on geography. When living in Oxford, or in his Somerset home of Ansford, Woodforde was tended by a barber. When he moved to his Norfolk parish of Weston Longville he took up the razor himself, although he continued to use a barber when away from home, particularly on his regular overnight visits to nearby Norwich. It seems likely therefore that Weston was too small to sport a resident barber. If a gentleman could pay for it he could buy the convenience of a home visit (see Chapter 2). If this were the case, it is probable that the client supplied the shaving equipment, including the razor, taking responsibility also for keeping the edge honed. Throughout the years during which Woodforde was being visited by a barber, his diaries record purchases of a full range of shaving equipment.

As with self-shaving though, professional barbering was not a daily experience. Woodforde entered into contracts with his barbers to visit him at first twice, and then three times a week. For a labourer or working man a weekly trip to the barbershop would be more likely, and we therefore need to note that class difference, apparent in so many ways, was also embodied in a man's stubble. Casual single shaves could of course also be bought, and as was discussed in the previous chapter it was also common to find barbers attached to inns. Although portable cases of grooming equipment were available – indeed, in remaining fundamentally unchanged from at least the seventeenth to the nineteenth century they reflected a long continuity in shaving practices[34] – it is easy to envisage that when travelling, a man needing linen, hot water, mirror, razor, soap and shaving brush might well prefer the convenience of a resident barber.

A surprising amount of what was felt by Pepys, Swift and Woodforde in early modernity is also articulated by much later sources. The nature of shaving as a time-consuming, difficult chore as likely to produce discomfort as a smooth chin appears frequently. Although often it is implicit – as in advertising claims that promise the ease, speed and comfort of shaving products, a strategy as commonly used in the nineteenth century as in the twentieth and twenty-first – there are also many occasions when such experiences are described overtly. Two (admittedly pro-beard) Victorian tracts dwell on this point. *Why Shave?* describes a man's chore of 'daily scraping', which does suggest that the frequency of self-shaving had increased since the eighteenth century. However, the anonymous author goes on to declare that if the razor is dull, the soap unsatisfactory and the water not boiling, it is a 'misery'.[35] That it is also labour-intensive toil is emphasized by *Shaving: A Breach of the Sabbath* (1860): 'Is not shaving work? The softening of the hair with soap and water, the process of sharpening the razor on the strop, and the actual employment of it on the skin, do they not constitute altogether an operation of work? . . . and to some among us it is work of a very painful and trying nature.'[36]

Although clearly partisan, with a pro-beard agenda, it seems likely that these two tracts were exaggerating little if at all, for it is corroborated by a report from the Mass Observation Archives produced on the eve of the Second World War. Although for many of the interviewed men shaving was a daily routine accomplished with relative ease and speed (around fifteen minutes), even following the advent of the safety razor, modern soaps and running hot water, some still found it vexing and unpleasant. For a secretary aged twenty-nine, 'all the time taken up in shaving seems such a waste of valuable time. Shaving is one of the things I hate about the daily routine.' A twenty-five-year-old commercial traveller admitted that 'Shaving is an aversion of mine, I have tender skin and however carefully I shave, I always get a sore face.' The report states that of those men under thirty who were interviewed, half shaved daily and 27 per cent every other day; for men over thirty the proportion of daily shavers rose to 75 per cent, with 12 per cent wielding a razor on alternate days. The remainder of the sample had no consistent routine. Thus, assuming the sample to be representative, in 1939 a sizeable number of men were, like Swift, putting off shaving for another day. Although conditions and equipment had improved considerably and the task was more likely to take a quarter of the time, shaving could still be experienced as a 'boring and arduous business'.[37]

It was also still a skill that needed to be learnt and a practice that could tie men into networks of family and friendship: in the Mass Observation survey, one man was using a razor that had belonged to his father; another had been given one by the father of his girlfriend. And, as with any skill, some achieved it to a higher degree than others: 'Shaving I detest because I'm no good at it', explained a respondent who cut himself frequently.[38] Perhaps most noticeable of all, however, is the consistency with which shaving is articulated as a social necessity, something that has to be done before a man is properly groomed and fit for society. Pepys, Swift and Woodforde in the seventeenth and eighteenth century were all explicit on this point; so too were their counterparts in 1939. In words that repeat their early modern predecessors almost verbatim, they talked of their sense of discomfort if inadequately shaved, their unpreparedness for the demands of the day, and even that it gave some 'an inferiority complex'. There was widespread agreement that women in particular disliked an unshaven look – 'they always describe the offending male as "horrid" or "beastly"' – and as with Parson Woodforde, who in his stubble avoided being seen by the squire's wife, there was a feeling that a man was only fit for polite, female company after having wielded a razor.[39]

One difference between modern and early modern experiences, however, concerns perceptions of cleanliness. According to Dene October, late nineteenth- and early twentieth-century hygiene movements, given impetus by the development of germ theory, saw facial hair as a dangerous, lurking home for microbes. This is borne out by the large number of Mass Observation respondents who described sensations of looking and feeling dirty when unshaved. A further development that ought to be noted concerns the corporeal geography of depilation, or of what hair is taken off where. Pepys, Swift and Woodforde, we need to remember, all shaved (or had shaved for them) their head as well as their facial hair. Like most men of their time they wore wigs, whose fit and comfort was achieved by a cropped scalp. To take another example, in the early years of the twenty-first century there was a marked vogue for all over depilation.[40] Influenced perhaps by longer-term trends amongst gay men, in the wider male population the zones of hair removal also expanded, to encompass for some the groin, chest, abdomen and back (Fig. 3.8). As is no surprise given the rapidity and plurality of contemporary fashions, the waxing (pun intended) and waning of this trend occurred relatively quickly. Another common variant of 'manscaping' has been the cropping of head and facial hair to the same length. Placed in conjunction with the shaved heads of the eighteenth century, these more recent developments remind us that the terrain of what is to be plucked, pulled, cut and cropped can shift its boundaries, and that masculinity can be emphatically glabrous.

FIGURE 3.8.
Increasing the zones of male depilation: waxing a man's hairy back.

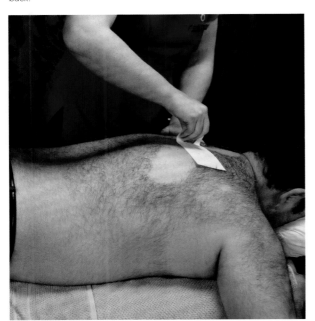

A closer shave?

Much in the shaving experience demonstrates a marked continuity over the centuries. Naturally there were some differences, with advances in technology improving the tools and accessories of shaving, but even then the equipment remained fundamentally the same, it just performed better: blades held a sharper edge, superior soaps and brushes lathered and lubricated, hot water came from taps and drains took away the waste, and with better lighting and mirrors a man could see what he was doing. Although all this undoubtedly made the process faster and more comfortable, still many continued to experience shaving negatively. On this, the development of the safety razor had less impact than might be imagined, though, as we shall see, it had other, far-reaching consequences.

Safety razors as we know them first appeared in the opening years of the twentieth century. The best known, made by the American company Gillette, started selling in 1903 (Fig. 3.9). While guards had been applied to the open edge of a traditional razor before, making it into a 'safety' razor, what was different about this new type was the upright design of handle and head, and that the blades were removable for re-sharpening and replacement. The uptake of the new technology was faster in the United States – by 1904 Gillette had sold 90,000 razors and 123,000 blades.[41] In the UK the change to shaving habits was more gradual, depending on generational turnover and the hesitant alteration of personal habits. The British Army's decision in 1926 to issue safety razors to all recruits was certainly influential, as had been the much earlier move by the US forces to give to their First World War soldiers a Gillette razor and blades (thereby profiting the company to the tune of 3.5 million razors and 36 million blades).[42] By the time of the British Mass Observation survey in 1939, by far the biggest majority of the men were using a safety razor and the market was dominated by a few still-familiar brands of global reach. By 1950, for instance, over a quarter of the world's shaving purchases were bought from Gillette.[43]

It has been said that the safety razor revolutionized shaving. Certainly, it was easier to use than a traditional razor – less skill was involved, it was less daunting to handle and simple to maintain. It also, as a consequence, greatly increased the prevalence of home shaving and likewise decreased the use of a barber, thereafter trips to a barbershop being only for haircutting rather than barbering in its strictest sense. Looking closely, however, it doesn't seem as though the safety razor was *necessarily* safer. In a marketing coup and with dubious claims, it managed to place itself as the harmless alternative: 'Impossible to cut yourself', declared

FIGURE 3.9.
Shaving with a safety razor: so easy and safe even a baby could do it. Gillette advertisement, c.1910.

one advertisement; 'Shave in the dark', shouted another in the very large font of a full-page spread (Fig. 3.10).[44] By comparison, and in a remarkable instance of denigratory hindsight, the traditional alternative became demonized as the 'cut-throat'. Until then, the straight-edge open blade was simply and neutrally a razor. The *Oxford English Dictionary*'s first example of the 'cut-throat' is only from 1932; in fact it cites Sayer's *Have His Carcase*, mentioned above, in which the razor acts up to its new name, slicing open the victim's throat. However, Sayers was

not responsible for the term and it was certainly in use before Harriet Vane nicked her fingers while groping for the murder weapon. An editorial in *The Times* of 1929 gives it as one name among several, as though it was a fairly recent term and still settling.[45] The point is that until it was in the process of being ousted by the safety razor, the cut-throat was not perceived as being murderously lethal. I am not, of course, suggesting that using a straight razor was not without risk or that it was never involved in violence. Browsing through newspaper reportage of the nineteenth century there are plenty of cases where a razor had been used to hideously harm either others or the self. What I am saying though, is that this danger and violence did not disappear with the coming of the safety alternative.

The reasons are not hard to discover. A traditional straight razor was obviously dangerous, and care was taken in its handling and use. After stropping and shaving, the blade folded away into the handle. And with many men still using a barber, or owning just one blade, their numbers were limited – common, but not ubiquitous. By contrast, the safety razor's name, and its easy use and touted harmlessness instilled a false sense of security. Coupled to this, the small removable blades were little two-edged hazards, which unlike the blade of a straight razor did not fold away, and when finished with were just discarded. Easy to buy, cheap and disposable, once safety razors were in widespread use there was an unimaginably huge number of these nasty little blades everywhere. According to preliminary research for a wartime scheme that in the context of shortages proposed re-sharpening them, every adult male in Britain threw away between one and two blades per week, and these were 'piling up all the time all over the country'.[46] As weapons then, they were simple to obtain, extremely portable and a cinch to wield. Newspapers report assailants of all ages and both sexes, carrying blades in handbags, in pockets, in handkerchiefs. Their tiny dimensions could equally make them slivers of accidental harm. In 1910, Captain Bryan Cooper trod on the blade of a safety razor that had fallen on the floor, severing an artery; a verdict of accidental death was brought in for another man in 1933 who swallowed a blade.[47] There was criticism in 1966 when a magazine included a free gift of razor blades with one of its issues, the brightly wrapped present dropping onto the door mat in 500,000 homes. As one mother said, 'I shudder to think what might have happened if the kids had got hold of them.' The publisher was unrepentant: 'Frankly, I have no idea why anybody should be complaining', said the editorial manager.[48]

Not only were the blades of the safety razor an unforeseen danger, they also presented an unanticipated problem in disposal. The throw-away consumption on which their success was based meant that very soon there were millions of blades to be got rid of. Questions began to be asked about what to do with them all. By 1929 it was an ironic joke (Fig. 3.11), although real responses seem only marginally less bizarre, like stringing them on a wire to cut the weeds from a canal.[49] Some new-build homes, particularly in the United States, had

What are we to do with them? Our readers have been making a few suggestions, some of which are illustrated here.

a built-in disposal device of a slot set into the wall. According to Howard Mansfield it was first developed by the Pullman Company for their rolling stock washrooms, but thereafter became a feature in domestic bathrooms.[50] Fitted into the back of the medicine cabinet, the used sharps dropped into the wall cavity or foundations. A British example can be found in the brochure for one up-market complex of flats aimed at those 'whose names may grace Debrett', which boasted that 'There is a used razor-blade receptacle wall-fitting, where discarded blades disappear for ever.'[51] Such out-of-sight-out-of-mind thinking is so misguided as to be almost as endearing; as many within the American construction industry know, piles of rusting old blades are a common find beneath and within older homes. The disposal of used blades continues, of course, to be a feature of the practice of shaving today, albeit with the added problem of throw-away plastic handles and heads. The ultimate destination of landfill is not too dissimilar a solution from the naive and hopeful slot in the wall.

The truly qualitative shift in shaving practices came with the invention of the electric razor. Needing no soap or shaving cream, brushes, hot water or towels, and needing no skill either, the only thing required for a safe and quick shave was a plug socket on the wall (Fig. 3.12). Developed in the 1930s, again the driving impulse was American, with Schick, Remington and Sunbeam all being early on the market. In Holland, Philips began selling the Philishave in 1939, just before the war. After millennia of a relatively stable technology, then, the twentieth century saw the use of three different kinds of razor: the traditional, the safety and the electric. Indeed, in a personal recollection emblematic of this wider context, my husband remembers three generations in his family home in the early sixties: he, a young man, with a 'new' electric shaver; his father with a safety razor; his grandfather using a cut-throat. The most recent of these technologies, however, has been the slowest to catch on. In 1966 Gillette reckoned that six million of Britain's twenty million shavers used an electric

FIGURE 3.12.
Electric shavers for the modern man, 1950s.

razor, which is just over 30 per cent.[52] Today the figure is even slightly lower, at a little over 25 per cent.[53]

   No doubt these statistics reveal something about the performance of electric razors – there is widespread agreement that they produce a less close shave and that they may be less suited to harder hair. However, there may be more going on here and we should consider how razors are perceived as well as how they perform. As we saw above, the association of razors with masculinity has historically been very close: 'A razor is surely the emblem of manhood.'[54] With the introduction of the safety razor, this association was disrupted. Compared to the traditional open blade, the safety razor was seen by some as soft and fussy, a namby-pamby option not suitable for a mature man. In an editorial of 1926 in support of the Army's move to equip its recruits with a safety razor, the leader writer in *The Times* thus defended the decision against those who

> will see in it, perhaps, yet another sign of a universal and deplorable effeminacy, another evidence of the innate depravity of youth and of its desire to avoid all and every kind of hazard. 'The Empire,' they will say, 'was built up by men who were not afraid of a naked blade.'[55]

This defence was not misplaced, for just as the straight-edge blade became known as the cut-throat, the safety variety was also popularly called a boy's razor: 'the straight, cut-throat, negro or man's razor and the safety or boy's razor'.[56] The juxtaposition of hard and untamed masculinity (with racist undertones of danger or animal vigour?) beside one that lacks potency could not be clearer. Such associations persisted, however tenuously, for a whole generation, as those who were brought up to the straight-edged open blade gradually dwindled in number. Thus, on the eve of the Second World War, at exactly the same time as the Mass Observation survey whose respondents almost uniformly used a safety razor, an article on the history of shaving declared that 'The man's or "straight," razor . . . was superseded on a million dressing-tables by the boy's, or safety, razor, with its dainty little duplicate cutting edge, its easily gripped handle, and its neat box.'[57] (Parenthetically, it is also worth noting the writer's comment on the problems of the latter's used blades: 'True it is almost as difficult and dangerous to dispose of the discarded blades as it is to dispose of newly murdered bodies.') Undoubtedly the fact that women had by now turned to the safety razor (to which we will return below) did not at this point help in its image struggle. With the passage of time, as we know, the safety razor was repositioned as manly, and the straight-edged blade became merely old-fashioned: a relic in a shaving mug, used by grey-stubbled old men in flannel underclothes. An estimate in 1966 suggests that of twenty million British shavers, only 200,000 still used the traditional razor (just 1 per cent), and these were mainly in the over fifty-five age group.[58]

I suggest that several generations on again, there may be something similar at work in the relationship between the wet shave and the electric. Although self-consciously entering the market as representing a modern, stylish masculinity, used on the big and small screens by culturally influential figures like Humphrey Bogart and *The Avengers'* John Steed (played by Patrick Macnee), it has not continued to fulfil this initial promise.[59] Instead, the cut-throat is experiencing a renaissance, its hard edge, pedigree and retro chic appealing to a new, younger demographic. At the same time the safety razor – by now, as formerly with its traditional counterpart, known primarily as just a 'razor' – also sports along with its blade more than a whiff of testosterone: 'There is arguably no activity more masculine than the wet shave.'[60] Both require a whole raft of supporting items that bulk out this performance of masculinity. Again, the soaps, creams and lathers, the brushes and the aftershaves deeply embed the repeated ritual of shaving. Perhaps by comparison, the electric razor, to all intents and purposes blade and paraphernalia free, is for current perceptions too convenient, too anodyne a grooming tool to gain the purchase on men's shaving habits that its technological ease would suggest we could expect. While shaving has a long history of being experienced as time-consuming and difficult, maybe those very aspects that demand discipline also produce loyalty and give it added meaning. With the full sensory engagement of scented and foaming soaps, the pleasure of hot water and the subtle pull of steel against skin, the wet shave is a powerful arena for the repeated performance of masculinity.

Hairless women

The idea of smooth femininity has a powerful and tenacious hold on our society. For Darwin, viewing the matter amidst the assumptions of Victorian England, this idea had solidified into a fact, indeed into an evolutionary imperative. Darwin believed the sexual preferences of the human male had weeded out the hairy female in favour of the bare-skinned. In evolutionary terms the hairy woman was to wither; natural selection favoured the smooth.[61] Yet although often interpreted as aberrant, women do have body and facial hair, and it has been in a marked and prolonged instance of wilful blindness that the idea of a naturally hairless femininity has existed side-by-side with the cultural practices of female depilation. In conjunction with the changing nuances of the smooth-skinned ideal, therefore, female hair has had a long history of removal. It is to this history that we will now turn.

Although the straight-edged razor may have been emblematic of manhood, tweezers were a unisex grooming tool most certainly used by women. They are also an ancient device whose form has barely changed and that links us to thousands of years of the management of appearances. In early modernity, women could use them alone, or in conjunction with concocted mixtures that aimed to remove unwanted hair, or once plucked prevent its regrowth. As we saw in Chapter 1, the recipes for these depilatories were recorded in manuscript collections whose (usually female) compilers clearly considered them suitable, though not necessarily limited, to women's use. Most often the texts are not specific as to the type or whereabouts of the hair that was to be removed, however one handwritten recipe advises anyone with 'many long hayrs on their armes' to singe them with a candle at every wane of the moon.[62] Printed recipe books are sometimes a little more forthcoming, describing in addition to the generalized mentions of 'face' and 'body', specific sites like eyebrows, lip, and – in a reminder that notions of beauty are subject to change – the forehead:

> Some that have the hair of their forehead growing too low, others the hair of their eyebrows growing too thick; and some women that have haire growing on their lips, (an unseemly sight to see) would give any thing for this Secret.[63]

Often the ingredients recommended by this recipe genre are pretty outré by our standards. The chapter on depilation in Thomas Jeamson's beauty manual of 1665 begins with inflated rhetoric – 'When the Lillies and Roses of your Faces Elysium, are oretopt by the hastie growth of superfluous excrescencies' – goes on to explain the products and processes that will 'eradicate those aspiring weeds that disturb you', and comes down to ground with ingredients that include an arsenic compound called orpiment, quicklime, opium, the gall of a hedgehog, the blood of bats and frogs, henbane extract (a type of nightshade so poisonous that Dr Crippen used it to murder his wife) and burnt leeches.[64] There is no doubt that at least some of these substances would have been highly effective in dissolving the protein bonds in hair and chemically burning it from the body, notably the quicklime combined with the orpiment (a mixture known as rhumsa). Note also that a quicklime derivative, calcium hydroxide, is an active ingredient in modern depilatory products. Interestingly, the recipe tradition also gives evidence of a form of 'waxing' for hair removal, for use particularly on the relatively large surface of the forehead. Take a mastic (perhaps gum arabic), heat until it is soft, then apply. Bind the applied area with ribbon or cloth and leave overnight. In the morning, just like a waxing strip, 'twitch it off'. The 'hair will come up by the roots' and 'the forehead will appear very comely'.[65]

Of course, we have no way of knowing how often these recipes were actually used – how much, in other words, they represent real practice as opposed to an ideal appearance. These kinds of recipes are also greatly outnumbered by preparations for hair growth rather than its removal. Furthermore, the numbers of women who transcribed recipes or owned their own published manual will never have been big in terms of the total population – the elite in the earlier part of the period, though rapidly growing to include women from the middle orders. By the late eighteenth century, however, we find manufactured depilatory products being advertised readymade in newspapers (Fig. 3.13). As the nineteenth century progressed, we can infer that depilatories found a growing market, for by 1898 the trade handbook *Pharmaceutical Formulas* informed its readers that 'there is a brisk demand for them'. Ten years later the 1908 edition was even more forthcoming: 'Superfluous hairs on the faces of women are a fruitful source of profit.'[66]

The Victorian emphasis (some might say fixation) on luxurious and abundant female head hair was thus balanced by its erasure on the face and body. Conduct and etiquette guides, whose numbers were burgeoning for the rapidly expanding middle classes, began to canvass the subject for readers on both sides of the Atlantic. Along with medical literature, these guides advised specifically on the what and how of removal. Not only did they cover different methods – from tweezing and depilatories, to the newly invented galvanic process, electrolysis – but for the first time specifically brought older women into the frame. Thus they differentiated between, and variously recommended how to remove, the soft downy growth that may be found on even the youthful (particularly noticeable in the dark-haired), but also advised on those sparse but tough hairs typical of the 'mature' (for which read post-menopausal) woman. Such a market invited a range of competitors. While some advertisements were for branded products

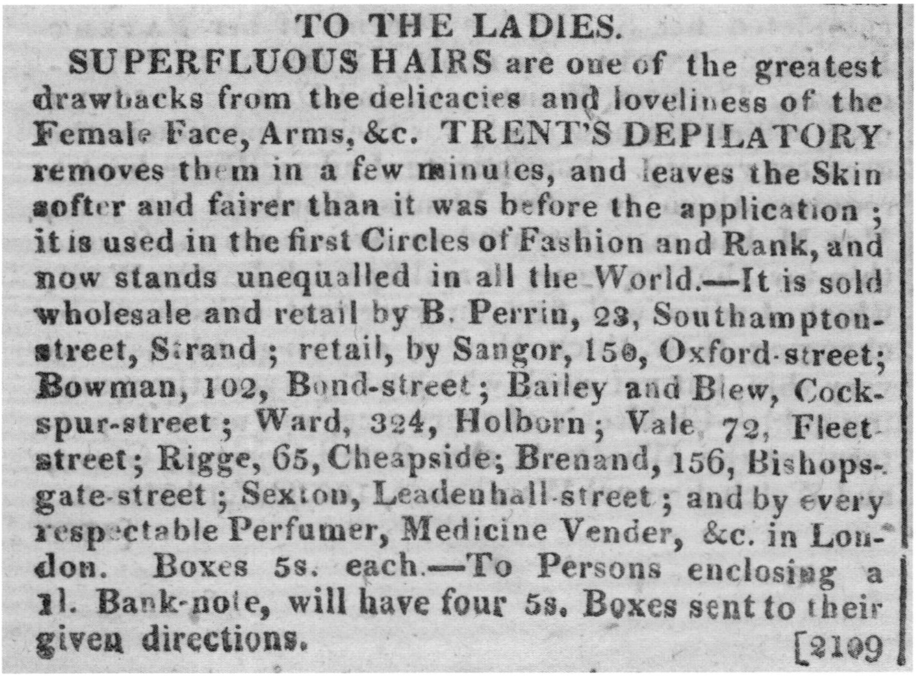

TO THE LADIES.
SUPERFLUOUS HAIRS are one of the greatest drawbacks from the delicacies and loveliness of the Female Face, Arms, &c. TRENT'S DEPILATORY removes them in a few minutes, and leaves the Skin softer and fairer than it was before the application; it is used in the first Circles of Fashion and Rank, and now stands unequalled in all the World.—It is sold wholesale and retail by B. Perrin, 23, Southampton-street, Strand; retail, by Sangor, 150, Oxford-street; Bowman, 102, Bond-street; Bailey and Blew, Cockspur-street; Ward, 324, Holborn; Vale, 72, Fleet-street; Rigge, 65, Cheapside; Brenand, 156, Bishops-gate-street; Sexton, Leadenhall-street; and by every respectable Perfumer, Medicine Vender, &c. in London. Boxes 5s. each.—To Persons enclosing a 1l. Bank-note, will have four 5s. Boxes sent to their given directions. [2109]

FIGURE 3.13.
Newspaper advertisement for Trent's Depilatory, effective at removing ladies' 'superfluous hairs', late eighteenth/early nineteenth century.

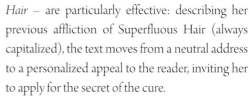

FIGURE 3.14.
John Singer Sargent's
famous portrait of
Madame Pierre
Gautreau (Madame
X), in which she wears
a daringly revealing
evening gown,
1883–4.

available from outlets like Boots, some were presented as confessionals by those (always ladies of good social background) who, having suffered, wished for nothing else but to share (at a price) their miraculous treatment and alleviate the burden for others. One such was 'Madame Constance Hall', under whose name a standalone pamphlet was issued, as well as column-length newspaper advertisements. The pamphlet's strategies – *How I Cured My Superfluous Hair* – are particularly effective: describing her previous affliction of Superfluous Hair (always capitalized), the text moves from a neutral address to a personalized appeal to the reader, inviting her to apply for the secret of the cure.

> Nobody but a woman who has experienced the mortification of having to show herself in public with hair on her face can realise what a cloud is lifted from her life when she gets rid of the hair. *I ask you to let this joy be yours.*[67]

Another reason for the steady growth in depilation, and one that is key to its history as a female practice, concerns contemporary fashions. The zones of a woman's body subject to hair removal bear a strong relationship to dress forms, with increasingly revelatory clothing bringing into public view new areas of potentially hairy skin. Thus we find that the early recipes, when they do specify the areas on which unsightly hair grows, generally talk in terms of the brows, forehead, lip and perhaps (fore)arms – the only parts of a woman's body that were exposed to public gaze. By the late nineteenth century however, evening wear was beginning to feature a sleeveless cut, for the first time ever revealing a woman's shoulders, upper arm and, most importantly in this context, hairy underarm (Fig. 3.14). An illustrated advertisement for Decoltene liquid hair remover from 1919 makes this link explicit (Fig. 3.15). The drawing shows a woman with her arms raised in a kind of inviting abandon, her breasts and upper body almost falling out of an exceptionally low-cut, strapless dress. The accompanying text explains: 'The vogue of the décolleté gown and transparent sleeve makes the smooth underarm a matter of importance to the woman who prides herself on a dainty personality.' During the 1920s and 1930s, legs also began to feature as needing management. Rising hemlines, the gradual shedding of stockings, the beginnings of beach culture, and a growing belief in the benefits of sunshine and outdoor exercise all combined around then to give women's legs an unprecedented visibility (Fig. 3.16). The public declaration that they might need grooming followed swiftly.

FIGURE 3.15.
Newspaper advertisement for Decoltene liquid hair remover, 1919.

FIGURE 3.16.
Four young women
on the beach at
Aldeburgh, Suffolk,
c.1927.

It is within this developing social context that the safety razor proved to be truly revolutionary. Breaking a centuries-old masculine monopoly over the sharpened metal blade, the safety razor began to be designed specifically for women, boasting functional adaptations like a curved edge for underarms and feminizing decorative features like pastel-coloured cases. They were also marketed as modern, chic, young and decidedly upper-class. Their names – the Debutante razor, the Duchess, the Milady – suggest users of privilege, a selling strategy obviously of appeal to an aspirational demographic as much as to an actual client base. It is likely, however, that the uptake was initially amongst well-off young women, whose wardrobes and lifestyles dovetailed with the corporeal and social sites where depilation was routinely practised. Something of this can be seen in a passage from *The Man in the Brown Suit*, published in 1924. In this early novel by Agatha Christie, a single conversation reveals the modernity of women's shaving, its social cachet and the fact that despite the naivety of the old-fashioned, everyone – including the reader – knows about it. In this conversation, Sir Eustace Pagett is convinced that a woman called Miss Pettigrew is a man in disguise. His interlocutor, the narrator of the piece, is not so sure. Pagett is speaking:

'I went straight up and searched her room. What do you think I found?'
I shook my head.
'This!'
Pagett held up a safety razor and a stick of shaving soap.
'What should a woman want with these?'
I don't suppose Pagett ever reads the advertisements in the high-class ladies' papers. I do. Whilst not proposing to argue with him on the subject, I refused to accept that presence of the razor as proof positive of Miss Pettigrew's sex. Pagett is hopelessly behind the times.[68]

The last area of bodily disclosure and depilation has been the pubis. Incorporating the upper legs, labia, perianum and mons pubis, grooming of this zone was given impetus by the high-cut swim and gym wear that appeared in the 1980s and 1990s (Fig. 3.17): indeed, the 'bikini line' came to denote both the borderline of revelation in these garments and the activity of depilation. In little more than a single generation, the trimming and removal of pubic hair has become unforeseeably widespread (Fig. 3.18). In the swinging sixties, fashion designer Mary Quant prophesied that 'pubic hair . . . will become a fashion emphasis . . . I think it is a very pretty part of the female anatomy'.[69] Instead, the very opposite has happened. According to a survey taken in 2003 in the United States and Canada, about 30 per cent of women completely removed their pubic hair, 60 per cent trimmed it, and only 10 per cent left it in its natural state.[70] Since then, there is no indication that the number of women removing their

FIGURE 3.17.
Supermodel Marie
Helvin modelling a
silver bikini, c.1980.

FIGURE 3.18.
Increasing the zones of female depilation: a woman shaving her pubic hair with a ladies' disposable razor.

pubic hair has done anything but increase. The Brazilian full depilatory treatment (and less thorough-going variations) has grabbed hold of cultural practice as tenaciously as solidifying wax seizes onto hair (Fig. 3.19).

The name given to the Brazilian is but the latest in a long association that links female hair removal with distant and exotic cultures. It is visible in a depilatory recipe published in 1650 that advertised itself as a secret known to 'the Moores', as also in the Exeter surgeon Caleb Lowdham's handwritten recipe from the late seventeenth/early eighteenth century for a substance used by Turkish women.[71] We can also see it at work in a long-running advertising campaign for a hair-removing product sold from at least 1916 to 1940, under the persona

FIGURE 3.19.
Hairs on a wax strip.

of Frederica Hudson. Of a high-society family, this widow of an army officer had for years been tortured by a hideous growth of unwanted hair, until her husband, saving 'a poor Hindoo soldier from death', was in gratitude given 'the preciously guarded secret which keeps Hindoo women free from any trace of superfluous hair'.[72] In part, this orientalizing theme reflects the actuality of cultural difference and the longer history to the removal of female body hair in, for example, Muslim societies (applied also to pubic and armpit hair

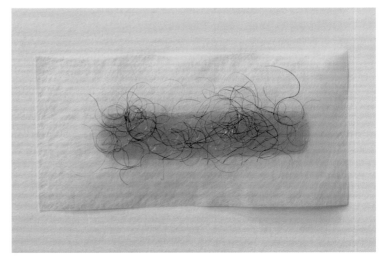

on men) and certain Hindu castes. However, it also freights the Western practice with a potentially transgressive allure, a frisson of sexual exoticism.

The removal of hair has been, and continues to be, an important part of the normative gender performance, and regardless of difficulties and discomforts, individuals have felt compelled to practise depilation in order to achieve the appearance that at any given historical moment has been considered appropriate for their sex. For men, it has been primarily a story of grooming the mature male into a state of civility, politeness and hygiene. For women, the emphasis has been on beauty and, articulated with particular clarity in modern advertising, sex. For both, depilation has been tied to boundaries between public and private – physically in terms of zones of the body, but also socially, where an engagement away requires different standards of grooming from a day spent at home. Whether James Woodforde in 1785 avoiding the squire's wife while unshaven, or a woman today refusing to go swimming until she has waxed, what is acceptable in private is accounted unacceptable abroad. For women, the boundary of acceptability has moved with the changing outline of fashionable dress, body hair becoming newly shameful as it becomes newly visible.

But the management of facial and body hair has not been confined to its removal. At certain historical moments it has been the fostering of growth that has been of importance. As we will see in the next chapter, at these times both individuals and wider society have been energetically engaged in the practice of being hairy.

Chapter 4

The practice of being hairy

The ensign of manhood

In 1533 an unknown Englishman translated a work by an Italian churchman written in defence of beard-wearing by the clergy. In a heartfelt preface addressed to the 'gentyll reder', he explained that his motivation in making the translation was by way of a personal vindication. As a habitual beard wearer, he had suffered from anti-beard prejudice – 'I haue euer vsed to weare a Bearde, and haue ben many tymes challenged and rebuked for the same' – and wished to prove that if facial hair was acceptable for a priest, there could be no valid reason whereby a layman should not also wear it.[1] Coming at the end of the predominantly clean-shaven years of the Middle Ages, this unknown translator was in the vanguard of a fashion that, if he only knew, would soon sweep the country. For a sizeable portion of the sixteenth and seventeenth centuries, facial hair was the norm. It became the shorthand for masculine identity, and far from being disparaged it was the *lack* of a beard that following generations would find derisory.

Tudor and Stuart portraits show both the ubiquity of facial hair and the wide variety of its styling (Fig. 4.1). They suggest that not only were beards (here taken to mean any facial hair, not only that worn on the chin) customary, but that their shaping and presentation was a matter of self-conscious design. Beards, in other words, participated in fashion. Thus by the end of the sixteenth century we find them the target of writers whose critical commentary sought

FIGURE 4.1.
This painting, *The Somerset House Conference*, celebrates a peace treaty negotiated between England and Spain in 1604. The Spanish delegation sits on the left of the table, the English on the right. All of the men have facial hair of some sort and in some degree, styled in recognizable ways.

to expose fashionable excess – that is, extremes of style and behaviour that were considered to be an immoral misuse of time, money and resources. Like other aspects of contemporary fashion, beards were in this context understood as evidence of pride. And pride, we need to realize, was no mere personal foible but a mortal sin that reared itself between the sinner and God, setting an individual over his (in this context) maker, refashioning what the Divine had already made good and leading the individual to self-worship. In satirical pen portraits whose burgeoning excess mirrored their targets' creative variety, beard styles were enumerated and lampooned:

> Some seeme as they were starched stiffe and fine,
> Like to the bristles of some angry swine:
> And some (to set their loues [love's] desire on edge)
> Are cut and prun'de like to a quickset hedge.
> Some like a spade, some like a forke, some square,
> Some round, some mow'd like stuble, some starke bare,
> Some sharpe Steletto fashion, dagger like,
> That may with whispering a mans eyes out pike;
> Some with the hammer cut, or Romane T,
> Their beards extrauagant reform'd must be,
> Some with the quadrate, some triangle fashion,
> Some circular, some ouall [oval] in translation,
> Some perpendicular in longitude,
> Some like a thicket for their crassitude [thickness, density],
> That heights, depths, bredths, triform, square, oual, round,
> And rules Geo'metricall in beards are found.[2]

In this type of critique, barbers – those responsible for the 'fashioning' of facial hair – were likened to tailors, whose inventive fancy with shears and needle was blamed for the changing novelty of garment forms. In an unusual casting of the barber's character that prefigured the effete hairdresser of the eighteenth century and later (see Chapter 2), his active engagement with fashion stripped his manliness, leaving a style-conscious simpering fellow, a finicking pander to fashionable desires. With a cringe of the knee, a wave of the curling irons and a ceaseless chatter of styles, these characters snipped and pimped their customers into the latest trends.[3]

Although the service industry that (over) tended facial hair was subject to an effeminizing discourse, the beard itself was resoundingly masculine. In the words of an early anthropological work that explored the body modifications of different cultures (including contemporary English practices), the beard was 'the naturall Ensigne of manhood'.[4] It was an all but universal signifier of gender, and the proof of a manliness that was virile and able to procreate.[5] So culturally significant was facial hair that some historians have even considered its presence or absence to have been *constitutive* of gendered identity:[6] the beard made the man. This gendered identity, however, was also strongly inflected by age: beards connoted – or helped construct – manly maturity; the chins of youths were smooth and hairless. We can see this exemplified in two portraits of Charles I's nephew, Prince Charles Louis, Elector Palatine (Figs 4.2 and 4.3). In both he is dressed almost identically in the manly accoutrements of armour, sword and a baton of command. In the earlier, however, painted when Charles Louis was nineteen, he is noticeably clean shaven. In the portrait from four years later he has reached full maturity and is now depicted with facial hair.

It is useful to put the cultural desirability of beards in dialogue with the contemporary receipt tradition, whose recipes for haircare included many products and substances for facial hair (see Chapter 1). These included dyes to darken or re-colour unwanted shades, and products that promised to stimulate growth. A recipe of 1588, for example, gives instructions for making a lineament: after steeping various plants and substances in wine, the whole is heated with the addition of butter, honey and resin. When applied to the chin and cheeks, this mixture 'will become heare'.[7] In the cultural context out of which this recipe arose, it is

FIGURES 4.2 AND 4.3.
Portraits of Charles I's nephew, Prince Charles Louis, Elector Palatine. The present an almost identically martial image, with only the addition of a moustache in the later portrait to depict the subject has achieved a mature masculinity.

easy to see how products to promote beard growth might have found a ready market of young men wanting to bring one on, or older men who found their sparse whiskers unsatisfactory.

The significance attached to beards as markers of male maturity and the concern an individual might feel about inadequate growth comes into even greater focus when we consider the insights gained by comparative physiology.[8] Evidence suggests that the onset of facial hair occurred up to six or seven years later in the early modern period than it does in our own time, with young men even in their early twenties with youthful smooth cheeks. Rembrandt, for instance, was somewhere between twenty-three and twenty-four when his facial hair began to grow. Appreciating this physiological change over time makes much more sense of the importance of the beard, rather than age, as a marker of full maturity. A man in his twenties was 'old' enough to be active in the adult world and yet in lacking facial hair was clearly still to reach full maturity. (This, of course, is the exact opposite of our own experience, which sees on average a much earlier onset of biological maturation coupled with a more delayed onset of performative adulthood.) Felix Platter (1536–1614), a Swiss physician, felt this keenly. Although having completed his studies, at the age of twenty-one he was worried lest his lack of a beard prevent him from being licensed to practice. Most interesting of all in light of the recipe tradition, Platter's diary records his efforts to bring his beard growth on. Aged nineteen years and nine months, in desperation he and a fellow student obtained just such a preparation as those whose recipes appear within the pages of household manuals and medical texts. They applied it in hope, but unfortunately it was only effective in dirtying their bed linen. In his own words:

> We were still bare around the mouth and would have liked thereby to improve our appearances. We applied it repeatedly at night to our faces and messed up the pillows; sometimes we had ourselves shaved with a razor around the mouth, but it did not help in any way.[9]

More than a window onto the adolescent anxiety of the past, Platter's diary shows both the recipe tradition to have been a practical resource and is also witness to a masculinity specifically embedded within the cultural and biological conditions of its time.

We can take this still further by looking at two different portraits of Charles I, both of them by Daniel Mytens. The first (Fig. 4.4) is dated to 1629, in other words when Charles was nearing thirty: a husband, soon to be a father, a king. The other (Fig. 4.5) was painted the year he turned twenty-three. In what we now can assume was the norm for his age, in this portrait of the younger Charles we see only a trace of the facial hair that came to be so much a part of his painted representations – a thin growth just on his upper lip. We can add to our understanding of this second image as a portrayal of a man not yet come to full maturity by

FIGURE 4.4.
King Charles I, 1629.

FIGURE 4.5.
Charles I in 1623 as
the Prince of Wales: a
faint trace of hair on his
upper lip.

considering it alongside an incident that occurred earlier in the same year. The heir to the throne, accompanied by attendants, planned a secret trip to Catholic Spain to forward marriage negotiations with the Infanta. Owing to the hazards of the enterprise, the risk of alienating public opinion, and the danger of being taken hostage if recognized, they planned to travel incognito. In fact, overcoming the disadvantages of youth they decided to disguise themselves by donning false beards. On the morning of 18 February 1623, Prince Charles and his companion George Villiers (soon Duke of Buckingham) put on their beards, decided on the fake and lamentably unimaginative names of John and Tom Smith, and set off for Dover. They got, however, only as far as Tilbury before things started to go wrong. Crossing to Gravesend on the ferry, one of the false beards fell off, causing the ferryman to become even more suspicious of his finely clad but dubiously named passengers.[10]

There is a macabre coda from the end of Charles's reign, which finished on the axeman's block. It was reported that on that bitterly cold January day in 1649, when Charles was lead through the Banqueting House to the scaffold he was faced by an executioner and assistant wearing not only a mask – customary at some executions – but also wigs and false beards. According to eyewitness accounts, the man who wielded the axe had a 'grey grisled periwig which hung down very low' and 'a grey beard'. The man who afterwards held Charles I's head aloft was said by one to have been wearing false hair that was black; another reported it was a 'flaxen' beard.[11] The reason for this grotesque-sounding mummery was to keep hidden the executioners' identity, to prevent anyone from recognizing them as the men who had decapitated the king. And the object of the disguise was achieved; to this day their identity remains open to speculation.[12] This background explains an otherwise bewildering inclusion in a Dutch broadside of Sir Thomas Fairfax and Oliver Cromwell, the chief leaders of the Parliamentary forces opposed to the king (Fig. 4.6). Fairfax, identified as the *Beul* (or executioner), holds Charles's severed head. However, the *Preek-heer* (preacher) Cromwell is no less guilty. In clasping the false beard and whiskers of the executioner, he reveals himself to be the man who was really responsible for bringing the king to his death.

Odd though such stories of false beards may strike us, they are far from being isolated cases. Such was the significance and associative power of beards, that their appearance as a prosthetic device was relatively common in all sorts of contexts that required impersonation or disguise. The chief of these was the theatre, where records show beards were routinely bought and hired for performances. For example, for a play performed by Oxford students before Charles's father, James I, twenty-two beards were rented. These included: a blue beard

PREEKHEER. BEUL.

FIGURE 4.6.
't Moordadigh Trevrtoneel (The Murderous Tragedy), 1649. Thomas Fairfax holds the severed head of Charles I, and Oliver Cromwell the disguising false beard of the anonymous executioner.

for Neptune, a black one for a magician, two hermits' beards – one grey, one white – three more beards, red, black and flaxen, and ten satyr's beards.[13] As Bottom in *A Midsummer Night's Dream* comically enquired of the part of Pyramus, which he had been assigned to play: 'What beard were I best to play it in? . . . I will discharge it in either your straw-colour beard, your orange-tawny beard, your purple-in-grain beard, or your French-crown-colour beard, your perfect yellow.'[14] Likewise false beards were used in masques, those theatrical pageants that entertained the court. The extent to which they were an accepted shorthand for evoking character generally, and masculine character specifically, can be seen in their striking appearance in the Shrovetide masque of 1626, in which Queen Henrietta Maria and her women dressed up and acted at Somerset House. As a contemporary eyewitness put it: 'On Shrovetuisday the Quene and her women had a maske or pastorall play . . . wherein herself acted a part, and some of the rest were disguised like men with beards.'[15] The accounts for the performance record the payment of 4l. 3s. 6d. to a John Walker 'for Lawrell wreaths heire and beards'.[16] The apparent unlikelihood of ladies of the Caroline court being disguised as men and wearing false facial hair collapses the historical distance between us, making those unapproachable subjects of portraiture seem altogether more 'like us'.

Of interest and relevance here, especially to Charles's experience with the treacherous beard on the Tilbury ferry, are the findings of The Shakespeare and the Queen's Men Project undertaken in Toronto in 2006. Named after the Elizabethan troupe The Queen's Men, the project followed as far as possible original theatrical practice in the performance and touring of three plays from the repertoire of its namesake. The aim was to illuminate through praxis the available evidence on early modern dramaturgy and stagecraft.[17] Among many other things, the project explored what the use of wigs and prosthetic facial hair could tell us. These, as we have seen, were invaluable props on the early modern stage for quickly establishing character, particularly useful given the common practice of role doubling in which one actor played two or more parts and needed both rapid and effective costume changes. What the project discovered, however, echoed the fate of Charles and Buckingham: false beards were found to be difficult to attach, and the hair of the upper lip in particular was liable to come adrift and obscure the players' mouths as they spoke.[18]

The need for disguise also saw false beards adopted off the stage. While awaiting execution in prison, John Clavell (1601–43), a young gentry highwayman, wrote a verse recantation of his ill-led life. While ostensibly seeking to dissuade any would-be young villains from trying a life of highway robbery, it also revealed to the interested reader the tricks and habits of this criminal class, including their wearing of masks, hoods, wigs and false beards.[19] As another example, when William Seymour, the husband of Charles I's cousin, Lady Arbella Stuart, made his escape from the Tower of London, he did so by putting on a carter's clothing, a wig and a false beard.[20]

Just how people who wanted them got hold of false beards is not exactly clear. Literary historian Will Fisher suggests that haberdashers – or at least some haberdashers – made, sold and rented them, at least to theatrical companies.[21] When William Seymour escaped, he had the assistance of his barber, so it may have been this barber who supplied the prosthetic device. An intriguing German satirical print from 1641 sheds some uncertain light on the matter (Fig. 4.7). Entitled 'New Haberdashery' (*Newer Kram Laden*), the print depicts a shop devoted entirely to the selling of beards.[22] A queue of decidedly clean-shaven customers waits to be served with their selection, and at the back of the shop – in an inversion of the normative gendering of fashion consumption as feminine – two women help with the fitting, one combing a customer's newly affixed whiskers, the other holding a mirror for his satisfaction. Every kind, colour and shape of beard and moustache can be found here. Displayed on the shop's counter and hanging from a railing above they are even numbered, and the key above plays with the idea that for every character and every physical defect there is a beard to match the one and ameliorate the other. The print also makes clear the link between facial growth and mature manliness, reminding the reader that 'wit and hair don't come before their time' (*Daß Witz und Haar / Nicht kompt vor Jahr*). While the tone and appearance of this broadsheet are clearly caricature, to be at all meaningful, and of course funny, the satire must have been levelled at a recognizable target. The print, first, confirms the variety of contemporary beard fashions; second, suggests that some men at least made use of prosthetics, whether for the purposes of fashion, cosmetic improvement or disguise; and third, indicates that there were establishments where, or makers from whom, they could be purchased.

FIGURE 4.7.
Newer Kram Laden
(New Haberdashery),
1641: false beards for
every occasion.

Within a few decades of the publication of this print, however, facial hair had become unfashionable, and as we saw in the previous chapter, over the long eighteenth century men like Pepys, Swift and Woodforde turned their energies not to its cultivation but to its removal. It was not until the mid-nineteenth century that beards returned. However, as will become clear below, their size and cultural purchase more than made up for this long absence.

The 'Beard Movement'

Beards can provoke strong reactions. Perhaps it is because they fundamentally alter the face, a practice that, like veiling, can seem like a repudiation of a shared social contract of mutual visibility, a breach of the tacit understanding of what constitutes an appropriate expression of personhood. Certainly, as we saw above, in 1533 the anonymous translator of *Pro sacerdotum barbis* complained that it was on account of his beard that he had been many times challenged and rebuked. The case of Joseph Palmer three hundred years later presents us with an almost unbelievably antagonistic reaction to facial hair, under which reaction lies the weight of social norms and a fierce struggle for fundamental personal freedoms.

In 1830 Joseph Palmer moved to Fitchburg, a small town in Massachusetts.[23] Like his Tudor predecessor he was out of step with fashion, full-bearded when most faces were still clean-shaven. Immediately, the conservative New England townsfolk expressed their disapproval: children threw stones at him, women crossed the street in disapprobation, the windows of his house were repeatedly broken, and finally he was denied communion at his local church. Palmer refused to be intimidated and would not remove his beard. Eventually he was attacked by four men who threw him to the ground and attempted to shave him by force. Using a pocket knife Palmer managed to drive them off, but he was then arrested for what was termed 'an unprovoked assault' and fined. Refusing to pay, he was imprisoned in the county gaol in Worcester. Palmer – religious, courageous and highly principled – still would not back down. In prison for over a year and still bearded (he had to fight off attempts by both gaolers and prisoners to forcibly shave him), with the help of his family he smuggled out letters that when published in the press brought his plight to wider attention. His case and martyrial stance started to become embarrassing, and the local sheriff attempted to release him. Palmer, however, continuing to make his point about personal freedoms, refused to go. As a thorn in the side of authority, Palmer was digging himself in ever more publicly and ever deeper. In the end, the only way for the sheriff and warders to rid themselves of this turbulent pogonophile was to carry him from the gaol in his chair. Palmer went on to form friendships with Emerson and Thoreau, be active in the intellectual developments of New England, and to campaign against slavery. His grave is marked with a tombstone on which there is both a relief bust of his head and the simple epitaph: 'Persecuted for wearing the beard' (Fig. 4.8).

The irony, of course, is that by the time Joseph Palmer died in 1875, vast numbers of men in both the United States and Britain were wearing beards; what had provoked unease and violence in conservative Fitchburg forty-five years earlier was now the accepted norm. In the years between, society had witnessed what became known, even at the time, as the Beard Movement. Dating to the middle decades of the nineteenth century, it was articulated through social commentary, in tracts for and against, in humorous cartoons, in medical discussion. It is evidenced by a cluster of new words that entered the lexicon, such as pogonotrophy (the cultivation or growing of a beard, first dated by the *OED* to 1854), pogonotomy (the cutting or shaving of a beard, from 1896), and pogonic (of or relating to a beard, first citation 1858).[24] Most of all, it was embodied on the faces of countless Victorian men, those patriarchal-looking figures whose full and flowing beards seem so paradigmatic of their age.

After the bewigged and clean-shaven years of the 1700s, the progress towards the full, 'Victorian' beard was at first modest. Although starting in the first decades of the nineteenth century with side whiskers, it was not until the 1840s that the idea of a more enveloping look really gained traction. An early commentary of 1841 on the prevalence of beards appearing in France shrewdly foretold that before long the fashion would spread to England and beyond, and even more shrewdly predicted that custom would convert the nay-sayers, turning repugnance into approval: 'We are always disaffected towards any habit or custom which is unfashionable but fashion converts our dislikes into likes, and shows us all up in our true characters as the creatures of prejudice.'[25] As well as giving us a sound description of the contingent and constructed nature of taste, the writer proved an accurate trend forecaster. Before the decade was out, beards were appearing in increasing numbers. One early champion of facial hair, Charles Dickens, began experimenting with a moustache and was exceptionally taken by the new look (Fig. 4.9). As he wrote with beguiling enthusiasm to a friend in 1844: 'The moustaches are glorious, glorious. I have cut them shorter and trimmed them a little at the ends to improve their shape. They are charming, charming. Without them Life would be a blank.'[26]

The emerging hirsute fashion was also given significant impetus by the Crimean War (1853–56). Owing to this campaign's extreme cold, gruelling conditions and difficulty of

FIGURE 4.8.
Joseph Palmer's tombstone, Evergreen Cemetery, Leominster, Massachusetts.

FIGURE 4.9.
Charles Dickens in
1855, enjoying
the experience
of cultivating a
moustache.

FIGURE 4.10.
Captain Dames of the
Royal Artillery, in camp
during the Crimean
War, 1855.

equipment supply, the military allowed its regulations on shaving to lapse (Fig. 4.10). The
bearded and seasoned soldiers who subsequently returned to England imbued the stirrings
of fashion with a heroic and martial manliness. Looking back from fifty years later, a writer
in *The Leeds Mercury* reminded readers 'how soldiers who went out to the Crimea, clean
shaven . . . returned full-bearded, and looking much more manly and vigorous than they had
done with shorn chins and cheeks.'[27] It was a sentiment that was articulated no less clearly
at the time. With swagger and verve, the popular press presented such figures as robustly
glorious, often depicted alongside puny civilians, whose imitative beards made them but pale

copies of the genuine article, and, moreover, whose wannabe status revealed a lack of true breeding (Fig. 4.11).

Such anxieties about the appropriation of signs of class and status appear frequently in the 1850s and 1860s in relation to beards, and not just in the context of the military. As the bearded fashion spread through the classes, satire repeatedly portrayed only the elite – the gentlemen, officers and toffs – as successful bearers of facial hair, with its adoption by lower-status men depicted as humorous or grotesque. From 1854, early in the bearded years, a *Punch* cartoon shows a hirsute railway guard trying to help a woman with her bags, who, in a fearful panic, thinks she has been set upon by brigands (Fig. 4.12). Likewise, comment inevitably surfaced as to whether beards were fitting for postmen, for the police, for the clergy, for office clerks and for the legal professions. One by one though, all ranks and trades fell to the sway of the new fashion for masculinity until, it was said, 'As far as the shape of

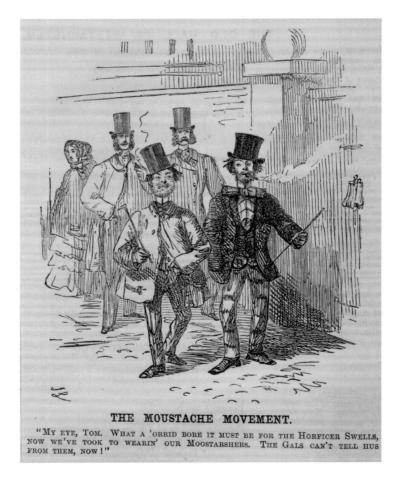

THE MOUSTACHE MOVEMENT.

"MY EYE, TOM. WHAT A 'ORRID BORE IT MUST BE FOR THE HORFICER SWELLS, NOW WE'VE TOOK TO WEARIN' OUR MOOSTARSHERS. THE GALS CAN'T TELL HUS FROM THEM, NOW!"

FIGURE 4.11.
'The Moustache Movement', cartoon from *Punch*, 1854.

THE BEARD AND MOUSTACHE MOVEMENT.

Railway Guard. "Now, Ma'am, is this your Luggage?"
Old Lady (who concludes she is attacked by Brigands). "Oh yes! Gentlemen, it's mine. Take it—take all I have; but
spare, oh spare our lives!!"

the beard is concerned, there is now nothing distinctive between the day labourer and the heir to a dukedom; between a hack driver and a Field-Marshal.'[28] Only one class of man remained beyond the pale as far as beard-wearing was concerned: the servant. In a period in which the visible distinctions between the different ranks within a household were at their most extreme – which invented the regalia and uniforms of service – and in which beards configured the normal appearance of masculinity, the servant was kept visibly subject to authority and debarred from full manliness by an enforced smoothness of skin. Quite simply, the shaven face of the servant marked him out from the bearded 'gentleman' he served. In the words of Eric Horne, a career servant from the 1860s until after the First World War, 'all those years in gentlemen's service, I had an intense desire to grow a moustache, which of course we were not allowed to do.'[29]

Although over the middle decades of the nineteenth century the Beard Movement seemed to sweep all before it, its triumph was neither uncontested nor silent. The commentary that accompanied its rise, and indeed that continued to preach to the converted throughout the years of its ascendancy, demonstrates the beard's ability to provoke strong reactions. Thus both apologists for facial hair and their detractors marshalled arguments whose very repetitiveness reveal them to be post-hoc justifications for personal preference and an inclination (or disinclination) for the fashionable norm. In the case of what was quickly to become the pro-beard majority, the continued reiteration of the same arguments soon rings with a congratulatory tone, as bearded commentators write for a bearded populace of the benefits of being bearded.

So what were the arguments adduced in favour of facial hair? As early as 1847 a pro-beard tract encapsulated in its title many of the declarations that were to follow, aggressively and emotively drawing the lines of battle from which the Beard Movement would emerge triumphant: *Beard Shaving and the Common Use of the Razor; an Unnatural, Irrational, Unmanly, Ungodly, and Fatal Fashion among Christians.* Unpacking this cluster of ideas reveals the following assertions and 'facts'.[30] First, beards acted as 'respirators', providing protection for the mouth and nose by preventing ingress of particulates like dust and smoke. They were therefore said to be of especial benefit to men like millers and stonemasons, who worked in dusty environments. Second, facial hair also protected the sensitive organs of its wearer from bitter winds and the chill air, guarding him against everything from colds to consumption. In keeping the mouth warm, beards were likewise said to prevent toothache and even help against tooth decay. Third, it was asserted that facial hair was more sanitary than clean-shaven skin, for it provided a covering against dirt. One wearer went so far as to claim that thanks to his beard his breath was now fresher and had 'quite a kissable tendency'.[31]

Another major strand to the apologists' argument was that facial hair was both natural and God-given. As such it had both a scientific and religious prerogative, intended by nature (and eventually, once the bearded Darwin's ideas gained widespread currency, by evolutionary selection) and the divine to be of ornament and use to the male of the species. Maned lions and bearded biblical patriarchs were adduced as evidence of this noble lineage. The nobility was further increased by some who made overt connections between beards and political freedoms: 'Speaking broadly, it may be said that with every popular struggle for freedom throughout the Continent of Europe the beard has reappeared'.[32] In the wake of such claims, it was a short step to the assertion that rationality also decreed that a beard be adopted, it being self-evidently foolish either to deprive oneself of a beard's advantages or to endure the wasted time and the misery of shaving. In support of this last, calculations were made of the number of days a man might save over a lifetime, and the amount of pain he might likewise spare himself. (The individual who asserted that the man 'who lived to be sixty had suffered more pain in littles in every day shaving, than a woman with a large family had from her lyings-in', obviously knew nothing about childbirth.)[33] Growing a beard was thus something that 'all thinking men will approve'.[34]

Finally, there were reasons of aesthetics and sensation. Time and time again, beards were described as a 'manly beauty'. Using the same language as was also employed with regards to a woman's head hair, male facial hair was understood as a 'glory' and an adornment to the sex. Beards were an acceptable way for men to engage with those narcissistic impulses of self-beautifying, permitting the wearer to spend time on personal grooming and self-presentation without the negative connotations of effeminacy or pettiness that so often haunt any masculine engagement with fashion. Furthermore, beards not only looked good, but their apologists claimed for them a haptic pleasure whereby a fine growth felt good too: 'it must be delightful to stroke a natural beard'.[35]

If the beard was taken to be of such resounding excellence – had assumed a stature that could even be said to be heroic – it is easy to see how its absence could connote the opposing set of characteristics. Thus, tapping into contemporary ideas of racial supremacy, hirsute peoples were found to be physiologically and morally superior to those 'degenerate tribes' whose men were by nature less hairy, and in whom the inability to grow a beard accompanied 'a want of manly dignity' and 'a low physical, moral, and intellectual condition'.[36] Equally, if a man, such as any who walked the streets of London, *could* grow a beard and did not, then his glabrous skin condemned him as an inferior, effeminate and dubious creature: it is 'plain fact' that 'the shaved man is unmanned, irresolute, and nervous'.[37] In short, for the vocal pro-beard lobby, facial hair was masculinity's silver bullet, a panacea for anything that might assail him. The call to action for such partisans was therefore simple: 'grow your beards! a habit most natural, scriptural, manly, and beneficial'.[38]

But what of the female half of the population, how did they view this rallying cry? It is interesting, but unsurprising for an apologist voice, to find that the Beard Movement often appropriated the female view to depict women as positively disposed towards facial hair. While they might be portrayed as evincing initial misgivings, inevitably they soon come to delight in its manly attractions, perhaps won over by the simple expedient of being kissed:

> Women of cultivation . . . do not quite approve, yet are ready to remember that all the worthies of antiquity . . . wore beards, and they do think a bearded man is more manly in appearance; but with a smile they ask, 'How will you ever manage to kiss your sweetheart?' If this question is answered by a smart practical illustration, almost any of them will admit that the beard is not so objectionable after all.[39]

As this passage suggests, in such commentary facial hair is often overtly sexualized. One story that appeared in a popular periodical in 1879 is remarkable for its evocation of the intimate physicality of facial hair, and the frisson of being kissed by a moustachioed suitor. As two of the young female characters coyly remark:

> 'Isn't Charles Winthrop just as nice as he can be? . . . And such a splendid moustache! And then he always has it so delicately perfumed!'

'That, indeed! But how should you know anything about Charles Winthrop's moustache and its perfumery unless he has held it close under your nose?'[40]

This fictional account (which was, incidentally, written by a woman) is mirrored by real-life evidence that suggests facial hair could indeed be experienced by women as a manly charm. In the memoirs of artist Gwen Raverat (1885–1957), Charles Darwin's granddaughter, she uses the experiences and letters of her mother and aunt to describe 'those maned and bearded lions, who had roared and tossed their tangled doormats' in the second half of the nineteenth century. Raverat says that her aunt 'wrote with pride' of Uncle Richard's 'unusually long thick brown beard', and that 'my mother still thought that Mr. T's [a former suitor] plentiful hair and "nice *soft* brown beard" were attractions'.[41] It seems safe to assume then that women as much as men were subject to the normalizing power of this, as any other fashion, and that along with the majority of males, their womenfolk agreed that facial hair was a manly ornament and possessed its own allure.

Is it possible to speculate on the causes of the Beard Movement? Historian Christopher Oldstone-Moore suggests that it arose in tandem with a shift in masculine identity, itself caused by changes in work practices, the feminization of the home space and the emergence of the women's movement.[42] In this light, beards can be seen as an assertion of masculinity, the staking of a claim to male certainty in the face of uncertain realignments of power and authority. However, these conclusions are by no means self-evident, and indeed in England at least, the timing and nature of these large-scale social developments does not correspond to the rise and fall of facial hair. Thus the rapid industrialization that took place in the early nineteenth century did indeed cause male labour to move from rural fields to urban factories, but the demographic among which beards first became popular was drawn from the middle to upper echelons, the sector of society which, being professionals, merchants and landowners, experienced no change in employment. Similarly, the domestication of the home space in which it was construed as the site of comfort and family leisure, the management of which was primarily a female responsibility, was a development of the eighteenth century – resoundingly clean-shaven and bewigged decades. And the rise of women's rights is more properly located in the later years of the nineteenth century, when beards had in fact substantially declined from fashion. The 'New Woman' was a phenomenon of the 1890s; the Married Women's Property Act, whereby a married woman had the legal right to money she had earned, was only passed in 1870 and then in 1882 was extended to cover all property she owned, earned or inherited. Likewise, only with the Infant Custody Act, passed in 1873, was a woman allowed to petition for custody of children under sixteen in the event of a divorce or separation. Other milestones in women's emancipation were equally late. The agitation for women's right to vote, for instance, began to gain momentum from 1872 with the establishment of the National Society for Women's Suffrage, but until the activities of Millicent Fawcett and the Pankhursts twenty to thirty years later remained fairly ineffectual and easily ignored by a wider society; full franchise was not granted to women until 1928. All of these momentous happenings and the groundswell of discussion and argument that accompanied and followed them therefore clearly post-dated the rise of beards and the highest point of their popularity. What *is* noteworthy about the timing of the Beard Movement is that its high point actually coincided not with the swell of women's emancipation, but with those decades that witnessed the maximum swell of her skirts. The fashion for beards matched the fashion for crinolines (Fig. 4.13). If there is any causal relationship it seems to be one of design and of the swelling and expansive outlook of mid-Victorian confidence, rather than politics or principles of changing male identity.

And speaking of design, as Dickens's enthusiastic letter to his friend shows, the great writer had discovered that just 'not-shaving' only took one so far, and that the appearance of facial hair could be altered and improved by tending it. Indeed, as thousands of other men made the same discovery a whole panoply of products and devices appeared to assist beard wearers in their self-presentation, and the individuals responsible for the invention and marketing of such items in their quest for profit. These accessories and substances were

FIGURE 4.13.
'Rather a Knowing Thing in Nets', cartoon from *Punch*, 1860. The gentlemen's full beards match the amplitude of the women's skirts as well as the abundance of their hair.

RATHER A KNOWING THING IN NETS.

Admiring Friend. "WHY, FRANK! WHAT A CAPITAL DODGE!"
Frank. "A—YA-AS. MY BEARD IS SUCH A BORE, THAT I HAVE TAKEN A HINT FROM THE FAIR SEX."

particularly designed to help wearers with the hair on their upper lips, which in more elaborate forms defied gravity in ways not expected of the beard. Combs, waxes and pomades teased, styled and set the hair into the required shape (Fig. 4.14). At night particularly, men could also don moustache guards, trainers and bands, devices secured around the head to either protect the moustache or set it in position (Fig. 4.15). Heated moustache curlers offered alternative ways of grooming. However, after taking such pains, the everyday and apparently anodyne activity of taking a cup of tea became surprisingly hazardous: the heat from the beverage risked softening the fixative, or more disastrously still the drink itself sopped into the hair. In response, around 1855 the Staffordshire potters Harvey Adams and Company developed the moustache cup. This was an ordinary item with the simple addition of a shelf or covering fixed near one section of the cup's lip, which protected the drinker's moustache (Fig. 4.16). They were popular until the end of the century, were frequently sold as souvenirs and came in both right- and left-handed styles.[43]

The fashion for facial hair could not, however, last forever. It had gradually appeared through the early decades of the nineteenth century, flowered vigorously from the late 1840s, then towards the century's close faded away. First to make the transition from being in fashion to being old-fashioned were beards. Although still favoured by many mature men, their younger fellows preferred to pair a dashing moustache with a shaven chin. This fall of the hirsute male can be seen in miniature within the pages of etiquette guides, those advisers to the aspirational on how to look and behave 'correctly'. As an advice text from 1887 declared:

> When a moustache is worn, pains should be taken to keep it neat and trim. Beards have quite gone out of fashion, so there is little occasion to descant upon the trouble they require; nobody now should wear a beard unless he have a preternaturally ugly mouth and chin. If whiskers are worn they should be kept as short as possible, any undue luxuriance in this direction giving a man a curious and old-fashioned appearance.[44]

As this short passage suggests, the mantras of the previous generation had begun to be reversed. Some of the very same reasons that had been cited in favour beard-wearing were now being used to attack the practice. No longer a practical convenience, they were in fact a trouble; instead of being an adornment, they made a man look odd; rather than manly, they were old-fashioned. The best that could be said of them was that they hid the worst cases of extreme ugliness. Rationality now required that facial hair, a characteristic shared with animals, be shaved off – the triumph of civilization over nature.

A main thrust of the anti-beard argument, however, concerned hygiene. A generation of public health campaigns, the rise of germ theory and greater knowledge of communicable diseases turned on its head the idea that beards were cleaner. Instead, they were now said

FIGURE 4.14.
Label for Pomade
Hongroise.

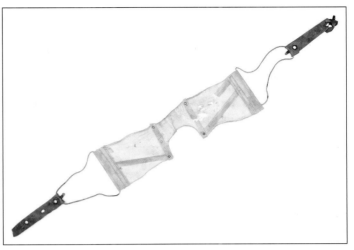

FIGURE 4.15.
Pre-1918 German
moustache trainer, left
behind when Australian
troops captured the
position during the First
World War. It is made
of celluloid, cotton and
leather, and the cut-out
semi-circle fits beneath
the wearer's nose.

FIGURE 4.16.
Moustache cup.

to harbour germs and bacteria (Fig. 4.17). The matter began to be debated in the pages of medical journals, although medical opinion – voiced by a profession that was renowned for being bearded – lagged conspicuously behind fashionable practice. For instance, in the 1890s a sprinkling of communications in the *British Medical Journal* began to discuss the hygiene of beards, with most correspondents gradually accepting that facial hair might harbour microbes, but as a consequence to insist on doctors and surgeons being clean-shaven was a counsel of unnecessary perfection, the logical end of which would be the removal of eyelashes and head hair.[45] While many doctors (more so in Britain than the United States) were dragging their heels, the awareness of possible microbial danger was being canvassed before a wider public. In 1901 New York authorities recommended that dairymen all be clean-shaven to prevent tubercular contamination of milk supplies. As Dr Park of the New York board of health explained:

> There is real menace to the milk if the dairyman is bearded. In the first place, the milker may be diseased himself. He may have tuberculosis and the dried sputum may accumulate on his beard and drop from it into the milk . . . The milker is forced to incline his head over the milk pail in order to get near enough to do his work and you have no doubt noticed that men with long beards have a habit of stroking them downward. That has the effect of brushing off any germs they may contain. Again, the milker may be perfectly healthy himself and yet accumulate bacteria from the dust of the stable. The beard, particularly when damp, may become an ideal germ carrier, and on an unclean man would have great facility for the transmission of disease.[46]

This one decision received widespread exposure, known not only to readers of the *BMJ*, but also to ordinary men and women in their daily papers. Substantially the same coverage, for example, was published in *The Atlanta Constitution, The*

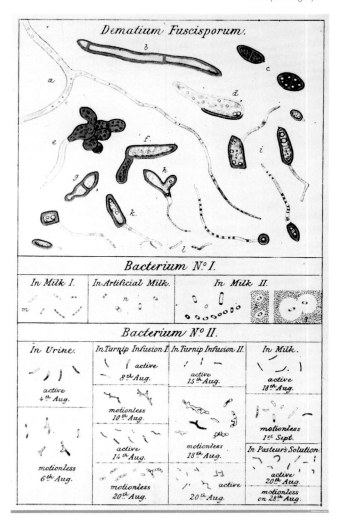

FIGURE 4.17.
Germ theory: illustration from Joseph Lister's *Collected Papers*, illustrating bacteria and putrefaction. Lister (1827–1912) pioneered the practice of antiseptic surgery.

Philadelphia Inquirer, and three months later, on the other side of the world, the *Star* in Christchurch, New Zealand.[47] While medical opinion remained divided, partly as a result of reportage like this the general populace increasingly tended to equate clean-shaven with hygienic. For much of the twentieth century facial hair, at least at the stubble stage, was thought to look, feel and be dirty. It is important to reiterate though that such feelings and beliefs most definitely post-date the decline in beards and were not a cause of this decline. Just as with the popularity of facial hair, arguments justified trends rather than being the reason for them. The beard had been spurned by fashion long before science further demonized it with germs.

Culture and counter-culture

Bearded bohemians

In June 1925 a review of D.H. Lawrence (1885–1930; Fig. 4.18) appeared in the *New York Herald Tribune* entitled 'Lawrence Cultivates his Beard'. In this, the critic Stuart P. Sherman not only treated his readers to an analysis of the writer's books, but also decoded the meanings of Lawrence's facial hair.

FIGURE 4.18.
D.H. Lawrence, c.1929: eyes 'glinting like a squirrel's' and 'a big bush of a beard'.

When he first faced the public he was open-faced, clean-shaven . . . Now he resembles a moujik [Russian peasant] . . . a shag of hair across the forehead, eyes alert, defiant, glinting like a squirrel's, snubby nose sniffing the air and a big bush of a beard. The beard is sacred. It is worn out of respect for the impulses from our 'lower' natures, out of reverence for the Dark Gods which inhabit the Dark Forest of one's being. As Mr. Lawrence wears the beard it is intended also to suggest and symbolize his isolate and inviolable 'otherness', 'separateness', 'maleness'.[48]

Lawrence himself was quite pleased with the review, taking the trouble to write to Sherman in person, although he seemed to disclaim the beard's self-conscious importance. 'Dear Mr Sherman', he wrote, 'I was amused by your article on me and my beard. But it isn't a beard needs "cultivating." It's a clean chin man has to work over.'[49] This was consistent with the sentiments expressed in a letter of eleven years earlier, back in 1914, when the then twenty-five-year-old explained to a friend the evolution of a self-presentation:

> Oh, by the way – I was so seedy and have grown a beard. I think I look hideous, but it is so warm and complete, and such a clothing to one's nakedness, that I like it and shall keep it. So when you see me don't laugh.[50]

It seems from this that Lawrence simply liked the practical and emotional benefits of a beard – the warmth, the convenience and the concealment – yet Sherman was also right. In a period in which fashion had banished beards, in which modernity was clean-cut, in which only the Victorian rearguard continued unshaven, in such a period growing a beard made a declaration beyond that of simple personal preference. Lawrence's beard may have given him a kind of emotional camouflage, but at the same time it paradoxically guaranteed him a resonating cultural visibility. The writer's facial hair unequivocally identified him with a particular set of meanings then being associated with the bearded younger man. It was a look that was knowingly outside fashion, outside polite society, wild and not tamed, beyond the normal conventions. In a word, Lawrence's beard was bohemian.

The degree to which Lawrence was running counter to the prevailing cultural norm can be seen by the popularity a short while earlier of a game called 'Beaver'. Ostensibly originating in Oxford and appearing in the early months of 1922, Beaver was the product of undergraduate humour that tapped into the sensibilities of the time. The rules, as explained in an article on the gossip page of the *Daily Mirror*, were simple: players watched out for a man with a beard and the first one to shout out 'Beaver' won the point. The scoring was the same as in tennis, with the difference that any player who successfully spotted a man with a red beard (called a King Beaver) immediately took the game. In other variations a black beard counted for one point, a full-length white beard four, a goatee six and a red beard a winning ten.[51] Although it is perhaps difficult to imagine such a pastime catching on, its widespread report in the press (including its recommendation on the children's pages) does seem to have ensured it an extensive if fleeting popularity. As one man remembered, looking back to his boyhood from the late 1950s, Beaver 'enjoyed a nation-wide vogue.'[52] Not everyone approved of the pastime – letters appeared in the papers from disgruntled beard-wearers – but such complaints by and large met with little sympathy. Whatever this says about the changing levels of acceptability as regards the making of personal comments based on body form and looks, it also suggests that for many, a bearded man was by then risible and fair game for mockery.

For D.H. Lawrence to grow a beard – wild, bushy and red to boot – was a bold statement and one that ran massively counter to the cultural norm. He was not, however, alone in making this statement. In 1895, the painter Augustus John (1878–1961) finished his first year at art school as a quiet, neat, painstaking and clean-shaven student. The eighteen-year-old returned to the Slade the following year as a larger than life and anarchic figure who was to stride through the art world in his signature flamboyant clothes, gypsy hat, earrings and large red beard (Fig. 4.19).[53] (In fact, as a celebrated red-bearded King Beaver he once received a postcard at his Chelsea studio with the message, 'Yah! Beaver!')[54] Together he and Lawrence, and many other writers, artists and musicians like them, formed a bohemian and counter-cultural style of which one of the key looks was a beard.[55]

The association between beardedness and edgy bohemianism was clear in the public consciousness. Lady Cynthia Asquith (1887–1960; Fig. 2.16), society matron and daughter-in-law to politician and Prime Minister Henry Asquith, mixed with this artistic cadre. Friends with Lawrence, painted by John and acquainted with many others of their ilk, she describes them in her diaries. She noted Lawrence's 'tawny beard'; the Irish poet A. E. [George William Russell] she called 'a strange, unkempt, bearded genius'; and meeting Augustus John for the first time she described him as 'very magnificent looking, huge and bearded'. Of the musician and composer Joseph Holbrook, Asquith's diary entry records that he exercised 'too many

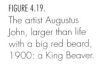

FIGURE 4.19.
The artist Augustus
John, larger than life
with a big red beard,
1900: a King Beaver.

privileges of genius – dirt, not dressing [formally], deafness, beard, and rudeness'.[56] Some of these connections and assumptions can be seen informing a cartoon that appeared in the *Daily Mirror* in 1913, which explicitly tied bohemianism to impatience with convention, bad manners, egoism, outré dress and an unshaven, ill-kempt presentation (Fig. 4.20). A bohemian apologist for the beard was found in the person of the multi-talented and controversial Eric Gill (1882–1940; Fig. 4.21), probably best remembered for his typefaces

THE GUESTS WE NEVER ASK AGAIN—NO. 2.

The Bohemian and without-ceremony guest, who makes free with everything in a noisy and intimate manner and suddenly retires when he has made a lot over bridge. He is a terrible person.—(By Mr. W. K. Haselden. Reprinted.)

FIGURE 4.20.
'The Guests We Never Ask Again – No. 2', 1913. The cartoon illustrates the boorishness of bohemianism in the popular mind and its association with outré dress, unkempt hair and beards.

FIGURE 4.21.
(Facing page) The bearded and unconventional Eric Gill in front of his sculpture at the front of the BBC's Broadcasting House in Langham Place, London, c.1925. He wears a robe rather than trousers, a dress choice he often preferred.

whose subtle influence continues to enrich our lives, as in the lettering so famously used on the London underground. Less well-known are his experiments in sexuality, which covered the gamut from incest to an experience with his dog.[57] In 1931 Gill published an eccentric and intriguing treatise on dress, which included a short tribute to beards, 'the proper clothing of the male chin'. For Gill, shaving was 'a sign of penitence and voluntary celibacy' and was 'naturally approved of by women', who, Delilah-like, 'desire nothing more than power over their husbands'.[58] As a newspaper correspondent summed it up in 1930, articulating the received wisdom of the time, 'Bohemians are more often than not inclined to beards.'[59]

From sexy to sleazy: the decline of the moustache

While the bohemians carried on in their creative, promiscuous and hirsute manner, society around them was becoming increasingly clean-shaven. Whereas the beard had long since become unfashionable, now the moustache began to be subject to multiple readings. Thus in the opening decade of the twentieth century newspapers saw the beginnings of a debate over its real desirability: did moustaches reveal character? Were features improved or made worse? What professions were suited to facial hair? Could a moustache spell social ruin? Women in particular were usually depicted as disliking them (though they were not as bad as a beard), citing as reasons their unhygienic nature, the untrustworthy way they obscured the mouth, the nastiness of being kissed by a moustachioed man, and the way a clean-cut male looked younger, more cultured and more intelligent.[60] From this point, more and more the manly norm was hairless. As a society hostess perspicaciously put it in 1912, 'The "ladies' man" of to-day' – for which, read young, modern and fashionable – 'has neither beard nor moustache. He must be a smart American type, that is to say, with regular features of the antique cast.'[61]

However, unbeknownst to all these men and women, a cataclysmic event waited in the wings whose overwhelming effect on Britain's social landscape would extend even so far as the minutiae of a man's self-presentation: into the lives of a whole generation of clean-shaven young men crashed the Great War. By the time the first shots were fired in Belgium, there had been a long association between moustache-wearing and the military. Starting with the Peninsula War a century earlier the martial moustache had quickly became incorporated into the British soldier's bravura, and although regulations changed from time to time and also the ranks and regiments to which they applied, generally speaking facial hair on the upper lip was allowed, and sometimes was compulsory. Although, under the influence of clean-shaven civilian fashions, this was becoming increasingly unpopular – and photographs by no means show all soldiers to have been moustached – on the eve of the First World War officers were theoretically required to have a neat, clipped growth. As a spokesman for the War Office stated in 1913, 'If an officer shaves his upper lip it is treated as a breach of discipline, and the matter is dealt with by the commanding officer.' Major General Sir Alfred Turner further explained:

FIGURE 4.22.
First World War
recruitment poster,
'Soldier Beckoning'.

'There is among officers undoubtedly a growing feeling against the moustache, which they are forced to wear. I have noticed an increasing number of Army men who have deliberately shaved the upper lip in defiance of regulations. The offence, of course, is only a trivial one, but it is a distinct breach of discipline.'[62] There are passages in Cynthia Asquith's diary of particular poignancy, as she sees for the first time her male friends and family bearing a 'military moustache'.[63] Along with the discipline of the new uniform, this changed facial look articulated a man's new status as subject to the authority and orders of an institution, his individuality subsumed in the great machine of war (Fig. 4.22). So many of those Asquith loved were never to return.

In October 1916 the order was rescinded and officially moustache-wearing in the military became optional, although it remained a customary and typical part of the officerial presentation.[64] What is unclear is the effect after the war of this institutionalization of shaving habits. Possibly, after the horrors of their experience, it made the demobbed even more resistant to facial hair; conceivably the reverse may be true, with the moustache connoting – in the midst of those wild post-war years – duty, discipline, patriotism and self-sacrifice. Perhaps what eventually occurred was a little of both, for through the twenties and thirties a pencil moustache was by no means unusual, although social practice tended far more to the clean-shaven.

One, very public, realm where the moustache did make a post-war impact was on the silver screen. Icons from the Golden Age of cinema stared moodily down at their audiences from behind a swoon-worthy moustache; for actors like Clark Gable, Ronald Colman, John Barrymore and both of the Douglas Fairbanks, it was a trademark look (Fig. 4.23). Christopher Oldstone-Moore has suggested that the moustache in this incarnation represented an edgy individuality; equally for scholar Joan Melling, the romantic leads of

FIGURE 4.23.
Pencil-moustached
screen idol Ronald
Colman with Vilma
Banky in *The Magic
Flame*, 1927.

the twenties were free-wheeling, passionate and intensely individualistic, with the 'small black moustache, a symbol of heroic virility'.[65] These screen idols were perhaps portraying the sort of characters of whom the famous dictum 'mad, bad, and dangerous to know' could be usefully employed. It is certainly interesting to consider the original of Caroline Lamb's notorious description alongside these later cultural icons. Byron in his most Corsair-like portrait (Fig. 4.24) bears an almost uncanny resemblance to these film stars of the following century. This image that was being cultivated was one that both the film studios and the individual actors themselves were careful to monitor and control. Twentieth Century Fox, for instance, putting the increase in fan mail for clean-shaven Tony Martin down to his new hairy upper lip in *Ali Baba Goes to Town* (1937), requested that he grow another moustache, and by 1932 Warren William had grown and shaved his moustache five times as required by his directors.[66] Duty to fans warred with a duty to history when Ronald Colman played Clive of India. When historical verisimilitude won the day and Colman decided to shave his trademark tash, it literally made headlines. 'Colman Shaves Moustache', declared the *Daily Mirror*, as did almost every other piece of reportage in connection with the movie, including

FIGURE 4.24.
A sultry Lord Byron in
Albanian dress, 1813.

FIGURE 4.25.
Actor George Cole
playing a quintessential
spiv in *Belles of St.
Trinians*, 1954.

simple theatre listings that advertised the week's films. Thus would-be viewers in May 1935 were warned what to expect if they visited the Dominion: '"Clive of India." Ronald Colman – without moustache – in great historic role.'[67]

Perhaps, however, the thin moustache – even though it did not, after all, materially disrupt the over-all clean-shaven look of the wearer's face – was more attractive on-screen than in person; a filmic fantasy more than a popular choice in real life. Detractors, after all, likened it to 'a piece of charred string', an 'extra eyebrow' or 'a fragment of tape'.[68] In time, even the on-screen rakish panache lost its verve, and what had been attractively dangerous became merely seedy. In Britain this decline is typified by the figure of the spiv, that oily small-time criminal who flourished in the black-market years around the Second World War (Fig. 4.25). By the 1950s, and no doubt influenced by those famous moustache-wearing dictators Hitler and Stalin, the comic genius P.G. Wodehouse could write: 'Never put anything on paper, my boy, and never trust a man with a small black moustache.'[69] Uncontested, the face of mainstream masculinity was now utterly hairless.

Hippies to hipsters

It was against this background of the clean-cut and smooth-planed that the youth culture of the late 1960s erupted in perhaps the most profound challenge to establishment looks and traditional mores that has ever occurred. While the more hard-core beliefs and practices of the hippie movement were only ever actively engaged in by a minority, the hippie style – the clothes and colours, the hair and accessories – swept through the younger generations the breadth of the western world. In an academic paper written within months of the hippie phenomenon becoming publicized to the wider public through the seminal events of the 1967 'Summer of Love', cultural theorist Stuart Hall marshalled an insightful analysis. One of his points was that hippies had not only defined a style, but had 'made the question of *style itself* a political issue'.[70] We will be returning to hippie style and its challenge to the status quo in the next chapter, for its penchant for facial hair needs to be seen within a larger focus on hair more generally, whether on the head, body or face. Here I want only to observe that the rapidity with which beards were espoused by all sorts of young men and the way they were worn was experienced by many as a repudiation of traditional values.

Consider, for instance, the case of Ken Bromfield, in 1969 a twenty-seven-year-old college lab technician. Ken, who was taking his holidays in Greece, arrived at the Bulgarian border only to be refused entry by the guards unless he shaved off his beard. Having no option but to comply he was sent to the nearby public toilets, where piled on the floor Ken found the shorn hair of other travellers like him. (Unlike them, however, Ken shrewdly kept his cut beard in a bag so as to be able to answer any future questions that might arise over the disparity between his bearded passport photo and his shaven face.) After Ken had returned to England and when taxed with what had happened, the Bulgarian embassy in London made the following statement:

> There is a new law that certain people like hippies must shave their beards and cut their hair. But this does not apply to respectable citizens. We would not advise people who are not hippies to shave their beards before going to Bulgaria.[71]

As the embassy made clear, context is everything. It was not facial hair per se, but the style of the beard and the face on which it appeared that constituted the unacceptable challenge. Respectable citizens – like Bulgarian Orthodox priests, say – could be bearded, but coupled with the wrong clothes, age and demeanour, facial hair made a counter-cultural statement.

It may not be coincidental that Ken worked in a college. In the 1960s and 1970s facial hair was especially prevalent within universities and colleges, partly owing to the youthful student demographic, and partly because, following the bohemian paradigm of the bearded intellectual and artist that had been established earlier, the academy had proved a 'natural' home. As a commentator in 1959 summed it up,

Beards are perfectly *comme il faut* for professors and other learned men; like absentmindedness, they are regarded almost as a trademark of the abstruser forms of scholarship. . . . The British are prepared to tolerate beards on sculptors, artists and writers . . . It is a sort of Philistine tradition that members of these professions . . . practically never wash; and, since they are already eccentrics by virtue of their vocations, it is felt that they have a certain right – almost, indeed, a duty – to emphasise the fact in their personal appearance.[72]

The idea that beards indicate mental preoccupation, a lack of hygiene, an impatience with conventional forms – in other words, that beards in some way run counter to the dominant and 'proper' culture – remained in place throughout the twentieth century. As Che Guevara and Fidel Castro taught us, revolutionaries are always hairy (Fig. 4.26). Recently, however, this has been challenged by the rise of the hipster beard. Although only time will tell for sure, it seems most likely that facial hair in this contemporary context is not so much counter-, as sub-cultural. It is style shorn of political meaning, a matter of personal choice that has quickly gained mainstream fashionable traction, rather than an oppositional statement. Following hard on the heels of the manscaping of the hairless metrosexual, the hipster beard

FIGURE 4.26.
Bearded revolutionaries parading in Havana, Cuba, 1959. On the far left is Fidel Castro, and next to him the moustache-wearing (but otherwise clean-shaven) President Osvaldo Dorticós Torrado. Beside the president is Che Guevara.

FIGURE 4.27.
Hipster beard.

is but the latest pulse in the constant arrhythmic beat that drives the plurality of modern fashion trends (Fig. 4.27).[73]

Interestingly, along with the rebirth of the beard has also come a return of that long-held concern over its cleanliness, as specialists wonder whether the hipster and his intimates are more at risk from illness and disease. There are some in the medical profession who say yes. Because of the structure of facial hair it traps germs and detritus – coming from saliva, nasal mucus, food debris and the habit of 'over-handling' – and these are also more resistant to subsequent washing than those found in shaven areas. Such bacteria can cause skin complaints in the wearer and increase the risk of contagious diseases for both him and those with whom he shares close contact. However, other experts, while acknowledging that bacteria cling to beard hairs, refute the idea that personal style comes at an increased risk to health.[74] Indeed, a piece of recent research suggests that some beard bacteria may even be beneficial. According to a comparative study of clean-shaven and bearded hospital staff in 2014, it was the former who were three times more likely to be carrying antibiotic-resistant bacteria. While the higher levels of such toxins might be explained by micro-abrasions to the skin caused by shaving, it is also possible that the microscopic inhabitants of beards include hitherto unknown microbes with anti-bacterial properties.[75] So who knows, it might just be that the answer to the antibiotic crisis that looms over our future lies in a hipster beard.

Saint, prodigy, freak and role model: the bearded woman

Sometime in the Middle Ages a story began to circulate through Europe. It spread far and it spread fast, travelling through Portugal and Spain, France, Italy, the German states, Holland

and England. Although the tale varied in its detail, the basic outline remained the same and concerned a devout young woman whose father was forcing her to marry a pagan ruler. Rather than submit, the woman prayed earnestly for some kind of disfigurement, which by making her unattractive would deliver her from her plight and allow her to remain chaste. The answer to her prayers came in the form of a moustache and beard. The woman's father, though, was so incensed that he had her tortured and, in imitation of the Christ she loved, finally crucified. Travelling in tandem with this story went an image of a bearded woman hanging on a cross – replicated in statuary, manuscript illumination, frescoes, paintings and woodcuts – and together they inspired an intense devotion (Fig. 4.28). The cult of St Wilgefortis (or Liberata,

FIGURE 4.28.
Statue of bearded female saint Wilgfortis in the Church of St Nicholas, Wissant, Pas-de-Calais.

Ste WILGEFORTE

Uncumber, Ontkommer or Kümmernis, among some of the names by which she was variously known in different parts of Europe) was popular with women but also with men, and among both the powerful and the poor, rivalling even Marian devotion in its following. Her feast day, until removed from the liturgical calendar by the Catholic church in 1969, was 20 July.[76] The legend of St Wilgefortis, one might say, has been erased in much the same way as has female facial hair.

Normative renderings of gender, both now and in the past, range the hairy male against smooth femininity, and this is so embedded that its constructed nature is all but invisible. It is so blindingly obvious to us that men are bearded and bristly and that women are hairless and soft, that, paradoxically, we are indeed blinded to the obvious – that all humans, in fact, are hairy. A very small proportion of both women and men are affected by a very rare condition called *hypertrichosis universalis*. In these cases the sufferer's body and facial hair grows so much thicker and longer that it gives an appearance more akin to fur. Historically famous cases include the Gonzales family, who moved in court circles in sixteenth- and seventeenth-century Europe; Mexican-born Julia Pastrana (Fig. 4.29), who was exhibited in Victorian England both in life and, embalmed, in death; and also Krao, originally from Thailand, who performed as the evolutionary 'missing link' from 1883 until her death from influenza in 1926. Such instances are, however, exceptionally rare – since the sixteenth century fewer than fifty such individuals have been documented.[77] More pertinent for this chapter is the broader physiological truth that all men and women have some degree of facial hair and its amount, quality and appearance is determined by an individual's age, ethnicity, hormone levels and genetic inheritance.

Facial hair on women, however, has been made 'unnatural', and its appearance has been physically removed from the body and metaphorically removed from our mental vision. As a newspaper strapline has put it, simultaneously endorsing the physical existence and the cultural absence of female facial hair: 'Millions of women suffer from it – but no one likes to talk about it. So what's the most effective way to beat this embarrassing problem?'[78] Nature, if left to its own devices, would pattern women with hair of varying densities and hues, from an all-but invisible

FIGURE 4.29.
Nineteenth-century poster advertising the exhibition of Julia Pastrana. She is described here as a nondescript, in biological terminology a member of a species that has not previously been recorded or identified. Julia suffered from *hypertrichosis universalis*.

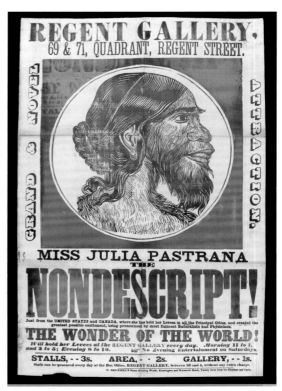

light down, to female moustaches and dark chin growths. But, as we saw in Chapter 3, removing this plumage is a project that has been pursued with great energy, from the ancient art of tweezing, the application of bleaches and depilatories, through to waxing, shaving, electrolysis and most recently, lasers. The net result has been to render any hair beneath a woman's eyelashes as problematic.

Yet for all this, the bearded lady can be glimpsed at the margins of the picture, and her voice – or the voice of someone who speaks of her – can be heard at the edges of the cultural conversation in every historical period. She has never been entirely invisible. In one guise, she is the bearer of sanctity. As in the story of Wilgefortis with which we started, bearded female saints of the medieval and early modern world bore facial hair as a sign of their devotion to a life of religion and to matters of the soul. Like a kind of internalized hair shirt, a female's beard in this case represented a triumph over rebellious flesh, bodily pleasures subdued to the imperatives of a spiritual union with Christ. Thus the legendary St Paula of Avila's tale is very similar to the story of Wilgefortis: to avoid unwanted sexual attention she prayed for disfigurement and thus deliverance, and was then 'blessed' with a beard.[79] The sanctity of St Galla is of a different order, as is her historical status. Without doubt a real woman of patrician background in late antique Rome, Galla was an honourable young wife. According to Gregory the Great, when her husband died, however, she refused to remarry, stating her intention instead to devote herself to God. In Galla's case her ensuing hirsutism was not caused by divine intervention but was seen as a medical issue, the result of her humoral imbalance. Doctors warned that unless she married (her abundance of heat dissipated through conjugal acts) she would grow a beard like a man. Galla, however, was unmoved, and knowing that God regarded not her outward appearance, remained steadfast in her determination to embrace a chaste life of devotion and prayer. And this was what happened. Galla grew a beard, retired to a nunnery and lived out her life in righteousness.[80]

In this model of sanctity, a woman's beard represents a triumph over her body and the confining limits of her gender. Instead, she is freed to rise above all such corporeal and earthly concerns to focus her energies on sexless matters of the soul. A second way in which the bearded woman entered the historical record, rather than transcending the feminine, expanded its shapes and forms. This is the bearded lady as prodigy, a phenomenon seen most emphatically in the sixteenth to eighteenth centuries. In this age of exploration and colonization, new creatures and peoples came flooding into the European worldview, revealing that nature teemed with variety and surprise as yet undreamt of. First Renaissance and then Enlightenment thought set about cataloguing these new wonders and renegotiating the boundary between the non-existent mythical and the rare but real. People and objects of wonder were collected: in cabinets of curiosity (the *wunderkammer* from which our museums

would grow); through the growing medium of print, in the news-sheets and broadsides that spread the word to the growing numbers of literate; and, in the tradition of the household fool or dwarf, in the retinues of the wealthy.

In this realm of marvels and monsters, the bearded woman found a sure place. Magdalena Ventura is just one of these women, and her name comes down to us today thanks to the Duke of Alcalá, who, in 1631, commissioned the artist Jusepe de Ribera to paint her portrait (Fig. 4.30). Hers was just one of many pictures in the duke's important collection, which comprised not only artworks, but more than nine thousand books and manuscripts that covered the range of scientific and humanist learning.[81] In this context, the painting of Magdalena functions as evidence of a wonder, a record of a phenomenon that had to be seen to be believed, and that demanded an explanation within the epistomological schema of the time. The Latin inscription to the right of Magdalena, which gives her age and history and the facts of the commission, makes this explicit by opening with the phrase: 'Behold a great wonder of nature'.[82] Magdalena's face has been depicted as entirely masculine – she and her husband share a receding hairline and a full beard and moustache. Indeed, Magdalena's facial hair is notably darker and more luxuriant than his. However, other aspects of her presentation underscore her femininity: the clothes she wears, the spindle to her left above the inscription, and, of course, her exposed breast suckling the child. Magdalena, who began growing pronounced facial hair around the age of thirty-six, was fifty-two at the time this portrait was painted, and the exposed lactating breast – hyper-real and anatomically impossible – does not tell the viewer the literal truth of her appearance, but the truth of her womanhood. Magdalena was a 'proper' female: a housewife and a woman who had borne three children. It is all these props and clues that, when set against her facial appearance, make her beard so shocking. Whereas some have argued that by depicting the unacceptable such strategies may actually work to further strengthen the normative gender binary from which it departs,[83] conceivably the opposite may also be true. Such a depiction – the bearded woman as prodigy – might also expand the gender category. After all, Magdalena is, as the inscription tells us, a wonder not outside, but *of* Nature.

Born in Liège in the sixteenth century, dwarf Helena Antonia is another bearded woman we know about, because she was taken into various European courts as part of the entourage of Maria of Austria. Like Magdalena her portrait was painted for inclusion in cabinets of curiosity, and printed engravings allowed multiple copies of her image to circulate to a wider audience. Interestingly, Samuel Pepys records in a diary entry for 1668 travelling to Holborne to see a lady with a beard: 'she is a little plain woman, a Dane, her name, Ursula Dyan, about forty years old, her voice like a little girl's, with a beard as much as any man I ever saw, as black almost, and grizzly'. Pepys was both utterly convinced of Ursula's gender and fascinated by the strangeness of her looks: 'there is no doubt but by her voice she is a woman . . . It was a strange sight to me, I confess, and what pleased me mightily.'[84]

It is easy to see how both recording the appearance of bearded women and their appropriation into the households of patrons, not to mention their presentation in taverns and fairs for more ordinary folk like Pepys, could easily slip into a wholesale display for the wider public. From around 1847 to 1914, both Europe and North America were caught in the grip of a fascination with unusual bodies and strange wonders, a fascination fed and fuelled by the freak show (Fig. 4.31). In earlier centuries only a few could experience such things in the flesh and verify with their own eyes the truth of the whiskered woman. With the achievements of modernity, however – better transport, mass media and increased leisure and spending power – bearded ladies and other 'grotesques' could be transported around the globe for the interest and amazement of vast crowds of beholders, and their stories could be published and their photographs taken to titillate a far wider and truly mass audience.[85] Madame Clofullia was but just one of these women. Born in Geneva around 1830, Josephine Clofullia (née Boisdechene) travelled in France before becoming a draw card in the 1851 Great Exhibition in London. Following this huge success – it is estimated that over a two-year period in England she was seen by two hundred thousand people[86] – she and her husband moved to America, where she was snapped up by Phineas Taylor Barnum. Promoted by him, she became America's original bearded lady, garnering fame and nationwide press coverage in the process.[87]

In some ways the freak show of the nineteenth and early twentieth century exhibits the same mix of education and entertainment as was evident in the collection and display of prodigies in earlier centuries. This was the meeting place of science and sensationalism, where credulity was tested and the unusual studied.[88] Indeed, sometimes the bearded women had their beards grasped and pulled by audience members, who not content with the evidence of their own eyes wanted the confirmation of touch. And such sceptics were right to doubt as fakes were not unknown, and thus sometimes, confusingly, the bearded woman turned out instead to be a man impersonating a woman who looked like a man. Perhaps in such sleights of truth, however, we can sense a shift from earlier centuries. The Victorian freak show raised – or lowered – the display of difference into a business, with all the profit, dubiety and showmanship that this entailed. Certainly livings had been made and money gained by the display of bearded women before: Helena Antonia's position at court was entirely due to her appearance, and although Pepys does not record paying to see Ursula Dyan, it is clear from his diary that she was being shown in an organized fashion and he certainly would have had to part with money in order to satisfy his curiosity. However, the techniques of mass marketing, publicity stunts and the idea that thousands of people would pay an entry price for the frisson of freakery was

FIGURE 4.31.
The bearded lady takes her place amongst other 'freaks' in this nineteenth-century poster for a Barnum and Bailey show. She is above the Skeleton Dude, and to the right of the Man with Two Bodies.

FIGURE 4.32.
Souvenir postcard of
Clementine Delait,
c.1910? The message
on the back of the
postcard is dated 10
February 1918 and
mentions both the
First World War and
Clementine's work for
the Red Cross. In 1928
Madame Delait went
on an international tour,
meeting royalty and
heads of state.

new. P.T. Barnum, for whom Madame Clofullia performed, was perhaps the most successful of these entertainment entrepreneurs, hyping his commercial enterprise to an incredible degree and dubbing his amalgam of circus, wild beast display and curiosity museum the 'greatest show on earth'. When it transferred in 1889 from its New York home to astound the population of Europe, it set up a new home at the Olympia in London. The recently built venue was enlarged so that for every show it could seat an audience of twelve thousand.[89]

While many of the bearded women who performed in such ventures may not have been willing and were undoubtedly exploited, some at least found self-determination. To appreciate this we need to consider the career of Madame Clementine Delait (Fig. 4.32). In her case we are privileged enough to have access to her story told through her own words, discovered in an unpublished memoir that came to light earlier this century in a garage sale in France. Clementine was born in 1865 in a small village in Lorraine. Aside from shaving her facial hair, which began to grow in her teenage years, she lived an unremarkable life, marrying a local baker and together with him setting up the Café Delait. It was sometime after this that things started to change, for she ended up making a bet with a customer and letting her beard grow: 'The success was immediate', she wrote, 'they were all crazy about me.'[90] As Clementine's fame spread, her beard became an attraction that was good for business, and she and her husband renamed their establishment the *Café de la Femme à Barbe* (Café of the Bearded Woman). Clementine's husband died in 1926, just before she turned forty, and the widow took her facial hair further afield, eventually achieving celebratory status in Parisian and London theatres. There are numerous postcards of her in many different poses and contexts, not only from her days of wider fame but also taken in front of her café, the establishment's eponymous bearded proprietor. She died in 1939, requesting that her tombstone bear the inscription, 'Here lies Clementine Delait, the bearded lady'.[91] Thus Clementine's memoir reveals that she deliberately put away her razor and chose to come out of the hirsute closet. She herself publicized her ability to grow whiskers, and it was a source of personal pride, as well as profit. As evidenced by the memorial inscription she chose, Clementine Delait's beard was a fundamental part of her identity and it gave her a social standing and degree of agency she would otherwise have been unable to attain. And she most certainly did not feel herself to be merely a curiosity for exhibit: 'I was much more and much better than that.'[92]

However, while it is important to bear her experience in mind, it is also important to remember that there were women who were neither empowered, nor who stood, however willingly or not, in the stage spotlight. These were the ordinary women whose only mark on history is a passing mention in the cramped columns of a provincial newspaper, and whose facial hair seems, at least to later readers, to have been part of their marginalized and pitiable status. Thus the sad tale of divorced and homeless Ann Lambert, 'a woman with a heavy moustache and a beard', who in 1894 was charged by the police with begging and sentenced to fourteen days in prison.[93] Similarly, the following year a Manchester woman named Carrol, 'whose chin was well bearded', was also accused of begging. She refuted the charge, saying that 'because of her whiskers people turned to look at her', and although she stopped to look back, she was not begging. She was advised by the court to shave, and sent to prison for a month.[94]

So far then, regardless of how they may have seen themselves, bearded females have been variously interpreted as saints, prodigies, money-making curiosities, or – as in these last cases – the pitiable on the fringes of decent society. Recently, however, individuals have been working to move this status in yet another direction. Jennifer Miller (b. 1961) is one such, whose routines as a performance artist are highly politicized and aim at normalizing female facial hair (Fig. 4.33). Billing herself as a woman with a beard, claiming the truth of her gender first and foremost, Miller's performance script explains that the power of facial hair is the reason why the patriarchy has staked its exclusive claim to it.[95] She challenges women to rise up from the subaltern state of hairlessness and assert their true and powerful hairy natures.

> The world is full of women who have beards, or at least, women who have the potential to have beards. If only they would live up to that potential, as I have done, instead of spending the time, the money, the energy on the waxing, the shaving, the electrolysis, the plucking. I mean we all know someone like this who's out there every day with the pluck pluck pluck! I'm talking about my mother, my grandmother, every day with the pluck-pluck- pluck-pla- pluck-pla- pluck-pla- pluck pluck pluck! As if they were 'chicken.'[96]

Miller started her career in the 1980s, and has appeared on television, has been the subject of a documentary, has had coverage in books, photographs, journals and newspapers. The advent of the internet, though, has given her and numerous others a much greater

FIGURE 4.33.
Jennifer Miller
performing with Circus
Amok in New York,
using the platform
for her politicized
performances.

presence. A quick search reveals that increasingly large numbers of women are finding the courage to put down their tweezers and take up their beard combs. If highly publicized bearded females in the past have been interpreted in varying ways, I suggest that we could term these modern individuals as role models. I have written 'individuals' here advisedly, as Tom Neuwirth (b. 1988), who achieved notoriety as the 2014 Eurovision Song winner Conchita Wurst (Fig. 4.34), is obviously working to blend the sexed body from the other side of the traditional gender divide. These women and men are the highly visible signs of a society that is busy debating and broadening its ideas on gender, breaking down the binary of gender roles, behaviours and looks, so that hair can be seen on anyone's face. Saint, prodigy, commodity, freak: it might just be that the next interpretation of the bearded female will be that s/he is merely ordinary.

This Exact representation of that Instrument of French refinement in Assassination, the GUILLOTINE is humbly submitted to the "Gentlemen of the Phalanx," & other well-wishers to the King & Constitution of Great-Britain,

by their devoted Servants at Com...
The Assassins of the King of Franc...

Whither; — O whither shall my Blood ascend for Justice! — my Throne is seized on, by my Murderers; my Brothers are driven into exile; — my unhappy Wife, & innocent Infants are shut up in the horrors of a Dungeon: — while Robbers & Assassins are sheathing their Daggers in the bowels of my Country! — what will become of thee! — Ah! ruined, desolated Country! vicegerents of eternal Justice; arbiters of the world. — look sharpest pang in death, festering in my own Blood! which flies to your august tribunal for Justice! — dispraved of Life & of Kingdom; — look down from that height of power to which you are raised, & behold me here! disproved of Life & of Kingdom; — look I lie; full low, festering in my own Blood! which flies to your august tribunal for Justice! — By your Liberty, which you possess by the Wives & Children, — rescue mine; — by your love for your Country, — revenge the blood of a Monarch most virtues which adorn the British Crown, — by all that is Sacred, & all that is dear to you, — from being the prey of Violence usurpation & Cruelty undeservedly butchered, — and rescue the Kingdom of France.

Chapter 5
The politics of appearance

This book began by looking at how and why people cared for their hair, and the professions that grew up around its tending. We then engaged with the long history of its removal, whether enforced in order to undermine identity, or voluntarily enacted in the (more or less) willing pursuit of different masculine and feminine ideals. The opposing practice of leaving facial hair to grow came next, with different periods and social groups proving to be particularly significant. The following two chapters, each with two case studies, consider what happens when it is the length of locks that is at issue. As it turns out, hair has been remarkably adept at both mobilizing and coming to stand for change and challenge. Hair can be adversarial. In what follows here, the confrontation is couched in primarily political terms and the fracture points are sited in the seventeenth and eighteenth centuries. In the last chapter we focus in on the twentieth century and the profound social upheavals in which hair played a leading role.

Civil War

In 1628, ardent moralist William Prynne (1600–69) published a short book about long hair. In eighty-four pages packed with spurious, repetitive argument and massively involved sentences far longer than the hair to which he objected, Prynne 'proved' that on men such styles were 'badges of infamie, effeminacy, vanitie, singularitie, pride, lasciuiousnesse, and shame'. Although the text laid a blanket condemnation over all such practices, his particular target were the lovelocks then in vogue amongst the fashionable. In this style a section of hair was grown longer than the rest to lie over the wearer's shoulder at the front (Fig. 5.1). It could either be worn loose, or braided and tied with a ribbon. In *The vnlouelinesse, of loue-lockes* Prynne showed how truly appalled he was at the fashion 'in which too many of our Nation haue of late begun to glory', throwing every epithet he could think of at those who nourished these 'vnnaturall, sinfull, and vnlawfull ornaments'. Declaiming the corrupted morality and unchristian behaviour of the men who fashioned themselves thus, in an extended metaphor he exposed the idolatrous vanity of those who had so turned from true religion: '*the* Barber *is their* Chaplaine: *his* Shop, *their* Chappell: *the* Looking-glasse, *their* Bible; *and their* Haire, *and* Lockes, *their* God'.[1]

It was perhaps unfortunate for Prynne that fashionable wearers of lovelocks included in their number the head of both state and church, Charles I (Fig. 4.4). But Prynne was not known for being conciliatory. Later writings – including an equally vehement and spectacularly lengthy attack on acting and the theatre – brought him into direct conflict with the crown, and saw him publicly denouncing female actors at the same time as Queen Henrietta Maria was preparing her performance for a court masque. Prynne was in fact found guilty of sedition twice (in 1633 and 1637), and was eventually fined, imprisoned, branded and maimed. Indeed, having his ears sliced off meant the cruel irony of thereafter having to wear his hair long enough to at least cover the disfigured parts of his head. Although

FIGURE 5.1.
The lovelocked Henry
Wriothesley, 3rd
Earl of Southampton,
in his late teens or
maybe aged twenty.
He continued to wear
a lovelock for some
years, as seen in further
portraits.

the representational accuracy of his portraits can be questioned – his appearance is airbrushed to the extent of showing neither his slit nose nor branded cheeks – all existing images show him with his hair either sitting just below his ears or an inch or two longer (Fig. 5.2).

William Prynne was not the first to be offended at the sight of men with long hair. Indeed, he himself makes a point of being part of this moral tradition, citing extensively everything from sermons and social commentary published over the preceding fifty years, to the writings of medieval church councils, to patristic texts and both testaments of the Bible; his densely packed sidenotes are a pedant's dream. Joining the chorus of these voices that had come before, Prynne argued that long hair was the sign of a man more given over to pampering his body than tending his soul, more concerned with his appearance than his moral worth, more taken up with himself than with others or with God. Added to this, long hair on a man ran counter to the laws of nature (equals God) and, being like women's hair, was fundamentally effeminizing. None of this was new; these were the familiar terms in which unease with appearances was often cast. Something that was to be new, however, occurred around thirteen years after the publication of Prynne's book, in those volatile months leading up to the outbreak of the Civil War. Sometime around 1641 to 1642 – no one quite knows how or when – hairstyles became deeply factionalized. Instead of hair length forming a minor part of the conservative moral arsenal, with traditional salvoes being fired at predictable targets, suddenly it was pushed centre stage and found to be bearing a heavy weight of new meanings. The customary moral certainties were swept aside; instead long and short hair were each linked to fundamentally opposed political and religious positions, with the divide between them quickly fracturing into bitter and prolonged violence. Long hair was the sign of loyalty, the index of political and religious orthodoxy; short hair the revolutionary challenge to the status quo. The cavaliers and roundheads were born.

Although the precise circumstances will never be certain, contemporary witnesses and modern historians agree that these names first appeared in the public consciousness in the winter of 1641–42.[2] It was a London-based phenomenon, most likely sparked by insults

Mr. William Prynne, for writing a booke againſt Stage-players called Hiſtrio—maſtix was firſt conſured in the Starr-Chamber to looſe both his Eares in the pillorie, fined 5000ˡⁱ & perpetuall impriſonment in the Towre of London. After this, on a meer ſuſpition of writing other bookes, but nothing at all proved againſt him, hee was again cenſured in the Starr-chamber to looſe the ſmall remainder of both his eares in the pillorie, to be Stigmatized on both his Cheekes with a firey-iron, was fined again 5000ˡⁱ and baniſhed into yᵉ Iſle of Ierſey, there to ſuffer perpetuall- Croſs- impriſonmᵗ; no freinds being permitted to ſee him, on pain of impriſonment,

FIGURE 5.2.
William Prynne, vehemently opposed to masculine long hair. Although his own hair seems quite lengthy in our eyes, it contrasts with the longer styles often worn by the elite. It also demonstrates the relativity of judgements about hair, and that what was seen in one period as short, in another might be considered as immoral in its length.

thrown during civil disturbances – clashes at Westminster between apprentices and other citizens on the one hand, and armed officers on the other. The hostility between the two became focussed on the politics of appearances: the crowd of ordinary folk in working apparel and plain hair; the officers in their martial finery, with the self-presentation of courtiers. An account first published ten years later, in 1651, described it in the following terms:

> Those people or citizens who used thus to flock unto Westminster were, most of them, men of mean or a middle quality themselves . . . but set on by some of better quality. . . . They were modest in their apparel, but not in language. They had the hair of their heads very few of them longer than their ears; whereupon it came to pass that those who usually with their cries attended at Westminster were by a nickname called *Roundheads*. The courtiers, again, wearing their hair and locks and always sworded, at last were called by these men *Cavaliers*; and so, after that this broken language had been used awhile, all that adhered unto the Parliament were termed *Roundheads*, and all that took part or that appeared for his Majesty, *Cavaliers*.[3]

From their initial appearance in the midst of the civil unrest in London, these names quickly gained traction and spread throughout the country. By June 1642, for example, Lady Brilliana Harley and her family at Brampton in rural Herefordshire were being openly abused by locals. In her words, 'they looked upon me and wished all puritans and Roundheads at Brampton hanged'.[4] The rapid and popular take off of the terms was spurred by a burst of pamphlets and broadsides that began to appear (Fig. 5.3), in which much mileage was made on both sides,

FIGURE 5.3.
A woodcut image from the title page of one of the many pamphlets produced in the Civil War. The cavaliers are on the left: long hair, feathered hats, sashes and spurred boots for riding. The roundheads have plainer garb and shorter hair. The confrontation between the two parties extends to the dogs in the centre. Prince Rupert's shaggy dog Puddle growls 'Roundhead Curr', while the shorthaired Pepper responds with 'Cavalier Dog'. They are egged on by their respective owners.

the names being variously adopted, contested, lampooned and manipulated. As we might put it today, 'cavalier' and 'roundhead' went viral.

On the royalist side 'cavalier' was quickly reclaimed, losing its absolutist connotations, including perhaps associations with the Spanish soldier (*cavaliero* or *cabalero*), a figure representing the Catholic nation with whom England had so long been enemies.[5] Instead the cavalier was refigured as the stylish swashbuckling hero, whose poster boy was the dashing and militarily effective Prince Rupert, the king's nephew (Fig. 5.4). As one pamphlet stated simply, a cavalier 'may be an honest man, though he wear skarlet and silver lace, and holds it no sin to be in fashion'.[6] As for 'roundhead', those on the loyalist benches played with it as a synonym for humourless stupidity: 'A *Round-head* is a man (though cut within a quarter of an inch to the skull) hath more hair than wit, and according to his daily distractions, may be titled *Hair-brain'd*.'[7] In some tracts the figure was quite literally demonized. Thus, in *The Devil turn'd Round-head* (1642) by John Taylor, Satan is so impressed with the rebels that he begins to imitate their beliefs, speech and appearance, including cropping 'his hair close to his ears, that he might more easily hear the blasphemy, which proceeded from them . . . And lastly, that he might be in a perfect opposition to the *Cavalier*'.[8]

On the other hand, those who were seeking political and religious change also attacked their opponents with verve. Cavaliers were delineated as sexually incontinent, bestial, foppish, over-fashioned and effeminate. Their long hair was associated both with the taint of Catholicism and the figure of the roaring boy, a louche destructive character whose debauched behaviour was already a long-established trope. Cavaliers were 'rattle heads' (pleasure-lovers with heads empty of ideas or morals) and shag-poll locusts, a plague of long-haired anti-socials who consumed all they lighted on, leaving in their wake only barren waste.[9] And in a masterly series of reversals, the label of roundhead was both rehabilitated and then flung in turn at the opposition. Thus the term was adopted with pride – 'your Puritan or Round-head was made by him who made the round world, and all that therein is, by *Iehovah Elohim* in most perfect beauty, shape, and form' – only to be turned back on detractors with the claim that the

FIGURE 5.4.
Cavalier poster boy, Prince Rupert, 1642.

true roundheads were in fact the tonsured monks whose papist image haunted the established church.[10] In a final reversal the label was applied to the cavaliers themselves, whose sexual incontinence and lax morality had led them to contract the pox and suffer syphilitic hair loss. Beneath the wig that the cavalier in his shame was forced to adopt, lay the bald glans-like pate of the real roundhead.[11]

The cavalier/roundhead designations were immensely potent, so much so that they still resonate today, neatly dividing up the chaos of the English Civil War into easily compassed categories just as they did over 370 years ago. Obviously this was not really a conflict over hair length, but rather physical appearances were mobilized to stand in for a raft of other, more serious matters concerning the nature of authority, the structure of the church, the role of the individual, and his or her relationship to God. Short hair, already typically worn by the non-elite, was thus made a signal of rebellion – a challenge to the traditional agents of power.

But what was the reality of the appearances that lay behind the increasingly frenzied name-calling and propaganda? In actuality it was much more complex and much less clear, as indeed was articulated by some at the time. In the words of a puritan-sympathizing pamphlet: 'we intend not a definitive sentence against any particular person for wearing of their hair . . . all that weare long hair are not Locusts; as also, all that weare not long hair, are not Round-heads'.[12] This echoed the views articulated by Lucy Hutchinson, wife of leading Parliamentarian John Hutchinson, who vigorously repudiated the roundhead label, seeing it as a self-identification espoused only by dangerous extremists. In her memoirs she pointed out that her husband had in fact 'a very fine thickset head of hair, kept it clean and handsome without any affectation, so that it was a great ornament to him' (Fig. 5.5). It angered her that 'the godly of those days' would 'not allow him to be religious because his hair was not in their cut'.[13] Alternatively, we might consider Archbishop Laud, whose perceived popish sympathies and crusade to purge the church of all puritan practices appalled and utterly alienated the godly. However, before he lost his head – found guilty of Parliament's charges of treason and spreading Catholicism – the hair that he wore upon it was habitually modest and closely cropped (Fig. 5.6). Without a doubt, it was much shorter than many of those who accused and sat in judgement on him.

That appearance did not in fact provide an infallible guide to identity was to some worrying. In 1644, the year before Laud was executed, godly preacher George Gipps delivered a Fast sermon before the House of Commons. In it he described his shock on arriving in roundhead-controlled London and seeing the appearance of notable men of the cloth; he could hardly believe, he says, their 'ruffianly haire' and 'Cavalerian garbe'.[14] Nine years later, in the middle years of the Interregnum, another godly cleric, Thomas Hall, published *The Loathesomeness of Long Haire* (1654). In the same tradition as Prynne's diatribe against lovelocks, Hall cites Prynne with great approval, musters the same line of moral and spiritual

FIGURE 5.5.
Long-haired puritan Colonel John Hutchinson, commander in the Parliamentarian army.

FIGURE 5.6.
Short-haired Archbishop Laud, whose church policies led to his execution by Parliament.

authorities, and calls for a reformation of long-haired abuses apparently current even under puritan government.

These continued calls against long hair witness the continuity of a particular ethical position, but also reveal the limits of stereotypes to adequately describe the complex nature of the actual beliefs and behaviours of real people. It is manifest that there has to be enough truth to a stereotype for it to have any power: the labels of roundhead and cavalier were not empty. Many who led the rebel cause did not sport the long curls of elite fashion, but then neither did all loyalists. And the rank and file of both sides were drawn from ordinary folk whose income and social position precluded them from having anything but a minor engagement with the questions that surrounded fashionable self-presentation. Rather than hair revealing the truth of a binary split in society, it was a powerfully emotive symbol that drew on an ancient pedigree of debate over its appearance. It provided an easy certainty in the midst of chaos; hair was a visual sign pressed into the service of faction.

Intriguingly, and in a way typical of the uncontrollable mechanisms of fashion, the roundhead political victory proved a dismal failure for short hair. Although monarchy was eventually restored, it was never again absolutist, and after the Glorious Revolution of 1688, the principle of parliamentary democracy was unassailable. However, despite the rise of the middle classes and the waning importance of the court as fashion's arbiter, hair just kept on getting longer. By the eighteenth century, not only was it longer than ever, it was often someone else's. And it was the powdered long hair and wigs of this new era that witnessed the next challenge.

The republican crop

As the 1790s dawned, the mood in Britain was uneasy. The loss of the American colonies to revolutionaries was a bitter and recent memory. King George, although recovered for the time being, had just suffered what was to be merely his first bout of madness. The Prince of Wales, heir to the throne and Regent waiting in the wings, was dissipated and debt-ridden, illegally married to a Catholic, and a drain on the public purse. In 1789 the French Revolution had sent shock waves across the Channel, followed by a tide of escaping émigrés. January 1793 was to witness the execution of Louis XVI, and a month later Britain would be at war with the new republic. At home, radicalism was increasingly vocal, with a range of individuals and societies agitating for political reform, universal male suffrage, workers' education and freedom for the press. Added to this, bad harvests meant that by early 1795 hunger would be an issue, with some conjuring the spectre of famine. In the midst of this unrest, turmoil and uncertainty, a shocking new fashion began to appear: people began to wear their hair short (Fig. 5.7). The matter of a new hairstyle seems ludicrously trivial when set beside this background of turbulence and sweeping social change. However, appreciating the visual and moral context in which the crop appeared makes clear that its impact and challenge were significant, and that to late eighteenth-century eyes, short-cut hair presented an implicit threat to the traditional order.

Powder

But first some background. By the last decade of the eighteenth century, no one could remember a time when elite hair had not been long. For around 170 years, fashion and status had agreed that privileged masculinity was connoted by hair reaching at least to the shoulder. Even more dramatically, for much of this time it was customary for a man's long hair either to come in the form of a wig, or to be crafted as though it did. Essential to this enterprise were the two giants of eighteenth-century haircare: powder and pomatum. By absorbing grease and oils powder was used as a cleanser, by making the hair's texture workable it enabled the styling of elaborate hairdos, and in either its white or tinted forms it altered the hair (or wig's) hue. Keeping long hair clean, styled and presentable, powder was essential to gentility, to social acceptance and to self-respect.

THE KNOWING CROPS

HA! JACK IS IT YOU___ HOW ARE YOU DAM-ME.

Publish'd 1st May 1791 by LAURIE & WHITTLE 53 Fleet Street London.

FIGURE 5.7.
The new short cut depicted here in *The Knowing Crops* of 1791. The print also features other new-fashioned, innovative dress forms with which the crop was often associated: pantaloons, a tight coat worn shrugged off the shoulders, steeple hat, and a short bludgeon. The quizzing glass held by the figure on the left is yet another pointer to dandyism.

FIGURE 5.8.
A hairdresser applying powder to a man's hair using a powder puff, 1770.

The amounts of hair powder used varied, but by the 1770s, when hairstyles for both men and women were at their largest and most complex, the quantities consumed were prodigious. Apart from that used directly by the hairdresser in combing, pinning and styling the hair, the finished headdress was dredged all over, like a cake with icing sugar (Figs 5.8 and 5.9). Because of the resulting clouds of white dust, typically this took place in a small designated room – a powder closet – where the sitter was swathed in linen covers and a protective mask put over his or her face. Powder was puffed all about with a special bellows device (see foreground of Fig. 2.19) or a shaker, and any excess that found its way between the mask and the powdering clothes to settle on the skin was scraped off with a powdering knife. Diarist Mary Frampton (1773–1846), in remembering the elaborate formal headdresses of her youth, suggested that 'one pound, and even two pounds' might be got through at a single sitting.[15] Certainly excise accounts from the period

The ENGLISHMAN in PARIS.

Un Perruquier
1780

FIGURE 5.9.
A hairdresser/wigmaker powders a woman's coiffure using a shaker, 1780.

before 1795 show that Britain produced over eight million pounds of starch every year, most of which went into hair powder.[16]

This starch, from which the best powders were made, was itself derived from cereal crops like wheat, corn and barley. Although poor-quality grain could be used in the process, manufacture was by no means confined to such stuff as was unsuitable for consumption. This gave rise to a long and enduring concern over both the economics and the morality of starch production, a concern that at times sharpened into public argument and government legislation.[17] When food was in short supply and the price of bread too high for the poor, then the 'wasting' of cereal crops to make starch, or its offspring hair powder, came into stark focus. Just such a moment occurred in the mid-1790s. Bad weather, poor growing seasons, meagre harvests and the resulting high prices boiled over into food riots throughout the period from 1794 to 1796.[18] Coupled with the crippling national expense of the war with France, Prime Minister William Pitt came up with a novel strategy to kill these two social problems with one legislative stone: a tax on hair powder.[19] The powder tax of 1795 required those who wished to wear powder to first purchase an annual licence, costing one guinea (£1 1s). Those that did so quickly became known as 'guinea pigs', a term deriving from politician Edmund Burke's notorious 'swinish multitude'. Coined in his attack on radicalism, *Reflections on the Revolution in France* (1790), the infamous phrase described the yobbish common lot, a stark contrast to the pigs of a different calibre who had paid their guinea to powder. The names of these licence holders were published in lists that were affixed to public places like church doors and market crosses, which – in keeping with the sumptuary laws with which the act shares certain features – enabled the policing of the law to be done by mutual surveillance. Again borrowing from earlier sumptuary legislation, the carrot to lure individuals to inform on their powder-wearing but unlicensed acquaintances and neighbours was half shares in the £20 fine levied on those found guilty. Gaining income from both compliance with or defiance of the powder act, and with little outlay required to police it, it seemed the government could not lose.

For a range of reasons, however, the tax proved massively contentious, generating a short-lived but extremely vigorous public debate waged through the medium of newspapers, pamphlets and prints (Fig. 5.10). The inherently funny nature of the tax only fuelled the furore, and both graphic and textual satirists had a field day, mining the subject for its considerable comic potential. It is often assumed that the powder act and its controversies caused the practice of powdering to die away and, by extension, that it was instrumental in establishing a new fashion for short hair. Certainly there was a rapid fall in the number of certificates sold and thus in the money the powder tax raised. When presenting the proposed measure to Parliament as part of his budget, Pitt estimated its annual revenue at £210,000.[20] In reality, over the first six years (1795–1800) the tax raised the considerably lower average annual sum of £158,000, and thereafter it plummeted: in 1801–02 the amount was £75,000,

FAVORITE GUINEA PIGS *going to Market.*

FIGURE 5.10.

Favorite Guinea Pigs Going to Market, 1795, is a satirical comment on the powder tax. In the centre, William Pitt is driving the powdered guinea pigs to market for sale (revenue from the tax) and slaughter (being bled dry) – the signs on the building indicate that it's an office selling guinea licences and also declare 'Pigs Meat sold Here!' 'Why don't you drive them in?' complains Pitt to Queen Charlotte on the right. The smock-clad George III, dealing with a recalcitrant swine who is noticeably unpowdered, points out that you can only drive people so far and tax them so hard before they rebel.

in 1814 it was under £700, and in 1820 the total net amount raised was just £12.[21] So within a very short time powder-wearing fell away from fashion completely, thereafter becoming a negligible practice confined to servants in liveried regalia. At first sight, it does indeed look as if the goose of taxation killed the golden egg of potential revenue. However, powder use had been declining and short hair raising eyebrows well before the 1795 tax polarized the nation's drawing rooms. The measure probably hastened the demise of powder and long hair, but emphatically did not cause it. Instead, the startling new look got caught up with, and immersed in, the furore caused by the act, which to a large degree has obscured its real origins. To fully understand the crop, therefore, we need now to examine it in this context of the politics and propaganda of powdering.

A crop of revolutionaries

In England, short hair seems to have first emerged in the 1780s and was part of a much broader and long-term trend towards the democratization of appearances and greater simplicity of fashionable dress forms. Contemporary Soame Jenyns (1704–87) noted this movement, observing with disapproval not only the levelling of distinction between servants and those they served (an age-old complaint) but even its reversal, whereby the footmen were in wigs and ruffles and the valet better dressed than his master. On hindsight we can see this as presaging the formal regalia of nineteenth-century servants' uniforms, whose decorative and ossified forms were a foil to the understated dress code of upper-class masculinity in the modern age. Jenyns, however, could only deplore such dressing down by gentlemen and ladies, which he saw as 'debasing ourselves' to the meanness of common folk 'by ridiculous imitation of their dresses and occupations'. It is from this misplaced desire to imitate working dress, Jenyns declares, that 'were derived the flapped hat, and cropped hair, the green frock [coat], the long staff, and buckskin breeches'.[22]

This early mention of the crop very clearly places the style in opposition to polite forms of both dress and comportment, and declares the fashion to have been inspired by the aping of a lower social register. Jenyns's sense is echoed by other commentators, who also made it clear that they considered short hair to be an oppositional style that pitted ill-breeding against the decently behaved norm and youth against tradition: cropped hair (the hair of the masses) was loutish and its wearers young slovenly boors unfit for genteel society. Thus that famed and astringent delineator of character Horace Walpole (1717–97) in 1791 described the non-attendance at a royal ball of 'Lord Lorn and seven other young men of fashion'. They 'now crop their hair short and wear no powder', which, 'not being the etiquette yet', means they are 'not fit to appear so docked'. In another letter, he commented further on what he saw as the ill-groomed and ungenteel nature of the fashion, and how it made all young people look the same: 'I pass by them in the streets . . . and the dirty shirts and shaggy hair of the young men, who have levelled nobility almost as much as the mobility [mob, rabble] in France have, have confounded all individuality.'[23]

Over the course of 1791, a rash of newspaper mentions and visual caricatures indicates that the crop had become a common enough sight in London society to merit it becoming a public target for jibes and comic criticism. Associated with a number of other signature dress items, the ensemble together became the identifier of loungers and other disreputable figures who existed on the edges of the genteel world. This typical description comes from a September issue of *The Times*:

The head hair cropped close all round, so as to make the head appear like an *inverted bason*, and no powder. The waistcoat tight with an high collar very stiff, so as to rub against the roots of the hair . . . The coat loosely made, and hanging off the shoulders about mid-way from the clavicle to the elbow. If it can be brought so as to make the skirts touch the ground – it will be more fashionable. The breeches extremely tight, long at the knees . . . Boots and spurs, and a stick about four inches long, peeping out of the right coat pocket . . . The gait must be awkward and the head carried as if nature had set it on in a crooked position – a kind of vacant stare is also requisite, and if the person aims at being very genteel indeed, he must be almost quite blind and deaf, neither seeing nor hearing any body . . . He must stretch and yawn and say the town's a bore – and that . . . he's engaged all the rest of the week with the *Barrys* at Brighton – with the Duke of Hamilton – with Mendoza, Ward, Big Ben, or the Tinman . . . He must be very consequential until he gets to the end of Bow-street – then taking off his spurs and putting up his coat, he must go home, and for fear of waking his master, give one gentle tap at the shop door in Cheapside, and go to bed supperless.[24]

The different elements in this lengthy passage appear repeatedly in conjunction with the crop throughout the early years of the 1790s: the clothes, the comportment, the ambivalent class status. The mention of specific named individuals is also significant. The 'Barrys of Brighton' refers to Richard, Henry and Augustus, the three cropped and notorious Barry brothers. Members of the Prince of Wales's dissipated set, who were at that time partying the obscure seaside town into fashionability, Richard 7th Earl of Barrymore (1769–93) was particularly infamous. Nicknamed 'Hellgate' for his scandalous behaviour, in his twenty-three short years he managed to run through his inheritance, elope with an underage girl, and die debt-laden in a shooting accident. Along with his short hair, the 8th Duke of Hamilton (1756–99) was known for his extra-marital affairs, to the extent that in 1794 his wife would take the then unusual step of suing for divorce. The papers openly speculated about the fate of his title if he should die without legitimate issue.[25] Mendoza, Ward, Big Ben and the Tinman were famed boxers, part of an up-and-coming but often brutal sport. Boxing matches drew huge crowds and constituted a classless and resolutely masculine space, where rough equality of gender trumped status and the dictates of polite society. Finally with regard to *The Times* piece, it implicitly connects the figure of the crop with the emerging idea of the dandy, which was to be given full rein in the first half of the following century.[26] In the tightness of his clothes, the height of his collar, and his studied disengagement and disinterest, we see an early form of dandiacal masculinity distinguishing itself from the brocaded and bewigged politesse of the previous generations (Fig. 5.11).

    As was apparent from the comments by both Horace Walpole and Soame Jenyns, right from the start the crop was felt by many to dangerously blur important social distinctions. In that historical context, moreover, it could not fail to call to mind the erasure of class difference in Revolutionary France, from where this fashion for short hair was (it seems erroneously) believed to have come. A passage that typically plays with these ideas appeared in *The Times* on Christmas Eve 1791, under the heading 'Society of Levellers'. The spoof article lists the resolutions taken at a supposed meeting of the 'friends of a General Revolution in Europe', who wished to remove all distinctions of birth, property and education. This was to be achieved, the society declared, by having everyone habited alike, most particularly with all

CROPS GOING TO QUOD!

young levellers having 'their hair cropped close round the head in the form of a semicircle'. By such measures, 'the Shop Boy shall not be known from the Peer – the Pickpocket from the Man of Fashion – or the Gentleman from the Blackguard'.[27] Sir Nathanial William Wraxall, musing in his historical memoirs on the collapse of complex dress formality, remembered something similar. Although he noted there had been a gradual undermining of standards beforehand (which certainly agrees with Jenyns's complaints from the 1780s),

> Dress never totally fell, till the Era of Jacobinism and of equality, in 1793, and 1794. It was then that Pantaloons, cropped hair, and shoe-strings, as well as the total abolition of buckles and ruffles, together with the disuse of hair-powder, characterized the men: while the ladies, having cut off those Tresses . . . exhibited heads rounded '*a la Victime et a la Guillotine,*' as if ready for the stroke of the axe.[28]

As short hair in England first appeared before 1789, its relationship with Revolutionary France is not as simple as direct borrowing. Yet as we can see here events and fashions over the Channel definitely added to the crop an extra edge, underlying the demotic fashion with hints of brutality and violence. Anyone who read the foreign news, for instance, would know about Louis Philippe duc d'Orléans (1747–93), radical in politics despite his royal blood

FIGURE 5.11.
Crops Going to Quod, 1791, again depicts the stereotypical figure of this fashion in short hair, tight tasselled pantaloons, tight coat worn off the shoulder, and a steeple hat.
It also plays on the idea that the crop is on the edge of polite society – of dubious manners and morals – as is indicated by the coming incarceration of the figures in prison, or quod.

and cousinship to the king. Eschewing his titles, Bourbon lineage and long hair, the duke was active in the revolution, in 1792 re-inventing himself with the new surname Egalité and a sans culotte-like crop.[29] His activity on behalf of the cause notwithstanding – a member of the National Convention, he voted in favour of Louis XVI's execution – during the Terror, Citoyen Egalité was in turn tried, found guilty and sentenced to the guillotine. It was his career that Edmund Burke no doubt had in mind when attacking the Duke of Bedford's reformist politics and powder tax-defying crop, warning the duke that the mob was no respecter of rank, role or appearance: 'They will not trouble *their* heads, with what part of *his* head, his hair is cut from; and they will look with equal respect on a tonsure and a crop. Their only questions will be . . . how he cuts up? how he tallows in the cawl or on the kidneys?' (Fig. 5.12).[30]

The semantic links that could so easily be forged between the guillotine's crop of victims, its cropping of their heads from their bodies and the cropping of hair were exploited to the full.

> Cutting off the hair, is the *extreme unction* of the High Priest of the Guillotine! It is always customary with the *Jack Ketch* [executioner] of *France*, previously to the victim's execution – as the *last* mark of *lively* attention – to make a *crop* of the unhappy *martyr* to *mobocracy!* Why should our *young Swells*, therefore, *play* with the *fashionable edge-tools* of *France*?[31]

As Wraxall reminds us above, there were even named styles (*à la Victime*, *à la Guillotine*) that played with the echoes of threat and bloodshed. If we consider for a moment what might be the reaction today of naming a – one can only say 'cutting-edge' – hairstyle after ritual beheadings, we can appreciate the shock of this (very grisly) new. Other, classically named styles conjured a republican Roman past. The *coiffure à la Titus* called to mind Titus Herminius Aquilinus (d. 498 BC), famous for defending the city against invading monarchical forces. The 'Brutus' was named for the assassin whose 'unkindest cut of all' referred not to his cropped hair, but to the plunge of his dagger as he killed the too-powerful Caesar.

It was into this context, in which short hair was edgy, confrontational, freighted with meaning – and also alluring – that in 1795 William Pitt launched his powder tax. The results were startling, and the unpowdered crop got drawn into the fray. Although generating little controversy in Parliament, once the measure came to the attention of the wider public the argument began. Some objected to the fact that it was a tax not on the purchase of powder but on the wearing of it (another similarity, incidentally, with earlier sumptuary laws). In addition, an individual who powdered only once a year was obliged to pay the same guinea sum as someone who powdered every day, which was considered to be manifestly unjust. Many thought that the tax was a burden that would therefore fall unfairly on those at the margins of respectability, the impoverished genteel and hard-working tradesmen. Another argument evolved over the relationship of starch with grain, and thus the likely effect of the powder tax on the food supply.

A further debate, and the one that concerns us here, was sparked over the measure's potentially divisive nature. Given that the tax was designed to raise money to bankroll, in Pitt's words, the ongoing 'just and necessary war',[32] some were aware that it created not only potential revenue but also an opportunity for silent, though eloquent, protest. From Parliament's front benches to agitators dodging charges of sedition, anyone opposing Britain's fight with the French republic could articulate their position by refusing to powder their hair. The Earl of Moira raised this concern in the House of Lords. In objecting to the proposed tax he warned of 'the distinctions it would introduce with respect to persons of different parties and political sentiments'. Pointing to contemporary events in France and to the roundheads and cavaliers of English history, he cautioned that outwards marks of difference were important in articulating partisan positions, and that in passing such an act Parliament would be handing to political dissidents 'a certain mode of distinguishing those of their own way of thinking'.[33] Furthermore, by clearly demarcating between those that could afford the guinea and those that could not, the hair powder tax politicized appearances in a reckless way, starkly materializing the divide between rich and poor with the puff of a powder-filled bellows. In such unsettled times, this was felt by some to be not only foolhardy but dangerous, creating a public show of privilege that could so easily invite violent reprisals. As the immediate contrast made between guinea pigs and the swinish multitude suggests, they were maybe right to be concerned.

An early high-profile individual to grasp the opportunity for dissent so opportunely offered by the tax was the Duke of Bedford. A Foxite whig opposed to Pitt, he not only stopped powdering but cropped his hair, a move that was widely understood as expressing his 'levelling' sympathies (Fig. 5.13). By September, *The Times* was declaring that 'Most of the Jacobins that have ears, have cropped off their hair.'[34] Four months later the liberal *Morning Chronicle* ran a defence of the crop, which concluded with a list of notable figures who had

Tis gone,—and like the baseless fabric of a Vision,—left not a wreck behind.

Doch d un, to be the go.'

Blefs me our John what hast then done with thy tail?

G Woodward del.

Whim of the Moment or the Bedford Level!!

S·W·F

FIGURE 5.13.

In *The Whim of the Moment or the Bedford Level!!*, 1795, the aristocratic Duke of Bedford crops off his long hair, or tail, as does the aspirant country fellow on the right. Although the working man wears old-fashioned breeches and the duke pantaloons, the stripes on the waistcoat of the one and the stockings of the other set up an echo, and underline the fact that the visual difference between them has effectively been levelled. The title also puns on the achievements of the duke's grandfather, the 4th Duke, who oversaw the draining of a large area of fenland, known as the Bedford Level.

sacrificed their locks. Joining Bedford and three more dukes were twenty-nine other titled or publicly significant men who had submitted to the cut. Two further named individuals – one of them being Pitt's political opponent Charles Fox – had 'not cut their Hair, but left off the use of Powder'. For this, declared the radical-sympathizing newspaper, 'they deserve the thanks of their Country for the example'.[35]

While there were jokes at the expense of those who cropped – word plays on the emasculating effects of cutting off the 'tail', as the pigtail or queue of hair was commonly called, and jibes about the dark-haired crops using coal dust rather than hair powder – supporters of political change embraced the idea of the short-haired fashion. Indeed, they seized on its political potential and ran with it. One striking instance of this appeared in *The Philanthropist*, a weekly tract published by Daniel Isaac Eaton (bap. 1753–1814), a radical printer. The issue for Monday 18 January 1796 included a song entitled 'The Republican Crop', whose opening lyrics declared short hair to be not only manly and natural but also moral, neatly calling on Pauline strictures against masculine long hair that the seventeenth-century moralists like William Prynne had also repeatedly wielded.[36] The song went on to claim a bold genealogy of political freedom, from Athenian heroes to liberty-loving Romans: 'Each Brutus, each Cato, were none of them fops, / But all to a man wore Republican crops.' The next verse turned to France and depicted the revolutionary triumph of the cropped over the despotic long-haired tyrants, before bringing the argument closer to home, with a résumé of the Civil War. Elliptically, and skirting a fine line around seditious incitement, the lyrics describe a roundhead fight against Charles I, and his eventual execution:

> In England's proud days no long hair was seen,
> Unless on the heads of base scoundrels I ween,
> The Aristocrats then to freedom sworn foes,
> To bind us in chains, with a tyrant arose.
> To repel the vile slaves and our rights to maintain,
> Up sprung the brave crops and subdued them amain.
> The tyrant himself they caught tho' he fled;
> And to end all his schemes they crop't off his head.

The final verse is a rallying call to action that essentializes societal fracture into a question of appearances, to the point where a simple haircut signifies the brave new utopian world to come:

> Britons off with your hair, and you are sure to prevail,
> For a crop strikes with terror, a slave with a tail,
> When your ancestors wore short hair on their head,
> They valiantly fought, and they nobly bled.
> For Equality's laws, and the freedom of man,
> Can you ever submit to betraying their plan,
> Then follow their steps, and no longer be fops,
> Your Hampdens, your Miltons, your Sydneys were crops.

It is the last line of this song that is the most interesting and the most audacious. The three men it refers to were important figures of the seventeenth century, highly influential in later political radicalism and reform movements in Britain, France and America.[37] John Milton (1608–74) was famed not only for his poetry but also his polemical writings, which after his death established him as a republican and posthumously enrolled him in the Whig camp. Algernon Sidney (or Sydney, 1623–83) was likewise a founding father of constitutional reform, whose tracts on political theory and plans for armed resistance led to his execution for treason, though he was survived by his associate John Hampden (bap. 1653–96). These three, who so vigorously advocated a shift in the uneven balance of privilege and power, have been co-opted here as crops. In actual fact, in real life they were all long-haired, as befitted the fashions of their time. Sidney's portraits depict him as the aristocrat he was, with abundant curled hair flowing down and over his shoulders (Fig. 5.14). In later life Hampden was

FIGURE 5.14.
The long-haired 'crop',
Algernon Sidney.

described as 'a beau [who] dresses and powders', that is, wore formal, elaborate outfits and hair powder.[38] However, here this is conveniently forgotten, or rather is subsumed under a greater truth. The 'crop' has unshackled itself from literal visual appearance, and instead articulates a set of beliefs that have actually nothing to do with outer looks. These three long-haired radicals are thus metaphorical crops, claimed as part of a spurious but inspiring genealogy to fight in a battle waged partly through visual signs and outward appearances.

Despite (or maybe because of) the crop's politicization, by the mid-1790s the fashion for shorter hair was unstoppable for both men and women: long powdered locks were clearly of the past; the cut was of the present. Less loaded comment began to appear, and even neutral fashion reportage. Thus in 1795 stalwart defender of hair powder, the powder manufacturer John Hart, had to admit that even before the tax young men and women of rank were powdering much less often and favouring simpler-looking styles, an observation that again accords with the evidence of Soame Jenyns and Nathaniel Wraxall.[39] A letter to *The Times* in January 1796 from 'Amicus Crop' not only laid claim to the fashion, but took it into new territory by aligning it with a personal moral reform, a New Year's resolution of cropping: 'I have begun the new year . . . with a resolute endeavour to *crop* my own vices, and to cultivate and cherish in their stead a *crop* of virtues.'[40] By 1797 the provincial papers were advising female readers as to this shift, the ladies of Norfolk learning that even for formal dress the hair was to be cropped.[41] Although the nineteenth century would see abundance of hair for women becoming a cultural preoccupation, in its early years a no-fuss simplicity was admired: 'no inconvenience . . . such as daubing it with greasy lard, and flour of the finest quality', was instead the goal.[42] As the *Lady's Monthly Museum* declared in 1801, 'Powder is universally out of use amongst the Ladies.'[43] As for men, by 1799 eighteenth-century established fashion had turned on its head, so that advertisements were appearing not for wigs as items of dress, but as devices to remediate a lack of hair. The naturalness of their appearance was touted, along with the fact that they did not need to be powdered. The selling of 'natural crop wigs' was a revolution indeed: instead of long hair being styled to look artificial, the artificial was now being finessed to appear like real and short-cut hair.[44] (Figs 5.15 and 5.16)

So the victory for short hair was in the end swift, and for men would prove to be extremely long lasting. Although the crop had been used by both sides of an ideological battle, this obscures its earlier appearance and its place in the unstoppable and long-term drift to greater simplicity of dress forms and a growing democratization of appearance. On hindsight, as societal structures changed, short hair was always going to happen, although the furore over the powder tax gave it an extra push. It remains to ask though, why did Pitt decide on the powder tax in the first place? He must have been aware that a few were already cropping their hair, and that many were using smaller quantities of powder on increasingly

FIGURES 5.15 AND 5.16.
Matching portraits of the Shurlock family, 1801. Both Robert and Henrietta Shurlock wear fashionable crops without a trace of powder. The long powdered hair and wigs of the eighteenth century are by now indisputably old-fashioned.

infrequent occasions. Why did he, as Fox observed in Parliament, choose to rely for revenue on such an uncertain source: 'for he who relied on the fashion of the day, built upon a slippery foundation'.[45] The matter becomes even more puzzling when put against the fact that ten years earlier, in 1785, a hair powder tax had been suggested by Lord Surrey in preference to Pitt's proposed tax on maid servants, and Pitt had opposed it. Indeed, he was eloquent in adducing the very same reasons as were later marshalled against him. Surrey's scheme was, he said, 'experimental and uncertain', and the revenue it generated would be unreliable. Moreover, it would be difficult to enforce, and it struck Pitt that this would 'depend chiefly on informers, which was not the most pleasant way for the collecting of any duty, as persons of that description were, of all others, the most detestable to the public'. He even expanded on how, given that powdering was so widespread, it would be easier to spot those who abstained rather than policing the generality of powdered heads. This lead to his next objection, which was that it was a poll tax – a charge that carried serious ideological weight and that a decade later was levelled against him in turn – and finally, that it would fall unfairly on those who could not necessarily afford it.[46]

For Pitt to enact a hair powder tax ten years later was an incredible volte-face. Nothing had changed to make a powder tax any more acceptable or certain – indeed, as by 1795 the custom of powdering had substantially decreased, as a source of revenue it was, if anything, an even less attractive proposition than before. The conclusion seems inescapable: in 1795 Pitt was deliberately trying to harness the crop's confrontational character to lever overt support. This appears implicit in the way he amusingly, lightly, introduced the measure for debate. If the whole business of governing and taxation were not so serious, he said, this would be a matter that 'the House would hardly hear with gravity'. Moreover, it was a measure 'which also applied to every member of that House'.[47] For in looking around the Commons' benches, Pitt would see row upon row of men with long, powdered hair, and in deliberately encompassing his fellow MPs in being liable for the one-guinea tax, he seems to have been drawing an implicit 'us and them' divide (Fig. 5.17). On one side of this silent comparison were the young and wayward with their unpowdered crops; on the other were the old values of formal dress and old-fashioned etiquette. Surely he must have hoped to have forced the issue, to have banked on a majority desire to avoid notoriety and newness by supporting the old practices of powdering. To powder on the side of the tax and of tradition, would also, by extension, be tacit approval of his broader policies, of which the powder tax was just an outrider of little intrinsic importance. Pitt miscalculated badly, but so too did those radical voices that championed the dark-haired crop as a badge of liberty. Short hair quickly became the hegemonic norm, not to be seriously challenged for nearly two hundred years. It is to this next confrontation that we will now turn.

Chapter 6

Social challenge: The long and the short of it

Youth revolution

The school where I received my secondary education sits under the open skies of New Zealand's Canterbury Plains. Bounded by the Southern Alps to the west and the Pacific Ocean to the east, 1970s rural Canterbury was a world away from Europe's student protests, the swinging London fashion scene and the demonstrations in the United States against the Vietnam War. Yet the ripples of youth rebellion eventually lapped across the globe even so far as this tiny country school. When my brother enrolled, in 1973, short hair for boys was mandatory: at the back of the neck it was not allowed to touch the collar. By the time I started four years later, a new and more liberal principal was in post. Among the many relaxations of the confining dress code, boys were now permitted to choose their hair length; one senior even wore a beard, which made him look more like a staff member than the schoolboy he still was. Unlike the other contexts explored in these last two chapters, in this case study the oppositional position – even in rural New Zealand – was articulated by *long* hair. The youth revolution of the 1960s reversed historical precedent and embodied social and political challenge in hair that was left to grow, its length countering the regulation short back and sides, becoming the most visible sign of a vast cultural confrontation.

The story begins in 1963 with the eruption into the public consciousness of four shaggy-haired young men from Liverpool (Fig. 6.1). The Beatles' first single had been released a few months previously, and in April they appeared on national television. It turned out to be a defining moment that not only changed Britain, but the world. By the following year their meteoric rise was part of the British pysche. In a December 1964 retrospective, the *Daily Mirror* described how 'the Mersey mopheads became the entertainment phenomenon of the age': society was already defining itself in relation to these men, busy making them into icons.[1] Of the many things that were said of the Beatles – in all the column inches devoted to the band, the tides of fan adoration and the dismissive barbs of establishment attacks – the most frequent comment in these early years concerned their hair. It seemed the Beatles could not be talked of without their mop tops also being evoked: the phenomenon of their music was inseparable from the spectacle of their appearance. For example, in May 1964 the American Tom Wolfe's article about John Lennon asked the question in its title: 'A highbrow under all that hair?' Three months earlier, the journalist Paul Johnson, writing a piece for the *New Statesman* called 'The Menace of Beatlism', had even claimed that the 'Queen expressed concern about the length of Ringo's hair'.[2]

Like a Werther Effect of personal style, copycat hair was everywhere. All over the country, boys and young men emulated the rising stars of the pop firmament, principally the Beatles, but also their seedier-looking peers The Rolling Stones. Schoolboys, students, apprentices and workers stopped visiting the barber and anxiously scrutinized the results in the mirror. There are three things of note about this. The first is the extreme youth of most of those

FIGURE 6.1.
(Facing page) The mop-haired Beatles as they erupted into the public consciousness in 1963. Here, backstage at the Finsbury Park Astoria, London.

involved. While the Republican crop of the 1790s had been associated with younger men as opposed to the old guard, here the agents were lads in school blazers and teens fresh out in the world. The youth revolution really *was* about the young.

The second thing, which from this vantage point seems the most surprising, is just how short this 'long' hair of the early sixties was. To modern eyes it seems the acme of respectability, and it is hard to recapture the sense of a traditional order under threat that was felt by many at the time. In positions where the young were subordinate, their

James Byrne, 14, covers his hair-trim as he leaves school with his mother. Haircuts for fifteen boys approved by the headmaster started a rumpus.

FIGURE 6.2.
A pupil at a Carlisle secondary school whose hair has been forcibly cut at the headmaster's order, 1964. Here reported in the *Daily Mirror*.

'long' hair was seen to embody rebellion and quickly led to clashes with authority. Thus Charles Hall, headmaster at a grammar school in Darlington, in the October of 1963 ordered his unwilling pupils to get a haircut. As he explained to the papers: 'Teaching standards of dress is an important part of the education we give at this school. We mustn't allow current crazes to lower these standards, Beatles or no Beatles. So I have asked the boys to keep their hair TIDY.'[3] The following June, educational colleagues at a secondary modern in Carlisle went a step further and forcibly cut the hair of fifteen of their pupils. The boys, aged between thirteen and fifteen, had been warned previously that, to quote the deputy head, their hair 'was far too long' and if they didn't do something about it themselves, it would be cut at school. True to his word, a month later the school recruited a barber who usually cut the hair of young soldiers, and without their consent lined the boys up to be barbered (Fig. 6.2).[4] Also in 1963 a commanding officer on HMS Bulwark, an aircraft carrier, issued the following communication: 'I note with alarm an increasing number of peculiar haircuts affected by teenaged members of the ship's company, attributable, I understand, to the influence of the Beatles.' The directive concluded with the order to 'Get de-Beatled now!' While the officer in question insisted he had nothing against the Beatles personally – indeed, they are probably nice young men, he conceded – 'there's nothing particularly nice about the way they wear their hair.'[5] Again, as it relates to the issue of length, it is important to be aware that what he was objecting to was a small number of young men, 'about four or five', combing their hair forward to make a fringe. The fringe was the infringement.

The third thing to bear in mind is the populist nature of this fashion challenge. It was not a change being led by the moneyed and elite, but – and this made it much more threatening to a stable social order – was a new style spreading from the grass roots up. Popularized by those Scouser boys made good, emulated by working class and provincial youths, long hair held two fingers to the trickle-down theory of fashion dissemination and instead asserted an impudent independence.

For those who voiced opposition to long hair, it touched on a number of sensitive points. It was interpreted as a lowering of standards, both personal and collective, and the actions of the senior teachers and the navy officer described above suggest that this perception was also accompanied by a fear that if not arrested forcibly, such a decline would be contagious. Long hair on boys was, furthermore, not only apostrophized as dirty and unkempt, but in an age-old charge of effeminacy and gender confusion, was said to make them look like girls. In the words of one newspaper columnist:

> In Britain – dear old Britain – the very sight of hair longer than two inches brought on widespread attacks of apoplexy. Fathers have banned long-haired sons from meals, publicans have banned students from pubs, headmasters have banned pupils from school.[6]

Not everyone was against the look, however. As early as 1964 the President of the National Hairdressers Federation, with shrewd business sense, suggested that most hairdressers did not object to youth wanting to wear its hair long, providing it was shaped. To recoup the financial loss of the regular trim, the Federation resolved to charge long-haired men more than those with short hair.[7] Others, more prescient as to future developments in street style and subculture, saw long hair as the most visible sign of a dynamic society that had plenty to offer the modern world. 'The mop hair, howling Merseyside culture, and pop' had grabbed global attention and enthusiasm:

> If we allow this kind of Britain to come to the fore we shall not be considered an old country, in spite of our traditions and paraphernalia of processions and castles, nor a middle-aged country that is trying to be modern, but a really young country which Britain is, can be, and will be.[8]

Before we trace the effects on this wider modern world of the Beatles and their hair, there is a further point to bear in mind. While it was boys whose long hair constituted the challenge, girls were also involved in the style politics of youth. Eschewing the set and teased styles of the 1950s, all bouffant and backcombed, girls also began to cultivate a long-haired look (Fig. 6.3). As a *Times* reporter wrote in 1967, the swinging London generation would be remembered 'because its girls were the first for 50 years who could sit on their hair'. As a case in point the article interviewed eighteen-year-old art student, Gerda Macdonald, whose hair was nearly a yard long. Gerda, whose decision was prompted by hearing that one of the Beatles liked girls with long hair, underlined the discipline of her regime. It was not a case of foregoing a grooming routine, but of substituting visits to the hairdresser with another kind of care regimen: a weekly wash with conditioner, an hour to dry her hair, a cleanser between washes, colouring products and one hundred brush strokes a night.[9] The message is, of course, clear. For boys long hair was lax and unkempt, undermining traditional values and a manly gender performance, but for girls it could be the opposite: both the crowning glory of her femininity and the means to articulate a stringent personal discipline.

While in the UK the long hair of the sixties mobilized opinion, engendered unease and sparked some grumbling confrontations with authority, its effects in the United States were considerably more dramatic. Lacking both a tradition of dissent and a tolerance of eccentricity, middle America was instead built on a deep and guarded conservatism. Fresh from the repressions of the McCarthy era with its persecution of difference and its neurotic invention of outward signs of inward subversion, long hair was a blinding revelation that there existed personal and political alternatives. In a 2016 interview, Bruce Springsteen described this effect of the Beatles as they erupted into the American psyche with their 1964 appearance on *The Ed Sullivan Show*. Then at the beginning of his musical and individual journey, he learned that with appearance you could 'physically distinguish yourself as part of a new philosophy'. He explained that while to today's eyes the band's hairstyle looks conservative, the cover of their first record '*outraged* people':

> They thought, you know, are you *gay*? You know? That was what my father asked me, you know, when I grew my hair like an inch, and he wasn't kidding, you know. And it was just something at the time that it's hard to explain but it immediately made you part of a very elite, and imperilled, club, where if you saw anyone else with that hair, they were immediately your soul brother. And it was very, very . . . it was very powerful. It was a very powerful statement at the time, and one that it took some balls to wear because there were a lotta guys who felt deeply threatened by your fashion choice. And let you know it.

So deeply was this threat felt, Springsteen says, that there were doctors who refused to treat you 'literally because – it's insane – but because your hair was long'. He himself suffered head injuries in a serious motorcycle accident and found he was not only the butt of jokes

FIGURE 6.3.
Two young women
on Carnaby Street,
London, wearing the
new-look long, straight
hair, 1967.

because of the length of his hair, but that some doctors were declining to give him follow-up treatment. His father's response was to call in a barber; 'but oh man', laughed the reminiscent Springsteen, 'I screamed bloody murder!'[10]

Some youths did more than scream bloody murder. While the United States was more rigid in its behavioural norms than Britain, it was also more litigious and quicker to defend a particular concept of the individual. Related to this was the absence of a tradition of school uniforms, a tradition whereby children and their parents, however unwillingly, expected individual appearance to be subsumed within the broader identity of the community, over which they had no say. All this meant that whereas schoolboys in Britain (and sometimes also their parents) might have complained when forced to cut their hair, in the United States some of them sued. In the face of high-school codes that enforced short hair, in the ten years between 1965 and 1975 'an astonishing number' sought justice from the courts, not just from the state judiciary but also through the federal system. Following unsuccessful hearings under state law, more than one hundred hair cases were taken to the federal Courts of Appeals, and nine tenacious schoolboy litigants even appealed to the highest judicial authority in America, the Supreme Court.[11] It makes the grumbling compliance of my brother and his friends in our rural New Zealand high school seem very tame indeed.

The opponents of long hair brought to bear similar arguments as were marshalled on the other side of the Atlantic, albeit with a greater disgust and vehemence: it was physically sloppy, morally lax, and confused the appearance of gender. Long hair, indeed, threatened the breakdown of society and its wearers were anti-social degenerates who had left decency behind them at the door of the hairdressers. One of the reasons for the ramping up of concern was that the values seen to be flouted were identified as specifically *American*. This meant that, regardless of the motivations of the long-haired, their appearance was in some deep and threatening way felt to be treasonous. For the enemies of long hair, it was a style that deliberately denied those beliefs and behaviours on which the nation was founded. Thus suddenly the stakes were raised and the divide was very clear: on one side was short-haired decency and order, on the other was moral perversity and chaos. As a principal from a small school in Wisconsin said, testifying in support of hair regulations: 'Whenever I see a long-hair youngster, he is usually leading a riot, he has gotten through committing a crime, he is a dope addict, or some such thing.' Long hair, he said, was 'un-American' and 'reflects a symbol that we feel is trying to disrupt everything we are trying to build up and by we I mean God-fearing Americans.'[12]

Demonized by its opponents, and idealized in equal measure by its supporters, masculine long hair became a symbol that carried the weight of a much broader politics. Worn increasingly long as the decade proceeded, as a badge it could stand for anything that ran counter to establishment structures, beliefs and policies; a badge that was pinned to escalating protests against the Vietnam War and to the emergence of a new and youthful repudiation of the accepted forms of citizenship (Fig. 6.4). Appropriated by the hippie phenomenon that had emerged into the wider consciousness through the 1967 Summer of Love, America viewed long hair as emblematic of social dysfunction – or, from the other side of the divide, it witnessed a coming utopia. In long, untrammelled locks were seen the autonomy of youth; freedom of expression, sex and drugs; an endorsement of nature over the artificial and the prescriptive; a rejection of patriotic war and a refusal of the imperatives of capitalism. It is difficult to overestimate the importance of hair in this regard as an embodied symbol: growing long hair was the 'coming out of the closet for the counterculture' (Fig. 6.5).[13]

FIGURE 6.4.
Hippie and armed guard, People's Park, Berkeley, California, 1969: a clash of more than appearances.

FIGURE 6.5.
A long-haired hippie, with beads and bells, at Detroit's first love-in at Belle Isle Park, 1967: a repudiation of traditional American values.

The apotheosis of all this was the stage musical, and then film, *Hair*. Seen by millions around the world, its single-word title summed up its moral message and its challenge. Two years after the debut performance, in 1969 John Lennon and Yoko Ono staged their own hairy protest by holding a series of bed events. Beginning with the celebration of their honeymoon, they capitalized on the inevitable media fascination by going public and living out their message of peaceful dissent: they stayed in bed and grew their hair. The invited reporters and photographers shared images with the world of the long-haired couple propped beatifically against pillows, the posters taped to the windows behind them declaring 'HAIR PEACE' and 'BED PEACE' (Fig. 6.6). 'Lennon was advocating a symbolic approach to politics. To him it was revolutionary to grow one's hair long as a symbol of one's rejection of the more conventional lifestyle.'[14] In an interview at the time, Lennon made this explicit: 'All we are saying is symbolically, instead of kickin' in a shop window, say, do something like grow your hair.'[15]

From nearly a half century later, what most stands out for me is the naive certainty of this counter-culture. Many of those involved really did believe that how they wore their hair mattered deeply, and that this would help change the world. According to Keith Carradine, whose subsequent acting career was launched by his roles in the original Broadway run of the *Hair* musical: 'Hair was important. It was important to have hair. It was part of the uniform, you know, part of the statement. . . . We were trying to manifest a utopian concept.'[16] Ironically, however, the commercial success of the *Hair* musical and film are a sign of the counter-culture quickly being both recuperated and exploited by an adaptable and greedy hegemony. As Dick Hebdige explains, the course of subcultures is an inevitable and continuing cycle of challenge, diffusion and then incorporation. Through the process of the commodification of style, in particular, a subcultural innovation will be taken from its original context, and mass produced to be made generally available, comprehensible, and of profit.[17] In Britain, the appropriation of long hair by the dominant culture happened earlier than in the more resistant context of the United States. As early as 1969, just a month before John and Yoko's first bed event, a columnist in the *Daily Mirror* declared:

> Unfortunately, as with all protest movements, long hair became so commonplace that it is now almost respectable. Judges, Government ministers, bank managers – the very pillars of our Establishment no less – can now be seen with sideboards reaching down their faces and long hair curling over their collars.[18]

And merely a year later, a disillusioned John Lennon said much the same thing. When asked what he thought was the effect of the Beatles on the history of Britain, he replied caustically:

FIGURE 6.6.
(Facing page) John and Yoko at their honeymoon bed event at the Hilton Hotel, Amsterdam, 1969.

The people who are in control and in power and the class system and the whole bullshit bourgeois scene is exactly the same except that there is a lot of middle-class kids with long hair . . . It's just the same only I'm thirty and a lot of people have got long hair, that's all.[19]

Thus by 1977, even the boys at my New Zealand school were no longer being disciplined for breaking a dress code on hair length, and pupils and teachers alike wore styles that were decidedly shaggy. However, while the long look had been incorporated into mainstream culture, punk and skinhead fashion was already gaining momentum. Gathering up its boots, safety pins and confrontational hair, this next subcultural challenge was already being issued (Fig. 6.7).

FIGURE 6.7.
Street looks in London, c.1970: the mohawks and spikes of the punk years.

The 'Bobbed Hair Controversy'

In early July 1922, New York stenographer Ruth Evans had her thick, nearly waist-length hair cut off. Two weeks later, back in her lodgings in Brooklyn, she wrote three letters to be read after she was found, turned the gas jet on full, then lay down fully clothed on the bed. Her death was reported not only in the New York press, but also eight hundred miles away in the *Chicago Daily Tribune*. Despite Miss Evans herself giving no reason for her suicide, both papers ascribed it to sadness over her bobbed hair. 'Girl Bobs Hair, Regrets It, and Commits Suicide', read one headline; 'Girl Kills Herself in Grief Because She Bobbed Her Hair', stated the other.[20] Ruth's was not the only suicide of this era to be attributed to the trauma of bobbed hair. Other young women in both America and Britain were said to have gassed or drowned themselves in bitter disappointment at the results of their haircuts. Somewhat differently, in Vienna a woman of middle age threw herself from a window in despair, a reconciliation with her divorced husband having foundered when he saw her new short style. Along slightly different lines, in 1926 *The Manchester Guardian* described the coroner's inquest into the drowning of eighteen-year-old Jane Walker, who lived near Wigan. The court was told that having had her 'beautiful head of hair' cut into a bob, Jane was attacked by her angry father. Although apparently in good spirits, Jane later jumped into the Leeds and Liverpool Canal, from where her body was pulled three hours later.[21]

The suicidal response was not confined to those whose hair was actually cut. A Polish woman in her sixties was reported to have swallowed poison when it was her daughter who had her hair bobbed. A teacher in rural Ohio took poison when his wife ignored his objections and did the same. He was found dead on the floor of the school premises. In France, a sacristan hung himself from the clapper of the church's largest bell because his daughter had bobbed her hair in disobedience to his wishes. In a macabre detail, it was explained that the worshippers came to find out what was wrong when the ordinary clanging of the bells turned suddenly to discord.[22] The press also reported instances where being *prevented* from following the new fashion caused women to take their lives. One such was fourteen-year-old Ruth Hornbaker, who was refused permission for a bob despite the fact that she was being teased at school. When Annabelle Lewis from New Jersey shot herself in 1926, the *New York Times* claimed it was in disappointment at having a trim for her already-bobbed hair postponed: 'Hair Bobbing Delayed, Girl of 15 Ends Life'.[23]

In these reports from the 1920s, the passions thought to have been aroused by bobbed hair are felt by young women, their mothers, fathers and husbands. Both the disobeyed and the disobedient are plunged into extreme distress, and they fall prey to hopelessness whether they live in Europe, Britain or the United States. In reality, of course, anger or grief over a haircut is by itself neither sufficient nor adequate as an explanation for taking one's life, and is, furthermore, unsubstantiated in nearly all these cases. In each and every one of them, there was a much more powerful underlying cause than bobbed hair. As the coroner reporting in 1925 on the drowning of a twenty-two-year-old woman from Preston commented, 'he had never before heard that worry about her hair could be sufficient to induce a girl in any ordinary frame of mind to commit suicide'.[24] However, what is important here is not the strict truth value of the claims that bobbing had led to suicide, but the fact that such claims were made in the first place. What was going on at the time whereby such reports were couched in these terms? Why was linking a hairstyle to the tragedy of self-killing deemed to be believable, or if not believable, then newsworthy? Bobbed hair had entered the psyche of the 1920s in a dramatic way.[25] In the remainder of this chapter we will explore how this occurred and what were the consequences.

Origins

The bob first emerged well before the Jazz Age with which it is now associated. Appearing originally as a unisex cut for children, it was adopted early by a few daring, bohemian-minded women. In marked contrast to the other case studies, the bob was an exclusively female style. Although the crop of the 1790s and the long hair of the 1960s had extended as far as women, the challenge they represented was carried primarily by male wearers. With the bob, the oppositional politics of self-presentation were embodied entirely in the feminine. One early wearer of short hair was Ellen Darwin, daughter-in-law to famous naturalist Charles. Her niece remembered her as modern and highbrow, both smoking and daringly 'cutting short her rough black hair'.[26] As Ellen died prematurely in 1903, hers was an unconventional and bold style choice, placing her in the vanguard of new ways of understanding femininity. Slightly later and higher-profile wearers of short hair included the French actress Eve Lavallière, who was bobbed by the famous hairdresser Antoine for a role in 1911, in which the forty-five-year-old Eve was to play a character of eighteen.[27] Another was the American dancer Irene Castle who was credited with bringing the style to the United States, although in a way typical of the mystery shrouding the bob's origins, stories differ as to exactly when and why she had her hair cut short.[28] However, with echoes of childhood and yet worn by such womanly trendsetters, the bob's associations with youthfulness, the avant-garde, and also with a certain physicality, were forged right from the start. Haute couture from the pre-War period likewise reveals glimpses of this style that was to come to full expression a decade later, with fashion illustrations showing turbaned figures or models with short clustered curls (Fig. 6.8). A few are even depicted with that sleek cap of hair plastered over a neat, androgynous head – an embodiment of the gleaming and spare Art Deco aesthetic, the haircut of modernity.

The contrast with nineteenth-century hair and femininity could not have been greater. Gone was the matronly and statuesque Edwardian beauty, to be replaced by a smaller and younger figure; instead of her hair being piled in a fulsome coiffure, it was cut or curled

FIGURE 6.8.
Pre-war fashions,
pointing the way
forward. The hair set
neatly framing the
head, often with a
turban as in this fashion
plate from 1913, was
a marked feature of this
new look.

Robe de charmeuse blanche à tunique de mousseline de soie violette brodée de vert et bordée de skungs. Manteau de velours étrusque.

tidily to the head (Figs 6.9 and 6.10). The Victorian and Edwardian passion for women's hair had led to styles that were dressed with postiches (hair pieces), padding and ornaments, the abundance that was not every woman's birthright being supplied by art and additions. Contemporaries remembered afterwards the 'hair-mindedness' of the time. 'In the nineteen hundreds', wrote Gwen Raverat (1885–1957), 'it had to be puffed out in hideous lumps and bumps, over cushions or frames.' Lady Violet Hardy also recalled the fashionable 'pyramid of hair, which if not possessed, was supplied, pads under the hair to puff it out, were universal and made heads unnaturally big'. She and her sister, being blessed with thick and plentiful hair of their own, refused to make use of such supports, but when on visits to less fortunate friends 'were amazed to see how much false hair and pads were shed at "brushing time"'.[29] After such abundance and artifice, the move to close-cut hair must have seemed revolutionary.

With the arrival of the First World War, however, came a context in which the practicality and restraint of shorter hair came into its own. For women working in men's jobs or nursing the wounded, or merely coping with the exigencies of a country plunged into conflict, its repudiation of a fulsome femininity came to strike the right note. Cynthia Asquith's (Fig. 2.16) war diaries chart the way attitudes and expectations could change in this regard. In 1915, when her sister-in-law had her hair cut short Cynthia wrote that it 'suits her as well as anyone, but I don't know that I really like it. I think it always looks a little uncanny or unpleasant – suggestive of prison, illness or suffragettes.' A year later, however, she noted that a friend's haircut made her 'astonishingly pretty and attractive'. And the year following that, when told by an artist that she had Victorian hair, recorded with a somewhat amused self-deprecation: 'It is hard to be such an anachronism.'[30] With the end of the conflict, though, at least some felt that female fashions ought to return to their pre-war forms, just as women themselves were returned from the male workplace to the domestic stage. The ambivalence felt towards the emerging woman of modernity is articulated in the following fashion forecast for the 'after-war woman' published just one week after Armistice Day. 'Women will become feminine again', it was declared.

FIGURE 6.9.
Camille Clifford (1885–1971), c.1905, whose voluptuous figure and thick, upswept hair made her a famed Edwardian beauty. Clifford became known as a Gibson Girl, an embodiment of the feminine ideal as drawn in illustrations by Charles Dana Gibson.

FIGURE 6.10.
(Facing page) Camille Clifford, 1916: the transformation of an ideal. Gone are Clifford's corsetry and curves, replaced with simpler verticals. While her hair is still long, it is arranged in a simple bun at the nape of her neck, and a bandeau gives the impression of short locks. Although taken around eleven years after the earlier photograph (Fig. 5.26), Clifford appears here to be much younger.

There may be a revolt against the mannish girl. Bobbed hair will disappear. Trailing draperies, ringlets and dressed hair will again become popular. Soft voices and charming manners will have as great vogue as they did in the Early Victorian age. The sports girl and the girl who motors or rides will hold her own, but the majority will turn to feminine pursuits.[31]

How wrong this prediction was. Victorian womanhood was gone for good, and despite recurrent claims that the days of the bob were over, as the twenties dawned the reports of its death turned out to have been greatly exaggerated. Instead, short hair spread like wildfire, and as it evolved from being an outré style to a mass fashion, so too was opinion mobilized and resistance articulated. As short hair for women of all ages swept the world – from New Zealand to New York, Birmingham to Beijing – so public argument and debate spread in its wake. The Bobbed Hair Controversy was alight.

Boom and backlash

As we have seen, right from the start the bob's associations were clear. The style gave visual expression to modernity and a new kind of womanhood. It connoted youth, sportiness, and that rapidly developing technology, the motor car. To ride or drive in an open-topped vehicle was much easier with a bob and a bandeau than with a full head of hair dressed with pads and postiches, topped off with a broad-brimmed hat. For role models daring enough to fly, like the pioneering Amelia Earhart, soaring above the clouds with aviator goggles and a short bob was an arrow flight to the future (Fig. 6.11). For women whose adventures were of a more mundane variety, the bob was convenient and efficient. There was a widely shared sense that it saved time and bother, and also that, in not requiring the frequent services of a hairdresser to style it, the cut was a fashion of equality, easily available to all and inexpensive to maintain. Rather than the luxuriously tressed 'angel in the house' of Victorian desire, the bob was the style for a busy working woman of the twentieth century, enfranchised, educated and rational. Such hair also matched the new look clothing, echoing the shorter hems and pared-down practicality of post-war dress (Fig. 6.12). It was absurd to contemplate long, dressed hair so definitively of the past teamed with clothing so emphatically of the future. The bob dovetailed, too, with contemporary developments in the field of hygiene. Just as a public informed about germ theory and the health benefits of washing had repudiated beards and stubble, so too it embraced the cleanliness of women's short hair. Time and again the ease and frequency with which it could be washed were adduced as benefits: it was 'neat, practical, cool, and sanitary'.[32] The importance of the bob for its supporters can perhaps best be summed up by the observations of Mary Garden, an internationally renowned singer who was in her 50s when she cropped her hair. While she found a short style both practical and flattering, there is a sense of epiphany in her explanation of its more profound consequences:

FIGURE 6.11.
Bob-haired Amelia
Earhart, a role model
for the modern woman,
1928.

FIGURE 6.12.
Fashion plate for 1922: a simple columnar look, short hems and short hair for an active life.

Bobbed hair is a state of mind and not merely a new manner of dressing my head. It typifies growth, alertness, up-to-dateness, and is part of the expression of the *élan vital*! . . . To my way of thinking, long hair belongs to the age of general feminine helplessness. Bobbed hair belongs to the age of freedom, frankness, and progressiveness.[33]

However, the conversation also included the voices of those for whom the bob signalled a more dystopian vision. For them modernity meant rising levels of unemployment, demobbed and damaged soldiers searching for jobs, increasing contraception and decreasing birth rates,[34] and the raw memory of a generation decimated on the battlefields. Set against this, the concept of the independent, working woman was less optimistic, and her short hair served as a lightning rod for this greater unease. We get a sense of the world turned upside-down in this newspaper report from 1924: 'Women have invaded all the sacred male precincts – they have cut their hair short and made themselves M.P.s and lawyers and candlestick-makers.' The author went on to paint a picture of the new world order of 'sex equality', warning that if they have just out-argued a man at a court of law and then beaten him at tennis, women should not expect any of the conventional courtesy formerly due the 'weaker sex'. When on the Tube 'I shall often', he therefore explained, 'have a little secret admiration for the little man who sits solidly on while the fierce bobbed young woman stands.'[35]

It is not surprising that the bob – and the even shorter shingle and Eton crop – were seen as mannish. Bobbed hair, unless fringed at the front, was cut to a single length. The shingle, which developed shortly after, was layered at the back in a way that, while familiar to our eyes, presented startled contemporaries with a vision of a woman with an even shorter and more tapered masculine cut. The Eton crop, appearing around mid-decade, was the most boyish of all, its sleek lines cut close to the skull in a knowingly androgynous manner. Yet closely related to this unsexed woman with her manly hair was the oversexed virago. In a new spin on what was a very old complaint, the adoption of male styles by women was also interpreted as hyper-sexual – the softly feminine replaced by predatory boldness. The bob, in other words, was worn by 'the provocative type'; it was 'fast'. The type of girl who sported it was without reticence, able to pursue a man, and was just 'waiting to send him a daring challenge in eyes and smile'.[36]

Today, the most obvious reading of the label 'manly' is as code for 'lesbian', but interestingly it is not one that was necessarily available to contemporaries.[37] In the early twenties the public awareness of homosexuality in women was low, and for most people lesbianism had neither a recognizable name, visual identity, nor pattern of behaviours. To a certain extent this was changed in 1928 by the trial for obscenity of Radclyffe Hall's novel of same-sex desire, *The Well of Loneliness*. A cause célèbre, it gave notoriety to the Eton-cropped Hall and her bob-haired lover Una Troubridge, their appearance providing the public with the template for an emergent lesbian subculture (Fig. 6.13). By the time the professional

FIGURE 6.13. (Facing page) Radclyffe Hall (1886–1943) and Lady Una Troubridge (1887–1963) in 1927.

manual *The Art and Craft of Hairdressing* was published in 1931, hindsight and knowledge had allowed the author to assess the crop's impact and popularity in a reasonably measured way, distinguishing different kinds of wearers and nodding in the direction of a lesbian minority: 'The vogue of the Eton crop did not, however, receive the universal approval of womankind. Its votaries were chiefly the fashionable mannequins, their less fashionable, but particularly imitative sisters, and the not too numerous masculine-minded type of woman.'[38]

One particular figure that electrified the American press at the time was the Bobbed Hair Bandit. Although most notably referring to a young New York woman called Celia Cooney (Fig. 6.14) who performed a series of armed holdups in 1924, she was not the first or the only bearer of the title. Indeed the media dubbed a number of women with the soubriquet, identifying as such different female criminals across America, in Britain, and even

in Russia and Turkey.[39] The idea of this gun-toting, cropped renegade captured and distilled several different facets of the new womanhood that many saw springing into being: unruly females with agency who threatened the status quo with an unfeminine hardness, yet were pervaded with a frisson of allure. The gangster girl even made it into jokes:

> He: Aren't you going to bob your hair?
> She: Well, you know, I can't decide whether to bob it or bandit.[40]

However, while the more literal-minded may have imagined a causal relationship between the coiffure and criminality, US Supreme Court judge Frank Katzenbach instructed a jury that this was not the case: it was wealth and alienation that was responsible for the modern crime wave, not bobbed hair and short skirts.[41]

One strategy for coping with the perceived disruption of bobbed hair was to provide it with a point of origin, a genealogy that in giving the bob antecedents also served to neutralize its threat. If the bob had a precedent, it would become merely one more flowering of that illogical, and often grotesque, force called feminine fashion. This might legitimate its presence but, by extension, it would also assure its disappearance. It was thus pointed out that Cleopatra and the other Egyptians had worn bobbed hair, as had that quintessential tomboy, the Maid of Orléans, Joan of Arc. Some marked the similarity to the cropped fashion that appeared in the 1790s, while another strand of thought sited the style's origins in another revolutionary context. The bob, it was suggested, had arisen with female comrades in Russia, and along with their Bolshevist politics had spread to the 'Greenwich Village lassies' in New York, or 'the "arty" female (of a Chelsea type)' in London.[42]

Another and more emphatic response was to forbid the short style. As it became clear that short hair was not going to be buried along with the casualties of the Great War but, on the contrary, was spreading like contagion – there were queues of women outside barbers and thousands of bobs were being cut every week – the backlash against this 'social menace' began to grow.[43] Principally this was a private phenomenon experienced in the closed world of family relationships, with husbands and parents forbidding the cutting of hair. This was the case in the famous Mitford family, where in 1925 the two second-eldest daughters, Diana and Pam, were consumed by their desire to get a bob. They even dragooned younger sister, eight-year-old Jessica, to the cause. 'Darling Muv', Jessica wrote in a letter,

> Diana and poor Pam want more than ever to have their hair off and Pam did not enjoy her visit at all because everyone says, 'Oh yes I like short hair best' and 'Why don't you have your hair off?' Please do let them have it. Please.

The year before, their eldest sister, twenty-year-old Nancy, had already defied parental wishes by bobbing without permission. 'Well, anyhow, no one will look at you twice now', had remarked their mother, and the sight of the short-haired Nancy in trousers made their father 'apoplectic with rage'.[44] Other private disputes were made public in newspaper reports of divorces and desertions, or the suicides with which we started. Here, in conjunction with broader experiences of dysfunction and coercion, a bob might apparently tip the emotional balance.[45] In 1923 an astonishing report appeared in the press, stating that some hairdressers were only consenting to bob a married woman's hair if she had her husband's permission, having been made wary by too many visits from irate spouses. And in 1922 an evangelist in Belfast advised the young men of his congregation never to marry a girl with bobbed hair.[46]

In some cases such tyranny was exercised at an institutional level. Seeking to halt this subversion 'of national morals', this 'symptom of post-war demoralisation', various organizations began to ban short hair. In 1923 the Salvation Army authorities made the attempt for its female membership. In November 1924 the Board of Guardians at Oldchurch hospital in Romford, Essex, forbade the bob for its nurses (Fig. 6.15). The style, the Board said, 'looked flighty and frivolous'.[47] In the United States there were similar contretemps, with those typically 'female' professions of nursing and teaching bearing the brunt. Thus in August 1922 the superintendent of Hagerstown hospital, Maryland, issued a rule that prohibited her nurses from cutting their hair. Like her colleagues in Romford, she

FIGURE 6.15.
Daily Mirror cartoon from 1924, poking fun at the decision by the Romford Board of Governors to ban nurses from bobbing their hair.

HOW WOMEN MIGHT RETALIATE

HOSPITAL COMMITTEE VOTING AGAINST NURSES BOBBING OR SHINGLING, AS BEING ALTOGETHER TOO NEAT AND HYGIENIC

STRANGE! — OUR IMPRESSION OF A NURSE'S HAIR IS THAT MOST OF IT IS CONCEALED.

WILL SHINGLED PATIENTS BE EJECTED?
YOU CAN'T STAY IN THIS HOSPITAL!

PERHAPS A DAY WILL COME WHEN THERE IS A COMMITTEE COMPOSED OF WOMEN
SHOULD DOCTORS BE ALLOWED TO SHAVE AND HAVE THEIR HAIR CUT?

THEN LET DOCTORS AND MEDICAL STUDENTS BEWARE!
IT'S VERY UNHYGIENIC AND ALL THAT, BUT WHAT CAN WE DO — THE COMMITTEE INSISTS ON HAIR!

Bobbed hair has been forbidden to nurses by the Romford Board of Guardians. The day may come when women will retort by insisting on beards and whiskers for men.

declared that bobbed hair had no place in the sick room, for it was 'frivolous' and undignified. 'I think it dreadful for young women to go among ill patients with bobbed hair.'[48] Earlier that year, a Boston teachers' agency had similarly made it clear that 'We do not encourage the bobbed-hair applicant for a teacher's position . . . School superintendents will not employ them.'[49] Over the months of 1921 there had also been debate amongst American businesses and department stores, no doubt fuelled by media coverage, as to whether it was appropriate for salesgirls and clerical staff to have short hair. While many were neutral on the subject, some, like the Chicago store Marshall Field & Co., were definitely opposed. In August the company served their thousands of female employees with notice that anyone with a short cut had to wear a hairnet over it until it grew out: 'They told us bobbed hair did not look dignified.'[50]

These, however, were extreme reactions, and they were opposed by the majority. Even if an individual did not like bobbed hair personally, most thought it an unacceptable infringement of a woman's rights to be dictated to on the matter of her own hair length, particularly by an employer. Furthermore, the tide of change was too strong to be halted by such rearguard action, and workplace prohibitions were short-lived. That British institution the Lyons tea shop was a case in point. In 1924 Lyons not only removed their ban on bobs, but redesigned the waitress uniforms to match. In place of the long maid's dress, full-length apron and cap, came a cloche-shaped headdress suited to short hair, a peter pan collar and a short-length frock (Figs 6.16 and 6.17). Even the waitress nickname was changed, 'Gladys' giving way to the much more modern-sounding 'Nippy'.[51]

Modernity came much less easily to some other countries though, and the backlash against the bob exacted a far higher toll. In Mexico City violent unrest erupted in July 1924. The Archbishop had already denounced the fashion, saying that bobbed women would be excluded from church. Then self-appointed student vigilantes began to target individual wearers, forcibly shearing them to the scalp as punishment. This polarized opinion across the city both for and against, and resulted in riots that involved armed soldiers, thousands of students, and the suspension of classes by the under secretary of education. Even worse, in the latter part of the decade in China 'The execution of women with short hair was widespread', the bob being interpreted as evidence of oppositional politics by both sides of a violent political divide.[52]

A transformative legacy

There is no doubt that the bob and its variants represented a challenge to traditional ideas of femininity the world over. On hindsight, however, there is a sense of inevitability to its triumph. So enmeshed was the bob with its context, that the early twentieth century seems unthinkable without it. Chiming with the growing emphasis on youth, fitness and hygiene,

FIGURE 6.16.
A Lyons tea shop in London, early twentieth century. The waitresses, dressed like Victorian maids, serve customers.

FIGURE 6.17.
A Lyons tea shop in London, 1926. Gone is the Gladys, replaced by the modern uniform and bobbed hair of the Nippy.

it also spoke to those developing modes of mass transport, the car and the aeroplane, and echoed the pared-down aesthetic of the machine age. It was the first mass fashion to be disseminated by the burgeoning motion picture industry, with early film stars like Clara Bow and Louise Brooks (Fig. 6.18) becoming role models for millions. In many places it roughly coincided with female suffrage, not to mention women's slowly increasing participation in higher education, the professions and politics. All of this seemed, even at the time, to be made manifest in the new short cut.

Repeatedly this sense of unfolding possibilities emerges from the recounted experiences of those who claimed the freedom of short hair. Watching their long hanks fall to the floor felt like a liberation: 'How nice and free and light I did feel', explained one woman. 'I'm not going to let my hair grow – I wouldn't do it now if a million dollars depended on it.' Henrietta Rodman, an American educationist, was eloquent – even proselytizing – when interviewed

FIGURE 6.18.
Film star Louise Brooks (1906–85) and her trademark shiny dark bob, 1920s.

on the subject: 'just try cutting your hair and you'll find that you wouldn't go back to long hair for the world'. She likened it to giving up corsets, and feeling so 'gloriously free and comfortable' that you would never climb back in to 'your suit of armor'. The bob was for the thinking and the active woman: 'Go on, cut your hair like a sensible girl and be clean and comfortable like the rest of us.'[53] This is not to suggest that every woman felt liberated and that none regretted the step. But as the bob's enormous, literally worldwide popularity indicates, most did find it was better than their long hair. And for *everyone* whose hair was cut, there was a profound sense of transformation. As one of them recounted:

> All the young women at the office were having their hair cut short . . . my mother and I went to the hairdresser's on Wardour Street, where we sat at the end of a long queue of women who, like us, were patiently waiting to let down their beautiful long hair. An hour later, with hats too large for our diminished heads, feeling very self-conscious, anxious to be home where we could make a minute, pitiless examination of our changed appearance, we emerged as new women.[54]

The long-term, systemic effect of the bob was also transformational. Its fashionability – its quality of being desirous and in the moment – has of course waxed and waned over the course of the following century. However, what the women immediately before and after the First World War did was to establish something much bigger than a mere fashion – they forged a change in dress practices. From then on, if she wanted, a woman could wear her hair short, even as short as a man's. The agency of all those countless women who grasped the scissors is also noteworthy, for the bob was not a style promoted by hairdressers – indeed initially they were both untrained in, and resistant to, the cut. According to Gilbert Foan's hairdressing manual published in 1931, the short hair fashion 'overtook the hairdresser', coming 'almost like "a thief in the night." The trade was not ready for it.' Women who wanted to bob had to insist; at the beginning, many had to visit a male barbering establishment (Fig. 6.19). As Foan pointed out, cautioning so that the lesson could be learned for the future, 'lucky were those of our confrères who were able to adapt themselves at once to the change, and secure the fruits of the boom'.[55]

This brings us to the second of the bob's transformative legacies: its consequences for the hairdressing profession. Practices changed entirely, so that instead of being a craft concerned almost solely with the 'dressing' of hair – its expert arrangement with ornaments, hair pieces, curls and waves – the stylist had to learn to cut. In little more than a decade, the profession completely reinvented itself with a new skill set. Although an ability with curling and colouring remained essential, increasingly these processes were applied to hair that was also styled with the scissors. By 1931, Foan's authoritative teaching text was alive to the possibilities of this change,

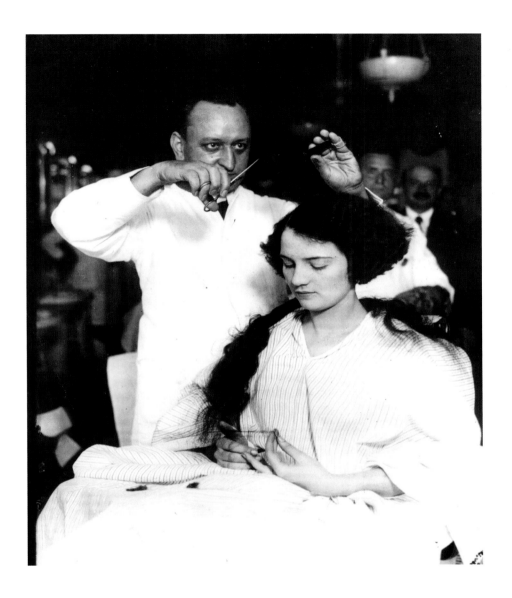

with not only full instruction on complex cutting techniques, but even a prescient sense of professional identity. Of the shingle, the manual stated, 'The hairdresser who is truly an artist will find in [it] plenty of scope to indulge in artistic conception.'[56] Such a sentiment surely set the stage for Vidal Sassoon, who eleven years later would enter the profession as a fourteen-year-old apprentice, and after him, the other hairdressing luminaries of the twentieth century.

But the hairdressing revolution did not stop there. Instead of catering only to a well-to-do clientele who had the money and leisure for elaborate hairstyles, suddenly huge numbers of women of all incomes and all ages were wanting their services. Rather than undermining the profession, the democratized bob dramatically increased demand, not only for the initial cut, but thereafter to keep it trimmed. Furthermore, the locus of service delivery shifted from the private home, where the hairdresser had visited elite clients, to the spaces of the salon. Together, these related developments added up to an explosion in hairdressing establishments – a vast and sudden expansion of the industry. In the United States, the years between 1922 and 1924 saw the number of salons rocket from around 5,000 to a nearly five-fold increase of 23,000.[57] In the ten years between 1921 and 1931 in England and Wales, the number of people employed in hairdressing nearly doubled.[58]

For women, these new salons offered not only the services of personal grooming, but were a public space that safely welcomed the feminine, representing another step away from life based in the domestic sphere, to agency in the wider domain outside the home. Nor was women's involvement limited to the role of client. The bob-driven increase in the number of hairdressers drove forward a trend that had first begun in the war, when women were drafted into the profession to replace a conscripted male workforce. What before the war – and indeed, since its inception in the eighteenth century – had been an almost entirely male profession, the increasing opportunities of the industry's growth began to transmute.

Thus while the 1920s had more or less doubled the size of the hairdressing industry in England and Wales, over the same period the numbers of women employed in the trade had increased by a factor of more than five: by 1931 they made up over a third of the workforce.[59] This feminization of the industry, begun with the bob in the early twentieth century, has continued: the statistics released by the UK's National Hairdressers' Federation revealing that in 2016, 88 per cent of the people working in hairdressing and barbering were female.[60]

Returning, then, to Ruth Evans, who gassed herself in her Brooklyn bedroom in 1922, why should the press seize on her recent haircut as the reason for her depression? Why was bobbed hair made to bear the brunt of suicides, divorce and violent crime? It was because this was reportage for a readership in the midst of social change, a powerful facilitator of which was short hair. Whether shocked or approving, people were aware of a new, post-war world order, of which the shifting appearance and behaviour of women was a significant element. Seeing so much laid at the door of the bob, people were ready and wanting to read of more, opening up their papers from the safety of the breakfast table to find further evidence of the style's disruption – news of fresh disasters to entertain, intrigue, or maybe validate their views. Such reportage was part of the process of becoming accustomed to modernity. The Bobbed Hair Controversy shows us a society thrashing out its views on how to move forward to the future.

Conclusion:
Histories and hair stories

For a time when I was a student I spent what seemed like a profligate amount of my limited income on perms. This was the era of big hair. Melanie Griffiths kicked executive ass in *Working Girl* (1988); Madonna strutted her nonchalant stuff in *Desperately Seeking Susan* (1985). And who could forget Jennifer Beals (and her dance body-double) in ankle warmers in *Flashdance* (1983)? Yes, I wanted to be them all. And yes, I definitely wanted their hair. I remember the weight of the rollers and the acrid burn of the perming solution as I sat in the salon chair, waiting for my emphatically straight, long hair to be transformed, even if my emphatically ordinary life remained pretty much the same. In the late 60s my hair would have been a fashionable blessing that any young woman could have been proud of, but as it was I was simply born too late. Besides, I really wanted the careless disorder of big locks; that was the person I wanted to be (Fig. 7.1a).

It was sometime after I started teaching that I gave up on the impossible. My hair was so straight – aggressively straight – that it laughed at chemical reshaping. Perms never lasted long and I reluctantly accepted the fact that big hair was never to be mine. Sadly, I was a person with boring straight hair. It was still long though, and being fine by the end of a day in the classroom it was escaping its customary braid or pony tail or twist. If it had a look, I would have to describe it as 'frazzled'. Thirty arrived and found me with a modicum of sense, for I had cut my hair short into a Louise Brooks-like bob. At last I had found something that my hair did well. Effortlessly it took the shape, swung as it ought, and even curved up at the front edges all by itself. And this was even before Victoria Beckham had made the bob so annoyingly popular. Also rather annoyingly, I look back at photos of myself as a little girl and find I had a bob then too (Fig. 7.1b). But then I didn't like it; if I concentrate I can still feel the cold scissors on my neck and the scrunch of the blades as they cut my fringe, my eyes screwed up in concentration as I am told to keep still.

Many years on and my hair is yet shorter. When I look in the mirror now I see another choice before me as the grey hairs become ever more numerous. Actually, I have no problems with this decision. Although I flirted with lowlights in my thirties, in my fifties I do not want to be yet another middle-aged woman with tastefully dyed hair. I like the way the silver catches

FIGURES 7.1A AND B.
Part of the author's hair
story: an aspirational
'big hair' perm,
c.1985; a short bob
as a child, c.1969.

the light and it's quite an interesting adventure watching the gradual change. Sometimes I even think of it as an opportunity to explore a whole new range of dress colour. This is my hair story, but we all have one. Throughout our lives we make and remake the decisions of our appearance. Working within the parameters of social norms, the constraints of cost and time, the shape of our individual desires and the nature of the stuff we grow on our head and body, we present a self. Out of this mix of the actual and the ideal comes our unique, yet constantly changing, appearance. As I hope this book has made clear, this is not a new phenomenon. Just as we all have our own hair story, so has had every person in history.

Some might argue that hair is a peripheral concern – something only on the fringe, pun intended. It is just a cosmetic add-on to both the weightier issues of cultural expression and the individual's place within such articulations. On the contrary, hair turns out to be central to both. Its relationship with selfhood is made manifest when hair is unwillingly lost or removed. Whether the victims of institutionalized or private abuse, those who have had their hair forcibly shorn experience it as a shocking violation that brutally dislocates existing identities.

Far less horrifically, but not without pain of its own, those who lose their hair through illness or age may also find themselves grieving for a lost self.

Such coercive and non-voluntary interventions make clear what is usually hidden: hair is hugely important to how we understand ourselves. Another truth that we usually forget is that everything done to it is a cultural act. There is no 'natural' hair: whether grooming, removing or even leaving it to grow, all engagement with our hair takes place within a wider cultural agenda. Often, however, the sheer hegemonic certainty of what we do confers a spurious naturalness, blinding us to the range of agendas and assumptions that trail in its wake. In simply reaching for the shampoo, for example, we engage with ideas of cleanliness that are so engrained that it is hard to remember they are very recent and will almost certainly change in the future. They rely on modern plumbing, the installation of showers, a chemical industry and water and power resources that we have only recently begun to take for granted. Without contact with India and ethnic borrowing, we would not even have a name for the soapy substance and the activity of massaging it into our scalps. In shampooing our hair, it turns out we unknowingly confront a colonizing past. The removal of female body and facial hair is another unexamined practice whose endless repetition creates an illusion of naturalness where really there is only arbitrary cultural habit. Likewise, at various times, has been the growing of beards for men, alternatively the removal of their facial hair, or even the shaving of their heads and the donning of wigs. Cultural norms, at the time, are invisible.

However, these norms and practices that concern hair extend so much further than just the individuals who embody them. They reflect society back to itself, giving form to ideas and reinforcing beliefs: how to be clean, for instance, how to be manly, how to be a member of the elite or of the masses. But they also provide a means by which the status quo can be challenged and changed can be fostered. Hair length has proved particularly amenable to this more subversive role, and at particular times in history has been utilized to enact protest or engineer social transformations. The politics of appearance, it turns out, is just as significant as any other kind of politics, and cannot be teased apart from more traditional understandings of the workings of power.

What a society does with its hair is therefore not frivolous. It is not an historical afterthought, but every bit as significant as more overtly important matters. Another thing that has become apparent during the course of this book is that our particular habits of hair have a long history. There have certainly been huge changes – fractures in the pattern of continuity – yet much of what we do has recognizable antecedents. As in the past, we cut, colour and curl our hair, and thanks to the Victorians we also brush it. We might have a raft of new chemical technologies, but our combs and tweezers, still in daily use, are virtually unchanged after thousands of years. Our responses to the process of grooming, moreover, seem rooted in a deeper, evolutionary past. Requiring trust and proximity, and giving pleasure, the activity has always been intimate. Probably because of this, the stereotypes clustering around its (particularly male) practitioners are recognizably the same after hundreds of years.

In writing this book I stopped taking hair for granted and began scrutinizing it more closely. I thought about my own hair choices and other people's, considered the subtext to shampoo and shaving advertisements, wondered about its afterlife as it clogs the drains. I fixated on the appearance of actors in costume dramas, noting the accommodation made between narrative needs, historical accuracy and modern preferences. I spied adverts on the Underground for baldness cures almost identical to claims I had read in manuscripts written four hundred years earlier. Simply walking down the street became an adventure in identity politics. Hair is fundamental to us all. It is part of being human. It is extraordinary stuff.

Endnotes

Introduction

[1] Geraldine Biddle-Perry and Sarah Cheang (eds), *Hair: Styling, Culture and Fashion* (Oxford: Berg, 2008), 246.

[2] Rose Weitz, *Rapunzel's Daughters: What Women's Hair Tell Us About Women's Lives* (New York: Farrar, Strauss and Giroux, 2004), 200–1.

[3] Joanna Pitman, *On Blondes. From Aphrodite to Madonna: Why Blondes Have More Fun* (London: Bloomsbury, 2003), 227.

[4] 'CoiffureGate: The High Cost of Hollande's Haircut', BBC News, http://www.bbc.=co.uk/news/blogs-trending-36784083, accessed 24 July 2016.

[5] Royce Mahawatte, 'Hair and Fashioned Femininity in Two Nineteenth-Century Novels', in Biddle-Perry and Cheang (eds), *Hair*, 193–203; Galia Ofek, *Representations of Hair in Victorian Literature and Culture* (Farnham: Ashgate, 2009).

[6] Charlotte Brontë, *Jane Eyre* (1847; London: Penguin, 2012), quote at 353.

[7] E.g. see Rachel Velody, 'Hair-"Dressing" in *Desperate Housewives*: Narration, Characterization and the Pleasures of Reading Hair', in Biddle-Perry and Cheang (eds), *Hair*, 215–27.

[8] Eric Sullivan and Andrew Wear, 'Materiality, Nature and the Body', in Catherine Richardson, Tara Hamling and David R.M. Gaimster (eds), *The Routledge Handbook of Material Culture in Early Modern Europe* (London: Routledge, 2017), 141–57, esp. 144.

[9] Ibid., 149–50.

[10] Also on this, Mark S. Dawson, 'First Impressions: Newspaper Advertisements and Early Modern English Body Imaging', *Journal of British Studies* 50 (2011): 277–306, esp. 295–6.

[11] See Irma Taavitsainen, '*Characters* and English Almanac Literature: Genre Development and Intertextuality', in Roger D. Sell and Peter Verdonk (eds), *Literature and the New Interdisciplinarity: Poetics, Linguistics, History* (Amsterdam and Atlanta: Rodopi, 1994), 168–9.

[12] Robert Copland, *The shepardes kalender* (London, 1570), sig. [Lvi verso].

[13] *The English Fortune-Teller* (London, 1670–9).

[14] *To her Brown Beard* ([London], 1670–96).

[15] E.g. Nicolas Andry de Bois-Regard, *Orthopædia: Or the Art of Correcting and Preventing Deformities in Children*, 2 vols (London, 1743), II, 11–17.

[16] *Crosby's royal fortune-telling almanack; or, Ladies universal pocket-book, for the year 1796* (London [1795]), 130.

[17] Sharrona Pearl, *About Faces: Physiognomy in Nineteenth-Century Britain* (Cambridge, MA: Harvard UP, 2010).

[18] Jacque Guillemeau, *Child-birth or, The happy deliuerie of vvomen* (London, 1612), sig. L1r, p. 3.

[19] Anon, *In Holborn over against Fetter-lane, at the sign of the last, liveth a physitian* (London, 1680).

[20] Giovanni Torriano, *The second alphabet consisting of proverbial phrases* (London, 1662), 211.

[21] Anon, *A new ballad of an amorous coachman* ([London], 1690).

[22] 'Bullied Anorexic is a Cut Above', *Metro*, 6 December 2011, 9.

[23] Reported in UK press widely, including 'Harriet Harman Says "Ginger Rodent" Comment Was Wrong', BBC News, http://www.bbc.co.uk/news/uk-scotland-scotland-politics-11658228, accessed 29 January 2017.

[24] Nelson Jones, 'Should Ginger-Bashing Be Considered a Hate Crime?', *New Statesman*, 10 January 2013, http://www.newstatesman.com/nelson-jones/2013/01/should-ginger-bashing-be-considered-a-hate-crime, accessed 29 January 2017.

[25] See events listings at the affirmative action site 'Ginger Parrot': http://gingerparrot.co.uk, accessed 29 January 2017.

[26] Statistics cited in Viren Swami and Seishin Barrett, 'British Men's Hair Color Preferences: An Assessment of Courtship Solicitation and Stimulus Ratings', *Scandinavian Journal of Psychology* 52.6 (2011): 595.

[27] Ibid.

[28] Pitman, *On Blondes*, 155–201.

[29] *Platinum Blonde* (1931); *Blonde Crazy* (1931); *Blonde Venus* (1932); *The Blonde Captive* (1932); *Blondie of the Follies* (1932); *Blonde Bombshell* (1933); *Don't Bet on Blondes* (1935); *Blond Cheat* (1938); *Blondie!* (1938); *Strawberry Blonde* (1941); *My Favourite Blonde* (1942); *Andy Hardy's Blonde Trouble* (1944); *Blonde Fever* (1944); *Incendiary Blonde* (1945); *Blondie's Big Moment* (1947); *The Beautiful Blonde from Bashful Bend* (1949); *Gentlemen Prefer Blondes* (1953). While the spate thereafter lessened, it never entirely stopped, and later 'blonde' movies include: *Three Blondes in His Life* (1961); *A Blonde in Love* (1965); *The Loves of a Blonde* (1965); *Blondes Have More Guns* (1995); *The Last of the Blonde Bombshells* (2000); *Legally Blonde* (2001); *Totally Blonde* (2001); *Blonde Ambition* (2007); *Blonde and Blonder* (2007); *Private Valentine: Blonde and Dangerous* (2008).

[30] Geoffrey Jones, 'Blonde and Blue-Eyed? Globalizing Beauty, c.1945–c.1980', *Economic History Review* 61 (2008): 125–54.

[31] Pitman, *On Blondes*, 4.

[32] Recent studies in psychology affirm the power of these stereotypes, demonstrating that blonde women get more attention, and that people react negatively to redheads of both sexes. See Swami and Barrett, 'British Men's Hair Color Preferences'; Nicolas Guéguen, 'Hair Color and Courtship: Blond Women Received More Courtship Solicitations and Redhead Men Received More Refusals', *Psychological Studies* 57 (2012): 369–75.

[33] *The Diaries of Lady Anne Clifford*, ed. D.J.H. Clifford (Stroud: Alan Sutton, 1990), 56.

[34] Clare Phillips, *Jewelry: From Antiquity to the Present* (London: Thames and Hudson, 1996), 81.

[35] *London Gazette*, 4 September 1701–8 September 1701. On eighteenth-century hair jewellery: Christine Holm, 'Sentimental Cuts: Eighteenth-Century Mourning Jewelry with Hair', *Eighteenth-Century Studies* 38 (2004): 139–43.

[36] Expanded afterwards, with longer versions appearing in 1714 and 1717: Alexander Pope, 'The Rape of the Lock', in Martin Price (ed.), *The Restoration and the Eighteenth Century*, The Oxford Anthology of Literature (Oxford: Oxford UP, 1973): 321–44 (quotes from 321, 337).

[37] Kenelm Digby, *Letter Book 1633–1635*, Smith College, Rare Book Room Cage, MS 134, pp. 40–1. My thanks to Peter Stallybrass for generously sharing this with me.

[38] On hair-work of the period: Helen Sheumaker, '"This Lock You See": Nineteenth-Century Hair Work as the Commodified Self', *Fashion Theory: The Journal of Dress, Body and Culture* 1 (1997): 421–45; Virginia L. Rahm, 'Human Hair Ornaments', *Minnesota History* 44 (1974): 70–4; Marcia Pointon, *Brilliant Effects: A Cultural History of Gem Stones and Jewellery* (New Haven and London: published for The Paul Mellon Centre for Studies in British Art by Yale UP, 2009), 293–311.

[39] Rosemary March, 'The Page Affair: Lady Caroline Lamb's Literary Cross-Dressing', 3, available at http://www.sjsu.edu/faculty/douglass/caro/PageAffair.pdf, accessed 22 January 2017.

[40] Elizabeth Gaskell, *North and South* (London: Penguin, 2012), 313.

[41] Quoted in Charlotte Gere and Judy Rudge, *Jewellery in the Age of Queen Victoria: A Mirror to the World* (London: British Museum Press, 2010), 73.

[42] Ibid., 167, 170 and Fig. 124.

[43] British Library references: Beethoven, RPS MS 406; Brontë, Egerton MS 3268 B; Dickens, RP 8738/3; Nelson, Add MS 56226; Goethe, Zweig MS 155; Hanoverians, Add MS 88883/4/8; Bolívar, Add MS 89075/12/1.

[44] Some of Che Guevara's hair, along with death photos and fingerprints, was sold by a CIA employee for $119,500: 'Most Expensive Lock of Hair', *Time*, http://content.time.com/time/specials/packages/article/0,28804,1917097_1917096_1917086,00.html, accessed 18 January 2017.

[45] Ofek, *Representations of Hair*, 43. On hair-work generally: Gere and Rudoe, *Jewellery in the Age of Queen Victoria*, 164–70.

[46] Ofek, *Representations of Hair*, 44.

[47] *General Advertiser (1744)*, 5 July 1748.

[48] *Reads Weekly Journal or British Gazetteer*, 23 September 1738.

[49] 'Hair', *London Chronicle or Universal Evening Post*, 24 March 1774–26 March 1774.

[50] E.g. Pepys, VI, 210.

[51] Margaret Spufford, *The Great Reclothing of Rural England: Petty Chapmen and their Wares in the Seventeenth Century* (London: Hambledon Press, 1984), 50–1.

[52] 'Country News Gloucester, Nov. 25', *Whitehall Evening Post or London Intelligencer*, 28 November 1749–30 November 1749.

[53] *St. James's Evening Post*, 10 March 1716–13 March 1716.

[54] *Daily Courant*, 5 October 1715. Calculation based on the currency converter supplied by Lawrence H. Officer and Samuel H. Williamson, 'Five Ways to Compute the Relative Value of a UK Pound Amount, 1270 to Present', MeasuringWorth, 2017, https://www.measuringworth.com/ukcompare/, accessed 12 February 2017.

[55] *Daily Post*, 24 December 1725.

[56] *Weekly Journal or British Gazetteer*, 9 August 1729.

[57] Steven Zdatny (ed.), *Hairstyles and Fashion: A Hairdresser's History of Paris* (Oxford: Berg, 1999), 15–16, 160. Calculation based on currency converter at https://www.measuringworth.com/ukcompare/, accessed 12 February 2017.

[58] *The Hairdressers' Journal, devoted to the Interests of the Profession* ([London, 1863, 1864]), 43–4.

[59] Georgiana Sitwell, *The Dew, It Lyes on the Wood*, in Osbert Sitwell (ed.), *Two Generations* (London: Macmillan, 1940), 3. A front was additional hair crafted into a piece to be worn at the front.

[60] 'Attempted Theft of a Lady's Hair', *Cincinnati Daily Gazette*, 30 October 1879, 6 (also reported in the *San Francisco Bulletin*, 5 November 1879, [1]. 'A Theft of Beautiful Hair', *Philadelphia Inquirer*, 8 December 1889, 2.

[61] *The Times*, 20 January 1870, 7.

[62] C. Willett Cunnington and Phillis Cunnington, *Handbook of English Costume in the Nineteenth Century*, 3rd edn (London: Faber, 1970), 480–1, 510–12.

[63] For what follows I have relied on Emma Tarlo, *Entanglement: The Secret Lives of Hair* (London: Oneworld Publications, 2016); and for temple hair and coercion, Eiluned Edwards, 'Hair, Devotion and Trade in India', in Biddle-Perry and Cheang (eds), *Hair*, 149–66.

Chapter 1

[1] *The Memoirs of Anne, Lady Halkett and Ann, Lady Fanshawe*, ed. John Loftis (Oxford: Oxford UP, 1979), 173.

[2] London, Wellcome Library, Fanshawe, Lady Ann (1625–1680), MS.7113/29. The reference to 'flies' may mean the substance Cantharides, the dried beetle *Cantharis vesicatoria*, also known as Spanish Fly. This was a common ingredient in hair preparations well into the twentieth century.

[3] John Partridge, *The widowes treasure plentifully furnished with sundry precious and approoued secretes in phisicke and chirurgery for the health and pleasure of mankind* (London, 1586), sig. Dvr–v; John Banister, *An antidotarie chyrurgicall containing great varietie and choice medicines* (London, 1589), 166–7.

[4] Peter Levens, *A right profitable booke for all disseases Called The pathway to health* (London, 1582), 2; Hannah Woolley, *The Accomplish'd lady's delight* (London, 1675), 174.

[5] W.M., *The Queens closet opened incomparable secrets in physic, chyrurgery, preserving, and candying &c.* (London, 1655), 212–14; London, Wellcome Library, Boyle Family, MS.1340/digitized image 154. Note that this may have been a pomatum for hair or face; the recipe does not specify.

[6] London, Wellcome Library, English Recipe Book, MS.7391/digitized image 5; London, Wellcome Library, Elizabeth Okeover (and others), MS.3712/digitized image 17. Also identical are two further hair-growth recipes, MS.7391/digitized image 67 and MS.3712/digitized image 105. According to Richard Aspin, 'Who Was Elizabeth Okeover?', *Medical History* 44 (2000): 531–40, MS.7391 was the exemplar for the later collection that carries Elizabeth Okeover's name. However, this does not explain the gaps in these two particular recipes. The problematic word is 're', presumably short for 'retort', a glass vessel used for distilling.

[7] See Virginia Smith, *Clean: A History of Personal Hygiene and Purity* (Oxford: Oxford UP, 2007), 51–3.

[8] Hilary Davidson, pers. comm.

[9] *Athenian Gazette or Casuistical Mercury*, 16 May 1693.

[10] On powder, see Chapter 5 below. Also Susan Vincent, *The Anatomy of Fashion: Dressing the Body from the Renaissance to Today* (Oxford: Berg, 2003), 15–17, 31–3.

[11] See Corbyn & Co., chemists and druggists, London, Manufacturing recipe books, 1748–1851: London, Wellcome Library, MS 5446–5450.

[12] London, Wellcome Library, Med. Ephemera EPH160B, Hair care ephemera, Box 9, Bear's Grease (Thomas Cross, Holborn, 1770).

[13] Alexander Ross, *A treatise on bear's grease* (London, 1795); Henry Beasley, *The Druggist's General Receipt Book* (London: John Churchill, 1850), 212–25, esp. 212, 216.

[14] *The Star Patent Medicine Stores* (Oxford, [c.1890]), p. 11, Oxford, Bodleian Library, John Johnson Collection of Printed Ephemera, Patent Medicines 14 (62), in *The John Johnson Collection: An Archive of Printed Ephemera*.

[15] Caution is urged in the successive editions of the chemists' formulary handbook *Pharmaceutical Formulas*, published in London every few years from 1898 (the 9th revised edition was reprinted in 1919). It is only the 10th edition of 1934 that states orpiment is no longer used because of its danger (p. 9).

[16] Geoffrey Jones, 'Blonde and Blue-eyed? Globalizing Beauty, c.1945–c.1980', *Economic History Review* 61 (2008); 128; *EH*, 253, 349, 382.

[17] John Jacob Wrecker, *Cosmeticks, or, the beautifying part of physic* (London, 1660), 74.

[18] Thomas Jeamson, *Artificiall embellishments, or Arts best directions how to preserve beauty or procure it* (Oxford, 1665), 108.

[19] Bridget Hyde (–1733), MS.2990/digitized image 20; Boyle Family, MS.1340/digitized image 109.

[20] Stevens Cox, s.v. 'curling irons' and variations; *EH*, 335, 366.

[21] Jeamson, *Artificiall embellishments*, 110.

[22] R.H. Gronow, *Captain Gronow's Recollections and Anecdotes of the Camp, the Court, and the Clubs, At the Close of the last War with France* (London: Smith, Elder and Co., 1864), 151–2.

[23] On perms, *EH*, 303–5.

[24] David Ritchie, *A Treatise on the Hair* (London, 1770), 26–7; William Moore, *The art of hair-dressing* (Bath, [1780]), 18–19.

[25] Foan, 295–6.

[26] Sali Hughes, 'Could Your Hair Dye Kill You', *The Guardian*, 28 November 2011, at https://www.theguardian.com/lifeandstyle/2011/nov/28/could-hair-dye-kill-you, accessed 31 January 2017.

[27] Felix Platter, *Platerus golden practice of physick fully and plainly disovering* (London, 1664), 539, 540.

[28] *Pückler's Progress: The Adventures of Prince Pückler-Muskau in England, Wales and Ireland as Told in Letters to his Former Wife, 1826–9*, trans. Flora Brennan (London: Collins, 1987), 177.

[29] Gail Durbin, *Wig, Hairdressing and Shaving Bygones* (Oxford: Shire, 1984), 12. Carolyn L. White, *American Artifacts of Personal Adornment 1680–1820: A Guide to Identification and Interpretation*

(Lanham, MD: Altamira Press, 2005), 104–10. See also *EH*, s.v. 'comb'.

[30] Pierre Erondell, *The French garden: for English ladyes and gentlewomen to walke in* (London, 1605), sig. E1v.

[31] Margaret Spufford, *The Great Reclothing of Rural England: Petty Chapmen and their Wares in the Seventeenth Century* (London: Hambledon Press, 1984), 94–5, 153, 188–9, 204–5.

[32] Durbin, *Wig, Hairdressing and Shaving*, 27. On celluloid vanity sets, Ariel Beaujot, *Victorian Fashion Accessories* (London: Berg, 2012), 139–77.

[33] See Galia Ofek, *Representations of Hair in Victorian Literature and Culture* (Farnham: Ashgate, 2009), esp. 34–5, 40–1.

[34] Durbin, *Wig, Hairdressing and Shaving*, 27.

[35] E.g., Balmanno Squire, Surgeon to the British Hospital for Diseases of the Skin, *Superfluous Hair and the Means of Removing It* (London: J.A. Churchill, 1893), 52 ff.

[36] *Vidal*, 32–3.

[37] *The Diary of John Evelyn*, ed. E.S. de Beer, 6 vols (Oxford: Oxford UP, 1955), III, 87 (13 August 1653).

[38] J. Liebault, *Trois Livres de l'embellissment et de l'ornement du corps humain*, 1632 (1st edn, 1582), quoted in George Vigarello, *Concepts of Cleanliness: Changing Attitudes in France since the Middle Ages* (Cambridge: Cambridge UP, 1988), 83.

[39] William Bullein, *The Government of Health* (1558), quoted in Smith, *Clean*, 209.

[40] On the bio-physicality of grooming, see Smith, *Clean*, 17–24. Note that Cynthia M. Hale and Jacqueline A. Polder, *ABCs of Safe and Healthy Child Care: A Handbook for Child Care Providers* (US Public Health Service, 1996), 91, even suggests a pet comb may be the most effective comb to use.

[41] E.g. Daniel Sennert, *The Art of chirurgery explained in six parts* (London, 1663), 2626; Jeamson, *Artificiall embellishments*, 123.

[42] Sennert, *Art of chirurgery*, 2626.

[43] *EH*, 102–3.

[44] Arthur Freeling (ed.), *Gracefulness: Being a Few Words Upon Form and Features* (London: Routledge, [1845]), 204.

[45] Georges Vigarello maintains that in France, washing the head continued to be a source of anxiety and that the essential tools for cleansing the hair remained the comb and drying powders until the second half of the nineteenth century: *Concepts of Cleanliness*, 174.

[46] Stevens Cox, s.v. 'shampoo'.

[47] *Pharmaceutical Formulas, Volume 2*, 11th edn (London: Chemist and Druggist, 1956), 804.

[48] Case and subsequent events and prosecutions: *The Times*, 22 July 1897, 7; 30 July 1897, 9; 9 August 1897, 10; 12 August 1897, 10; 16 September 1897, 2; 3 September 1898, 10. Two similar deaths and further events: *The Times*, 22 October 1909, 21; 28 October 1910, 4; 2 November 1909, 19; 5 February 1909, 10. Complete prohibition recommended: *The Times*, 31 May 1910, 7.

[49] *The Times*, 3 September 1898, 10.

[50] Case and subsequent events and prosecutions: *The Times*, 16 July 1909, 4; 25 August 1909, 2; 25 September 1909, 2; 29 September 1909, 2; 2 October 1909, 3; 6 October 1909, 14; 5 February 1910, 10; 25 March 1910, 4.

[51] *The Times*, 5 February 1910, 10. Caroline Cox, *Good Hair Days: A History of British Hairstyling* (London: Quartet Books, 1999), 35.

[52] London, Wellcome Library, Med. Ephemera EPH154, Hair care ephemera, Box 1.

[53] See Joseph R. Skoski, 'Public Baths and Washhouses in Victorian Britain, 1842–1914' (Ph.D. thesis, Indiana University, Bloomington, 2000).

[54] *Vidal*, 7, 27, 54.

[55] Jones, 'Globalizing Beauty', 138.

[56] W.F.F. Kemsley and David Ginsberg, *Expenditure on Hairdressing, Cosmetics and Toilet Necessities*, quoted in Smith, *Clean*, 338.

[57] Jones, 'Globalizing Beauty', 134 (table), 135.

Chapter 2

[1] Pepys, III, 213.

[2] Pepys, III, 213 (Elizabeth's hair dressed by maid). V, 72; VIII, 35 and IX, 424 (Samuel's hair cut by wife). VIII, 280 and IX, 201 (Samuel's hair cut by maid). E.g. III, 96; VI, 21 and VIII, 531 (Samuel's hair combed by maid). IX, 175 (Samuel's hair cut by Elizabeth's sister-in-law and brother).

[3] Pepys, III, 213. *The Letters and Journals of Lady Mary Coke*, ed. J.A. Home, 4 vols (1889–96; repr. Bath: Kingsmead Reprints, 1970), II, 303.

[4] Cecil Aspinall-Oglander, *Admiral's Widow: Being the Life and Letters of the Hon. Mrs. Edward Boscawen from 1761 to 1805* (London: Hogarth Press, 1942), 126, 20 December 1787.

[5] Isabella Beeton, *The Book of Household Management* (London: S.O. Beeton, 1861; facsimile repr. Jonathan Cape, 1977), 980, 978.

[6] John MacDonald, *Memoirs of an Eighteenth-Century Footman: John MacDonald's Travels (1745–1779)*, ed. John Beresford (London: Routledge, 1927).

[7] *Morning Herald and Daily Advertiser*, 4 January 1781.

[8] Ibid., 7 June 1783.

[9] Ibid., 11 June 1782; *Daily Advertiser*, 22 June 1778.

[10] SP 14/107 fol. 121, March(?) 1619.

[11] Pepys, IX, 454.

[12] R. Campbell, *The London tradesman. Being a compendious view of all the trades* (London, 1747), 209–10.

[13] Richard Corson, *Fashions in Hair: The First Five Thousand Years* (London: Peter Owen, 1971), 360; John Hart, *An address to the public, on the subject of the starch and hair-powder manufactures* (London, [1795]), 61, citing William Pitt's estimates in Parliament. On this latter, see John Barrell, *The Spirit of Despotism: Invasions of Privacy in the 1790s* (Oxford: Oxford UP, 2006), 165, n. 72.

[14] *Court and Private Life in the Time of Queen Charlotte: Being the Journals of Mrs Papendiek, Assistant Keeper of the Wardrobe and Reader to Her Majesty*, ed. Mrs Vernon Delves Broughton, 2 vols (London: Richard Bentley and Son, 1887), II, 5. J.B Suardy dressed Queen Charlotte's hair from at least 1784 to 1809. His name was obviously difficult. Papendiek gives it as 'Sonardi'; Fanny Burney, Charlotte's joint Keeper of the Robes, gives it as 'Swarthy': *The Court Journals and Letters of Frances Burney, vol. 1*, ed. Peter Sabor (Oxford: Clarendon Press, 2011), 25, n. 116; 104.

[15] Calculation based on the currency converter supplied by Lawrence H. Officer and Samuel H. Williamson, 'Five Ways to Compute the Relative Value of a UK Pound Amount, 1270 to Present', MeasuringWorth, 2017, https://www.measuring worth.com/ukcompare/, accessed 2 February 2017.

[16] *Journals of Mrs Papendiek*, II, 49.

[17] Ibid., I, 173; I, 222; I, 185; I, 199; I, 173, I, 222; I, 237, I, 292; II, 171. Mr 'Theilcke' may in fact be the husband of Mrs Thielcke, Queen Charlotte's wardrobe woman, on whom see, *Court Journals of Frances Burney*, 17, n. 75.

[18] *Journals of Mrs Papendiek*, II, 111; II, 142.

[19] Woodforde X, 27.

[20] *Court Journals of Frances Burney*, 96, 104 with n. 356.

[21] *The Memoirs of Richard Cumberland*, ed. Richard Dircks, 2 vols in 1 (New York: AMS Press, 2002), II, 14.

[22] Cecil Beaton, *The Glass of Fashion* (London: Weidenfeld and Nicolson, 1954), 13–14.

[23] Figures for 2016: 'Hair and Beauty Industry Statistics', National Hairdressers' Federation, http://www.nhf.info/about-the-nhf/hair-and -beauty-industry-statistics/, accessed 18 December 2016.

[24] 'How Many Famous Female Hairdressers Can you Name?', BBC News, http://bbc.co.uk/news /business-38267758, accessed 11 December 2016.

[25] Margaret Pelling, *The Common Lot: Sickness, Medical Occupations and the Urban Poor in Early Modern England* (London: Longman, 1998), 208. Doreen Evenden, 'Gender Difference in the Licensing and Practice of Female and Male Surgeons in Early Modern England', *Medical History* 42 (1998): 194–216.

[26] Calculation based on the currency converter supplied by Lawrence H. Officer and Samuel H. Williamson, 'Five Ways to Compute the Relative Value of a UK Pound Amount, 1270 to Present', MeasuringWorth, 2017, https://www.measuring worth.com/ukcompare/, accessed 13 February 2017.

[27] *Stuart Royal Proclamations*, vol. II *Royal Proclamations of King Charles I 1625–1646*, ed. James Larkin (Oxford: Clarendon Press, 1983), 88.

[28] Pepys, VII, 278 (shaved at the Swan); VIII, 133 (meets barber at the Swan); IV, 312 (Crown in

Huntington); VIII, 234 (Horseshoe in Bristol); I, 200 (shaved in street).

[29] Pepys, I, 298.

[30] SP 29/101 fol. 16.

[31] For more on disputed Sunday shaving, see Chapter 3. Also Richard Wright Proctor, *The Barber's Shop* (Manchester and London, 1883), esp. 135–6; Theologos, *Shaving: A Breach of the Sabbath* (London, 1860); William Andrews, *At the Sign of the Barber's Pole: Studies in Hirsute History* (1904; repr. [n.p.]: Dodo Press, [n.d.]), 15–17.

[32] Foan, 507.

[33] Proctor, *The Barber's Shop*, 56–7.

[34] After 1600, many barbers sold tobacco: Margaret Pelling, 'Appearance and Reality: Barber-surgeons, the Body and Disease', in A.L. Beier and Roger Finlay (eds), *London 1500–1700: The Making of a Metropolis* (London: Longman, 1986), 94. On music and barbers, see Laurie Maguire, 'Petruccio and the Barber's Shop', *Studies in Bibliography* 51 (1998), esp. 118–19; Pelling, *The Common Lot*, 222–3; Stevens Cox, s.v. 'barber music'.

[35] Pepys, I, 90; V, 352; IV, 237.

[36] Pepys, III, 233; III, 201.

[37] Woodforde, XI, 145.

[38] Evenden, 'Gender Difference in the Licensing and Practice of Female and Male Surgeons': 196–7, 201. Also Diane Willen, 'Guildswomen in the City of York, 1560–1700', *The Historian* 43 (1984): 217.

[39] I. Murray, 'The London Barbers', in Ian Burn (ed.), *The Company of Barbers and Surgeons* (London: Ferrand Press, 2000), 77.

[40] J.T. Smith, *Ancient Topography of London* (London: John Thomas Smith, 1815), 38.

[41] *DM*, 7 October 1936, 16; 22 September 1911, 11; 2 July 1951, 3.

[42] Pepys, I, 219.

[43] *Benjamin Franklin's Autobiography*, ed. J.A. Leo Lemay and P.M. Zall (New York: Norton, 1986), 108, n. 9.

[44] Shaun Lockes, *Cutting Confidential: True Confessions and Trade Secrets of a Celebrity Hairdresser* (London: Orion, 2007), 113.

[45] E.g. *Entry 3 / Level 1 VRQ in Hairdressing and Beauty Therapy*, The City & Guilds Textbook (London: City & Guilds, 2012), 19–24; Keryl Titmus, *Level 2 NVQ Diploma in Hairdressing*, The City & Guilds Textbook (London: City & Guilds, 2011), 31; Martin Green and Leo Palladino, *Professional Hairdressing: The Official Guide to Level 3*, 4th edn (London: Thomson, 2004), 9–11.

[46] Lockes, *Cutting Confidential*, 16.

[47] 'Hairdressing', Health and Safety Executive UK Government, http://www.hse.gov.uk /hairdressing/, accessed 5 March 2013.

[48] Kristan J. Aronson, Geoffrey R. Howe, Maureen Carpenter and Martha E. Fair, 'Surveillance of Potential Associations between Occupations and Causes of Death in Canada, 1965–91', *Occupational and Environmental Medicine* 56 (1999): 265–9. Also Foan, 472–6.

[49] Pelling, 'Appearance and Reality', 94–5.

[50] 'Assessment Strategy for Hairdressing NVQs and SVQs' (2010), and 'Assessment Strategy for Barbering NVQs and SVQs' (2010), both produced by Habia: Hair and Beauty Industry Authority, http://www.habia.org/, accessed 1 February 2017.

[51] E.g. oral history interview in Simon Szreter and Kate Fisher, *Sex before the Sexual Revolution: Intimate Life in England 1918–1963* (Cambridge: Cambridge UP, 2010), 240–1.

[52] E.g. David K. Jones, 'Promoting Cancer Prevention through Beauty Salons and Barbershops', *North Carolina Medical Journal* 69 (2008): 339–40; B.J. Releford et al., 'Cardiovascular Disease Control through Barbershops: Design of Nationwide Outreach Program', *Journal of the National Medical Association* 102 (2010): 336–45; J.L. Baker et al., 'Barbershops as Venues to Assess and Intervene in HIV/STI Risk among Young, Heterosexual African American Men', *American Journal of Men's Health* 6 (2012): 368–82; M. Fraser et al., 'Barbers as Lay Health Advocates: Developing a Prostate Cancer Curriculum', *Journal of the National Medical Association* 101 (2009): 690–7.

[53] *Vidal*, 98.

[54] Lockes, *Cutting Confidential*, 193–4.

[55] L. Paul Bremmer, *My Year in Iraq* (New York: Simon and Schuster, 2006), 151. My thanks to Barbara Vincent for this reference.

[56] On the cultural myth of Sweeney Todd, Robert L. Mack, *The Wonderful and Surprising History of Sweeney Todd* (London: Continuum, 2007).

[57] Lady Cynthia Asquith, *Diaries 1915–1918* (London: Hutchinson, 1968), 477. Other examples: 14, 128–9, 150, 158, 327, 329, 334, 339, 384. First published in 1918, *Married Love*, by Marie Stopes, was both infamous and influential. Among other things it championed equality within marriage and female desire. Stopes worked actively to educate on birth control.

[58] Andrea C. Beetles and Lloyd C. Harris, 'The Role of Intimacy in Service Relationships: An Exploration', *Journal of Services Marketing* 24 (2010): 351.

[59] *Vidal*, 4; Lockes, *Cutting Confidential*, 10.

[60] Interview quoted in Beetles and Harris, 'The Role of Intimacy', 353.

[61] In one study 72 per cent of respondents demonstrated a high level of personal loyalty to their stylist: Liliana L. Bove and Lester W. Johnson, 'Does "True" Personal or Service Loyalty Last? A Longitudinal Study', *Journal of Services Marketing* 23 (2009): 189.

[62] Mary Beard, *It's a Don's Life* (London: Profile Books, 2009), 237.

[63] Barbarossa [Alexander Ross], *A Slap at the Barbers* (London, [c.1825]), 9.

[64] Elizabeth Steele, *Memoirs of Sophia Baddeley*, 6 vols (London, 1787), V, 179.

[65] Lockes, *Cutting Confidential*, 15, 66.

[66] SP 34/12 fol. 110.

[67] SP 29/101 fol. 16.

[68] Athan Theoharis (ed.), *From the Secret Files of J. Edgar Hoover* (Chicago: I.R. Dee, 1991), 353–4. My thanks to Barbara Vincent for this reference.

[69] E.g. Pepys, IX, 20; IX, 48.

[70] Pepys, IX, 277.

[71] Pepys, IX, 337.

[72] MacDonald, *Memoirs*, 220, 80–1, 53–5. Don Herzog, 'The Trouble with Hairdressers', *Representations* 53 (1996): 25.

[73] Quoted in Herzog, 'The Trouble with Hairdressers': 25.

[74] Lockes, *Cutting Confidential*, 72.

[75] Mary Hays, *Appeal to the Men of Great Britain in Behalf of Women* (London, 1798), 200, 201.

[76] *Vidal*, 80, 79.

[77] *Vidal*, 91.

[78] Listed in the Polari dictionary appended to Paul Baker, *Polari: The Lost Language of Gay Men* (London: Routledge, 2002), 170. The *OED*'s first usage dates to 1966.

Chapter 3

[1] Henry Mayhew and John Binny, *The Criminal Prisons of London and Scenes of Prison Life* (1862; repr. London: Frank Cass and Co, 1971), 564, 273. Note that shaving would also have removed any lice infestation.

[2] Deborah Pergament, 'It's Not Just Hair: Historical and Cultural Considerations for an Emerging Technology', *Chicago-Kent Law Review* (75): 48–52.

[3] Quoted in ibid., 50.

[4] 'Justice for Magdalenes (JFM) Ireland. Submission to the United Nations Committee Against Torture, 46th Session, May 2011', hair-cutting as routine punishment, para 5.2.6; witness testimony, Appendices II, IV, https://www.magdalene laundries.com/jfm_comm_on_torture_210411 .pdf, accessed 28 September 2015.

[5] Sue Lloyd Roberts, 'Demanding Justice for Women and Children Abused by Irish Nuns', BBC News, 24 September 2014, http://www.bbc.co.uk/news /magazine-29307705, accessed 28 September 2015.

[6] Anthony Synnott, 'Hair: Shame and Glory', in *The Body Social: Symbolism, Self and Society* (London: Routledge, 1993), 122.

[7] Wendy Cooper, *Hair: Sex Society Symbolism* (London: Aldus Books, 1971), 68.

[8] Rodney Sinclair, 'Fortnightly Review: Male Pattern Androgenetic Alopecia', *British Medical Journal* 317, no. 7162 (26 September 1998): 867.

[9] Ibid., 865.

[10] Rebecca Emlinger Roberts, 'Hair Rules', *The Massachusetts Review* 44 (2003/2004): 714–15.

[11] Sacha Bonsor, 'A Tender Touch', *Harper's Bazaar* (October 2013): 127.

[12] Pepys, VII, 288.

[13] Some men wore thin, narrow moustaches, such as pictured in the portraits of Charles II in this period.

[14] Dene October, 'The Big Shave: Modernity and Fashions in Men's Facial Hair', in Geraldine Biddle-

Perry and Sarah Cheang (eds), *Hair: Styling, Culture and Fashion* (Oxford: Berg, 2008), 67.

[15] Pepys, III, 91.

[16] *Pharmaceutical Formulas, Volume 2*, 11th edn (London: Chemist and Druggist, 1956), 854.

[17] Balmanno Squire, *Superfluous Hair and the Means of Removing It* (London: Churchill, 1893), 49–50.

[18] Pepys, III, 96–7.

[19] Pepys, III, 196.

[20] Pepys, V, 6.

[21] Pepys, V, 29.

[22] For further information about the technical equipment required for shaving, see Stevens Cox, s.v. 'hone', 'strap', 'strop' and related entries.

[23] Woodforde, IV, 21.

[24] *Journal to Stella*, ed. H. Williams, 2 vols (Oxford: Blackwell, 1974), I, 13, 144, 223, 326, 355.

[25] *The Correspondence of Jonathan Swift*, ed. H. Williams, 5 vols (Oxford: Clarendon Press, 1963), III, 89.

[26] James Woodforde, *Woodforde at Oxford 1759–1776*, ed. W.N. Hargreaves-Mawdsley, Oxford Historical Society, n.s. 21 (1969), 87.

[27] Lawrence Wright, *Clean and Decent: The Fascinating History of the Bathroom and the Water Closet* (London: Routledge and Kegan Paul, 1960), 114–19.

[28] 'A Discourse on Barbers', *The Englishman's Magazine* 1 (1852): 48.

[29] Alun Withey, 'Shaving and Masculinity in Eighteenth-Century Britain', *Journal for Eighteenth-Century Studies* 36 (2013): 233.

[30] Woodforde, XIII, 35; VI, 186; XIV, 172.

[31] Woodforde, XI, 83.

[32] *Journal to Stella*, I, 155. Note that this was the same Charles Ford who later sent Swift some razors.

[33] Pepys, VIII, 247.

[34] For example, see from the V&A Museum: Gentleman's toilet set, 1640–50, 7201:1 to 20-1877, available at http://collections.vam.ac.uk /item/O10974/gentlemans-toilet-set-unknown / compared to the Dressing case, c.1850, AP.621:1 to 21, available at http://collections.vam.ac.uk /item/O77824/napoleon-napoleon-dressing-case -wilson-walker-co/, both accessed 17 January 2014.

[35] H.M. *Why Shave? or Beards v. Barbery* (London, [n.d.]), 9.

[36] Theologos, *Shaving: A Breach of the Sabbath* (London: Saunders and Otley, 1860), 20.

[37] MOA: FR A21 'Personal Appearance: Hands, Face and Nails', July 1939, 36, 37, 38–9, 47.

[38] Ibid., 29, 33, 34.

[39] Ibid., 34–9, quote at 39.

[40] Matthew Immergut, 'Manscaping: The Tangle of Nature, Culture, and Male Body Hair', in Lisa Jean Moore and Mary Kosut (eds), *The Body Reader* (New York and London: New York UP, 2010), 287–304; Shaun Cole, 'Hair and Male (Homo) Sexuality: "Up Top and Down Below"', in Geraldine Biddle-Perry and Sarah Cheang (eds), *Hair: Styling, Culture and Fashion* (Oxford: Berg, 2008), 81–95, esp. 86–90; Michael Boroughs, Guy Cafri

and J. Kevin Thompson, 'Male Body Depilation: Prevalence and Associated Features of Body Hair Removal', *Sex Roles* 52 (2005): 637–44, DOI: 10.1007/s11199-005-3731-9.

[41] *EH*, 355.

[42] 'Safety Razors for Recruits', *The Times*, 22 September 1926,12, 13 ; *EH*, 355.

[43] Geoffrey Jones, 'Blonde and Blue-Eyed? Globalizing Beauty, c.1945–c.1980', *Economic History Review* 61 (2008): 138.

[44] Simplex advertisement, *DM*, 11 November 1904, p. 13; Mulcato advertisement, *DM*, 11 June 1908, p. 15.

[45] Editorial, *The Times*, 19 April 1929, 17.

[46] MOB: FR 911 'Razor Blade Scheme', October 1941, 5.

[47] 'Court Circular', *The Times*, 10 September 1910, 11; *DM*, 26 August 1933, 2.

[48] 'Razor Blades "Hazard" in Magazine', *The Times*, 25 March 1966, 6.

[49] 'He Wants Old Razor Blades', *DM*, 1 June 1934, 24.

[50] Howard Mansfield, *The Same Axe, Twice: Restoration and Renewal in a Throwaway Age* (Hanover, NH: UP of New England, 2000), 123.

[51] 'New Flats', *The Times*, 20 February 1936, 24.

[52] 'Cut-Throat Competition for Shavers', *The Times*, 12 July 1966, 11.

[53] According to Mintel report, *Men's Grooming and Shaving Products – UK – October 2011*, 'Almost two thirds of men wet shave, whereas just over a quarter dry shave' (Section: The Consumer – Attitudes Towards Grooming Products, key points and graph).

[54] 'A Discourse on Barbers', 48.

[55] 'Safety Razors for Recruits'.

[56] 'Razors and Reason', *The Times*, 19 April 1929, 17.

[57] 'Shaving – Then and Now', *The Times*, 13 June 1939, 17.

[58] 'Cut-Throat Competition for Shavers'.

[59] Humphrey Bogart in *Sabrina Fair* (1954): Allan Peterkin, *One Thousand Beards: A Cultural History of Facial Hair* (Vancouver: Arsenal Pulp Press, 2001), 69. John Steed in *The Avengers* episodes 'The Golden Eggs' (1963), 'Too Many Christmas Trees' (1965) and 'Dead Man's Treasure' (1967), http:// www.johnsteedsflat.com/bio8.html, accessed 7 February 2017.

[60] Charlie Thomas, 'Wet Shave vs. Dry Shave – Which is Best?', *The Gentleman's Journal*, 16 July 2014, http://www.thegentlemansjournal.com/wet -shave-vs-electric-shave-best/, accessed 20 October 2015.

[61] Charles Darwin, *Descent of Man, and Selection in Relation to Sex, Part Two*, in *The Works of Charles Darwin*, ed. Paul Barrett and R.B. Freeman, 22 (London: William Pickering, 1989), esp. 624–5, 629.

[62] London, Wellcome Library, English Recipe Book, 17th–18th century, c.1675–c.1800, MS. 7721/ digitized image 139, 'To hinder haire from growing'.

[63] La Fountaine, *A brief collection of many rare secrets* ([n.p.], 1650), sig. Br.

[64] Thomas Jeamson, *Artificiall embellishments, or Arts best directions how to preserve beauty or procure it* (Oxford, 1665),157–9. On henbane, Richard Mabey, *Flora Britannica* (London: Sinclair-Stevenson, 1996), 301.

[65] Jeamson, *Artificiall embellishments*, 125–6; Amelia Chambers, *The ladies best companion; or A Golden Treasure for the Fair Sex* (London, [1775?]), 160.

[66] All editions of *Pharmaceutical Formulas* published in London by The Chemist and Druggist. Citations for: 3rd edn (1898), 108; 7th edn (1908), 127.

[67] London, Wellcome Library: Madame Constance Hall, *How I Cured my Superfluous Hair* (London, [1910?]), 8 (my emphasis). See also advertisements in *DM* on 18 October 1910, 17; 15 November 1910, 17; 9 February 1911, 11; 18 March 1911, 11; 17 October 1911, 13; 4 May 1912, 10.

[68] Agatha Christie, *The Man in the Brown Suit* (1924), in *Agatha Christie: 1920s Omnibus* (London: HarperCollins, 2006), 395–6.

[69] Quote from Mary Quant in 'Gone Too Far This Time?', *DM*, 16 October 1969, 17.

[70] *EH*, 316.

[71] La Fountaine, *A brief collection of many rare secrets*, sig. Br; London, Wellcome Library, Lowdham, Caleb (fl. 1665–1712), MS.7073/digitized image 74.

[72] *DM*, 24 October 1935, 17. The frequent advertisements repeat the same story over a period of twenty-four years.

Chapter 4

[1] Pierio Valeriano, *A treatise vvriten by Iohan Valerian a greatte clerke of Italie, which is intitled in latin Pro sacerdotum barbis translated in to Englysshe* ([London, 1533]), p. 2r, sig. A2r. Note that this date fits with Matthäus Schwarz's decision in 1535 to grow a beard, as recorded and depicted in his book of clothes: *The First Book of Fashion: The Books of Clothes of Matthäus and Veit Konrad Schwarz of Augsburg*, ed. Ulinka Rublack and Maria Hayward (London: Bloomsbury, 2015), 152.

[2] John Taylor, *Superbiae flagellum, or, The vvhip of pride* (London, 1621), sigs C7v–C8r.

[3] E.g. Philip Stubbes, *The second part of the anatomie of abuses conteining the display of corruptions* (London, 1583), sigs G8r–G8v.

[4] J.[ohn] B.[ulwer], *Anthropometamorphosis: man transform'd: or the artificiall changling* (London, 1653), Scene XII, p. 193.

[5] Sandra Cavallo, *Artisans of the Body in Early Modern Italy: Identities, Families and Masculinities* (Manchester: Manchester UP, 2007), 42.

[6] Will Fisher, *Materializing Gender in Early Modern English Literature and Culture* (Cambridge: Cambridge UP, 2006), esp. Chapter 3; Eleanor Rycroft, 'Facial Hair and the Performance of Adult Masculinity on the Early Modern English Stage', in Helen Ostovich, Holder Schott Syme and Andrew Griffin (eds), *Locating the Queen's Men, 1583–1603: Material Practices and Conditions of Playing*

(Aldershot: Ashgate, 2009), 217–28; also Mark Albert Johnston, 'Bearded Women in Early Modern England', *Studies in English Literature 1500–1900* 47 (2007): 1–28.

[7] John Partridge, *The widowes treasure* (London, 1588), 'To make the haire of the bearde to grow', sigs [D5r–D5v].

[8] For what follows, see Herbert Moller, 'The Accelerated Development of Youth: Beard Growth as a Biological Marker', *Comparative Studies in Society and History* 29 (1987): esp. 753–7.

[9] Quoted in ibid., 753, trans. by Moller.

[10] Gervas Huxley, *Endymion Porter: The Life of a Courtier 1587–1649* (London: Chatto and Windus, 1959), 76; *The Letters of John Chamberlain*, ed. Norman Egbert McClure, 2 vols (Philadelphia: American Philosophical Society, 1939), II, 480–1.

[11] Quoted in J.G. Muddiman, *Trial of King Charles the First* (Edinburgh and London: W. Hodge and Company, 1928), 150. Also C.V. Wedgwood, *The Trial of Charles I* (London: Collins, 1964), 189, and references at note 47 (p. 241).

[12] For example, Geoffrey Robertson, 'Who Killed the King?', *History Today* 56, no. 11 (2006), http://www.historytoday.com/geoffrey-robertson/who-killed-king, accessed 22 February 2015.

[13] Fisher, *Materializing Gender*, 83.

[14] William Shakespeare, *A Midsummer Night's Dream*, I.2, lines 83–9.

[15] *Letters of John Chamberlain*, ed. McClure, II, 630.

[16] Stephen Orgel and Roy Strong (eds), *Inigo Jones: The Theatre of the Stuart Court*, 2 vols ([London]: Sotheby Parke Bernet, 1973), I, 384.

[17] Available at http://thequeensmen.mcmaster.ca/index.htm, accessed 28 January 2015.

[18] Rycroft, 'Facial Hair and the Performance of Adult Masculinity', 225–6.

[19] J.H.P. Pafford, *John Clavell 1601–43: Highwayman, Author, Lawyer, Doctor. With a Reprint of his Poem 'A Recantation of an Ill Led Life, 1634* (Oxford: Leopard Press, 1993), 'Recantation', 6.

[20] *The Letters of Lady Arbella Stuart*, ed. Sara Jayne Steen (New York: Oxford UP, 1994), 69.

[21] Fisher, *Materializing Gender*, 85–6.

[22] My thanks to Alan Dunnett for his translation of this print.

[23] The following is drawn from Stuart Holbrook, 'The Beard of Joseph Palmer', *The American Scholar* 13, no. 4 (1944): 451–8.

[24] According to the *OED*, the 'pogon' prefix, taken from the Greek for beard, first appears in English in a rare usage from 1631.

[25] 'New Fashion of Wearing the Beard', *The Penny Satirist*, 16 January 1841, 1.

[26] Quoted in Richard Corson, *Fashions in Hair: The First Five Thousand Years* (London: Peter Owen, 1971), 405.

[27] 'The Hair and the Beard', *The Leeds Mercury*, 22 January 1881, 5.

[28] Ibid.

[29] Quoted in Lucy Lethbridge, *Servants: A Downstairs View of Twentieth-Century Britain* (London: Bloomsbury, 2013), 43.

[30] The following ideas stated in such publications as H.M., *Why Shave? or Beards v. Barbery* (London, [n.d., *c.*1888]); Theologos, *Shaving: A Breach of the Sabbath* (London, Saunders and Otley, 1860); Thomas S. Gowing, *The Philosophy of Beards* (Ipswich: J. Haddock, [1854]; repr. London: British Library, 2014).

[31] 'The Beard in Fog, Frost, and Snow', *Daily News*, 21 January 1854.

[32] *Why Shave?*, 29. However, linking Chartism with a bearded appearance (Christopher Oldstone-More, 'The Beard Movement in Victorian Britain', *Victorian Studies* 48 (2005): 7, 10, 16) seems flawed, as almost all Chartist leaders were clean-shaven or had side whiskers only (as did most men at of the period). Fergus O'Connor's famous and repeated address to the 'fustian jackets, blistered hands and unshorn chins' (see Paul Pickering, 'Class Without Words: Symbolic Communication in the Chartist Movement' *Past and Present* 112 (1986): 144–62) is more likely to refer to the stubble accruing from a typical once-a-week shave of the working man than it is to an actual bearded self-presentation.

[33] John Brown, *Plain Words on Health Addressed to Working People* ([n.p.], 1882), 79.

[34] 'Three Months' Experience of a Beard', *Daily News*, 29 November 1853.

[35] Brown, 'Plain Words', 80.

[36] Gowing, *Philosophy of Beards*, 14.

[37] 'The Beard Again', *The Sheffield and Rotherham Independent*, 14 January 1854.

[38] Quoted in Hely Hutchinson Almond, *The Difficulty of Health Reformers* ([n.p], 1884), 189.

[39] 'Three Months' Experience of a Beard'.

[40] M. Louise Hayden, 'Charles Winthrop's Moustache', *The Young Folk's Budget*, 21 June 1879, 396.

[41] Gwen Raverat, *Period Piece: A Victorian Childhood* (1952; repr. Bath: Clear Press, 2003), 261–2.

[42] Christopher Oldstone-Moore, *Of Beards and Men: The Revealing History of Facial Hair* (Chicago: University of Chicago Press, 2016), 189–91.

[43] Stevens Cox, 106, for entries related to moustache accessories and products; Corson, *Fashions in Hair*, 560–1, 562; *EH*, 280; Gail Durbin, *Wig, Hairdressing and Shaving Bygones* (Oxford: Shire, 1984), 21.

[44] *Modern Etiquette in Public and Private* (London: Frederick Warne and Co., [*c.*1887]), 39.

[45] For example: *British Medical Journal*, 'Beards and Bacteria', 1 February 1896, 295; 'Beards and Bacilli', 10 June 1899; 'Beards and Bacilli', 15 July 1905.

[46] 'Vanity, Greed and Hygiene Combine to Banish the Beard', *The Atlanta Constitution*, 23 February 1902, p. A4.

[47] Cited in 'The Passing of the Beard', *British Medical Journal*, 26 July 1902, 273. Full and substantially the same coverage in: 'Vanity, Greed and Hygiene'; 'Shave Microbe-Infested Beards', *The Philadelphia Inquirer*, 23 February 1902, 2; 'Danger Found in the Beard', *Star* (Christchurch, NZ), 10 May 1902, 2.

[48] Stuart P. Sherman, 'Lawrence Cultivates His Beard', *New York Herald Tribune*, Books section, 14 June 1926, reprinted in R.P. Draper (ed.), *D. H. Lawrence: The Critical Heritage* (London: Routledge and Kegan Paul, 1970), 250.

[49] *The Collected Letters of D. H. Lawrence*, ed. Harry T. Moore, 2 vols (London: Heinemann, 1962), II, 846.

[50] Ibid., I, 293.

[51] 'To-Day's Gossip: Beaver', *DM*, 6 April 1922, 9; 'London Letter: Beaver', *Hull Daily Mail*, 7 July 1922, 4.

[52] 'Beards and the British', *The Spectator*, 6 February 1959, 19, available at The Spectator Archive, http://archive.spectator.co.uk/article/6th-february-1959/19/beards-and-the-british, accessed 14 February 2017. Reports at the time include: 'London Letter: Beaver', *Devon and Exeter Daily Gazette*, 7 July 1922, 16; 'Mail: Mustard and Cress', *Hull Daily Mail*, 26 August 1922, 1.

[53] See Michael Holroyd, 'Augustus John', *ODNB*.

[54] 'London Letter: Beaver!', *Hull Daily Mail*, 21 November 1922, 4.

[55] See Virginia Nicolson, *Among the Bohemians: Experiments in Living 1900–1939* (London: Penguin, 2003), esp. 148–9 (also discusses 'Beaver').

[56] Lady Cynthia Asquith, *Diaries 1915–1918* (London: Hutchinson, 1968), 37, 62, 298, 479. See also 365.

[57] See his entry in the *ODNB*.

[58] Eric Gill, *Clothes: An Essay Upon the Nature and Significance of the Natural and Artificial Integuments Worn by Men and Women* (London: Jonathan Cape, 1931), 191–2.

[59] John English, 'As the World Goes By: Beards and Barbarism', *DM*, 18 September 1930, 9.

[60] For example, *DM*, 'Moustaches or Not', 20 July 1906, 5; 'Moustaches Unpopular', 14 July 1909, 4; 'Shaven "Ladies" Man', 24 February 1912, 5; 'Clean-Shaven Army', 8 July 1913, 4.

[61] 'Shaven Ladies' Man'.

[62] 'Clean-Shaven Army'; see also 'Military Men and Moustaches', *DM*, 21 July 1906, 6.

[63] Asquith, *Diaries*, e.g. 212, 223.

[64] 'The Army Moustache', *The Times*, 7 October 1916, 5.

[65] Christopher Oldstone-Moore, 'Moustaches and Masculine Codes in Early Twentieth-Century America', *Journal of Social History* 45 (2011): 47–60, esp. 54–6; Joan Melling, *Big Bad Wolves: Masculinity in the American Film* (New York: Pantheon Books, 1977), 44, 45.

[66] 'New Star Gets New Order – "Grow Moustache!"', *DM*, 28 December 1937, 16. 'Filmland Chatter', *DM*, 1 July 1932, 17.

[67] 'A Day with Ronald Colman', *DM*, 11 January 1935, 20; 'This Week's Film Shows', *DM*, 27 May 1935, 23.

[68] 'I'm a Hero at Last!', *Hull Daily Mail*, 4 March 1939, 4; 'Why I am Growing a Moustache', *Hull Daily Mail*, 7 May 1932, 4.

[69] Quoted in Lucinda Hawksley, *Moustaches, Whiskers and Beards* (London: National Portrait Gallery, 2014), 95.

[70] Stuart Hall, 'The Hippies: An American "Moment"', Occasional Paper, Sub and Popular Culture Series: SP No. 16, Centre for Cultural Studies, University of Birmingham (1968), 21. Emphasis original.

[71] George Fallows, 'A Banned Beard is Saved – In a Plastic Bag', *DM*, 15 September 1969, 11.

[72] 'Beards and The British'.

[73] On breakdown of unitary fashion cycle, Fred Davis, *Fashion, Culture and Identity* (Chicago and London: University of Chicago Press, 1992), e.g. 107–8.

[74] 'Are Hipster Beards Unhygienic?', Mail Online, http://www.dailymail.co.uk/health/article -2991865/Are-beards-unhygienic-Facial-hair -riddled-bacteria-spread-germs-trigger-infections -experts-claim.html, accessed 25 May 2016.

[75] 'Are Beards Good for Your Health?', BBC News, http://www.bbc.co.uk/news/magazine-35350886, accessed 25 May 2016.

[76] On St Wilgefortis: Ilse E. Friesen, *The Female Crucifix: Images of St. Wilgefortis Since the Middle Ages* (Waterloo, ON: Wilfrid Laurier UP, 2001); Elizabeth Nightlinger, 'The Female *Imitatio Christi* and Medieval Popular Religion: The Case of St Wilgefortis', in *Representations of the Feminine in the Middle Ages*, ed. Bonnie Wheeler (Dallas: Academia, 1993), 291–328.

[77] Merry Wiesner-Hanks, *The Marvelous Hairy Girls: The Gonzales Sisters and their Worlds* (New Haven: Yale UP, 2009), 5–6.

[78] Annie Shooter, 'Zap That Facial Hair!', Mail Online, http://www.dailymail.co.uk/femail/beauty/article -1331866/Revealed-Six-techniques-zapping-facial -hair.html, accessed 7 June 2016.

[79] Jane Tibbetts Schulenburg, *Forgetful of their Sex: Female Sanctity and Society ca. 500–1100* (Chicago: University of Chicago Press, 1998), 152–3.

[80] Gregory the Great, *Dialogues* 4.13; Schulenburg, *Forgetful of Their Sex*, 152.

[81] Jonathan Brown and Richard L. Kagan, 'The Duke of Alcalá: His Collection and Its Evolution', *The Art Bulletin* 69 (1987): 231–55. On this painting, and others of bearded women, Sherry Velasco, 'Women with Beards in Early Modern Spain', in Karín Lesnik-Oberstein (ed.), *The Last Taboo: Women and Body Hair* (Manchester: Manchester UP, 2006), 181–90.

[82] For the full inscription in Latin, a translation, and a modern medical explanation of Magdalena's condition, W. Michael G. Tunbridge, 'La Mujer Barbuda by Ribera, 1631: A Gender Bender', *QJM: An International Journal of Medicine* 104 (2011): 733–6, available at http://qjmed.oxfordjournals. org/content/qjm/104/8/733.full.pdf, accessed 9 June 2016.

[83] As Oldstone-Moore argues for the nineteenth-century, *Of Beards and Men*, 198.

[84] Pepys, IX, 398.

[85] Nadja Durbah, *Spectacle of Deformity: Freak Shows and Modern British Culture* (Berkeley: University of California Press, 2010), 1–6.

[86] Oldstone-Moore, *Of Beards and Men*, 191.

[87] Sean Trainor, 'Fair Bosom/Black Beard: Facial Hair, Gender Determination, and the Strange Career of Madame Clofullia, "Bearded Lady"', *Early American Studies* 12 (2014): 548–75.

[88] Rachel Adams, *Sideshow USA: Freaks and the American Cultural Imagination* (Chicago: University of Chicago Press, 2001), 27–31.

[89] 'Opening of Barnum's Show', *The Times*, 12 November 1889, 7.

[90] Quoted in Susan Bell, 'Memoirs of a Bearded Lady who Noted Barbed Comments in Ink', *The Scotsman*, 21 June 2005, http://www.scotsman .com/news/world/memoirs-of-a-bearded-lady -who-noted-barbed-comments-in-ink-1-716483, accessed 13 June 2016. See also for Clementine, Joe Nickell, *Secrets of the Sideshows* (Lexington: University of Kentucky Press, 2005), 152.

[91] Bell, 'Memoirs of a Bearded Lady'.

[92] Quoted in Bell, 'Memoirs of a Bearded Lady'. For similar arguments about the empowerment of freak performers more generally: Christopher R. Smit, 'A Collaborative Aesthetic: Levinas's Idea of Responsibility and the Photographs of Charles Eisenmann and the Late Nineteenth-Century Freak-Performer', in Marlene Tromp (ed.), *Victorian Freaks: The Social Context of Freakery in Britain* (Columbus: Ohio State UP, 2008), 283–311; Robert Bogdan, *Freak Show: Presenting Human Oddities for Amusement and Profit* (Chicago: University of Chicago Press, 1988), esp. 270–2.

[93] 'Strange Conduct of a Bearded Lady', *Evening Telegraph and Star and Sheffield Daily Times*, 25 August 1894, 2.

[94] 'A Bearded Woman', *The Evening News*, 11 May 1895, 2.

[95] The idea that facial hair represents power has been used by the French feminist group La Barbe, who don false whiskers to comment ironically on male supremacy.

[96] Quoted in Michael M. Chemers, *Staging Stigma: A Critical Examination of the American Freak Show* (New York: Palgrave Macmillan, 2008), 125. Also see Adams, *Sideshow*, 219–26.

Chapter 5

[1] William Prynne, *The vnlouelinesse, of loue-lockes* (London, 1628), sig. B2, p. 3; sig. A3v.

[2] On their origins, mobilization and meanings: Tristam Hunt, *The The English Civil War at First Hand* (London: Weidenfeld and Nicolson, 2002), 72–5; Jerome de Groot, *Royalist Identities* (Houndmills: Palgrave Macmillan, 2004), 90–107; Helen Pierce, *Unseemly Pictures: Graphic Satire and Politics in Early Modern England* (New Haven and London: Yale UP for the Paul Mellon Centre for Studies in British Art, 2008), 137–67; Jacqueline

Eales, *Puritans and Roundheads: The Harleys of Brampton Bryan and the Outbreak of the English Civil War* (Cambridge: Cambridge UP, 1990), 143–5; Tamsyn Williams, '"Magnetic Figures": Polemical Prints of the English Revolution', in Lucy Gent and Nigel Llewellyn (eds), *Renaissance Bodies: The Human Figure in English Culture, c. 1540–1660* (London: Reaktion, 1990), 88–94; Christopher Hill and Edmund Dell (eds), *The Good Old Cause: The English Revolution of 1640–1660*, rev. edn (London: Frank Cass, 1969), 245–6.

[3] W. Lilly, *The True History of King James I and Charles I*, quoted in Hill and Dell (eds), *The Good Old Cause*, 245–6.

[4] Letter of Lady Brilliana Harley, quoted in Eales, *Puritans and Roundheads*, 144.

[5] Hunt, *The English Civil War at First Hand*, 73, citing Veronica Wedgewood.

[6] T. J., *A Medicine for the Times. Or an antidote against Faction* (London, 1641), sig. A3v.

[7] Ibid. On puritanical joylessness, Humphrey Crouch, *My Bird is a Round-head* (London, 1642).

[8] John Taylor, *The Devil turn'd Round-head* ([London], 1642), sigs [A3v–A4r].

[9] E.g. Anon, *A short, compendious, and true description of the round-heads and the long-heads shag-polls briefly declared* (London, 1642).

[10] *A short, compendious, and true description of the round-heads*, 2; Anon, *See, heer, malignants foolerie retorted on them properly The Sound-Head, Round-Head, Rattle-Head well plac'd, where best is merited* ([London],1642).

[11] De Groot, *Royalist Identities*, 105; *The soundheads description of the roundhead. Or The roundhead exactly anatomized in his integralls and excrementalls* (London, 1642), 7.

[12] *A short, compendious, and true description of the round-heads*, 9.

[13] Lucy Hutchinson, *Memoirs of the Life of Colonel Hutchinson*, ed. N.H. Keeble (London: Dent, 1995), 86–7.

[14] George Gipps, *A Sermon preached (before God, and from him) to the Honourable House of Commons* (London, 1644), 9.

[15] *The Journal of Mary Frampton*, ed. Harriot Georgiana Mundy (London: S. Low, Marston, Searle and Rivington, 1885), 36.

[16] John Barrell, *The Spirit of Despotism: Invasions of Privacy in the 1790s* (Oxford: Oxford UP, 2006), 175.

[17] On starch, see Susan Vincent, *The Anatomy of Fashion: Dressing the Body from the Renaissance to Today* (Berg: Oxford, 2009), 29–34.

[18] John E. Archer, *Social Unrest and Popular Protest in England 1780–1840* (Cambridge: Cambridge UP, 2000), 28–41.

[19] 35 Geo. III, c. 49. Although Pitt did not publicly acknowledge the desire to ease grain shortage, John Barrell feels that this must have been a motivation for the tax. For an in-depth discussion of the tax see Barrell, *The Spirit of Despotism*, Chapter 4 (pp. 145–209), on whose expertise I draw on heavily for what follows, although also depart from.

[20] *Cobbett's Parliamentary History* 31, col. 1314, and *Parliamentary Register* 40, 488.

[21] See Barrell, *The Spirit of Despotism*, 207.

[22] Soame Jenyns, *The Works of Soame Jenyns, Esq.*, 4 vols (London, 1790), II, 116–17.

[23] Quoted in Norah Waugh, *The Cut of Men's Clothes, 1600–1900* (1964; repr. Abingdon: Routledge, 2015), 109; Horace Walpole, *Selected Letters*, ed. William Hadley (1926; repr. London: Dent, 1948), 524.

[24] 'Rules for the Box Lobby Puppies', *The Times*, 17 September 1791, 2.

[25] E.g. *Evening Mail*, 22–24 February 1796.

[26] On the development of the dandy, especially in relation to cropped hair and tailored restraint, see Elizabeth Amann, *Dandyism in the Age of Revolution: The Art of the Cut* (Chicago and London: University of Chicago Press, 2015). See particularly Chapter 5 'Crops', pp. 162–98, which deals with England and draws on much of the same material as is used here, though at times draws different conclusions.

[27] 'Society of Levellers', *The Times*, 24 December 1791, 2.

[28] Sir N. William Wraxall, *Historical Memoirs of my own Time* (1815; repr. London: Kegan Paul, Trench, Trubner and Co., 1904), 84.

[29] On his crop and others in the Republican government, see Jessica Larson, 'Usurping Masculinity: The Gender Dynamics of the coiffure à la Titus in Revolutionary France' (BA diss., University of Michigan, 2013), 12, available at https://deepblue.lib.umich.edu/bitstream/handle/2027.42/98928/jjlars.pdf?sequence=1, accessed 16 October 2016.

[30] 'Mr Burke's Letter to a Noble Lord', *Evening Mail*, 22–24 February 1796.

[31] *Oracle and Public Advertiser*, 17 October 1795.

[32] *Cobbett's Parliamentary History* 31, col. 1308, and *Parliamentary Register* 40, 476.

[33] *Parliamentary Register* 42, 449.

[34] 19 September 1795.

[35] *Morning Chronicle*, 6 January 1796.

[36] Notably I Cor. 11.14: 'Doth not even nature itself teach you, that, if a man have long hair, it is a shame unto him.'

[37] See their respective entries in the *ODNB*.

[38] Quoted in his *ODNB* entry.

[39] John Hart, *An address to the public, on the subject of the starch and hair-powder manufactures* (London, [1795]), 40–1, 66.

[40] 22 January 1796, 3.

[41] 'Female Fashions for May', *The Norfolk Chronicle: or, the Norwich Gazette*, 13 May 1797, 4.

[42] 'On Female Dress', *The Lady's Monthly Museum*, [1 October 1800], 303.

[43] 'Cabinet of Fashion', *The Lady's Monthly Museum*, [1 February 1801], 156.

[44] 'To Noblemen and Gentlemen of Fashion', *The Times*, 3 April 1799, 2.

[45] *Cobbett's Parliamentary History* 31, col. 1318, and *Parliamentary Register* 40, 493.

[46] *Cobbett's Parliamentary History* 25, cols 814–16, at col. 815, and *Parliamentary Register* 18, 484–7. Also reported in *The Gentleman's Magazine* 55 (1785): 864–5.

[47] *Cobbett's Parliamentary History* 31, col. 1313, and *Parliamentary Register* 40, 488.

Chapter 6

[1] 22 December 1964, 9.

[2] Tom Wolfe, 'A Highbrow Under all that Hair?', *Book Week*, 3 May 1964; and Paul Johnson, 'The Menace of Beatlism', *New Statesman*, 28 February 1964, both in Elizabeth Thomson and David Gutman (eds), *The Lennon Companion: Twenty-Five Years of Comment* (Houndmills and London: Macmillan Press, 1987), at 39–40 and 44–7 respectively.

[3] *DM*, 24 October 1963, 15.

[4] *DM*, 5 June 1964, 3.

[5] *DM*, 20 November 1963, 5.

[6] 'The Christopher Ward Page: After a While Short Hair Begins to Grow on You', *DM*, 12 February 1969, 7.

[7] 'Haircut Styles Analysed', *The Times*, 31 March 1964, 6.

[8] 'Beatle Haircut for the Lion', *The Times*, 15 April 1966, 7.

[9] 'The Hair', *The Times*, 10 October 1967, 11.

[10] Simon Mayo interview with Bruce Springsteen on 'Drivetime', first broadcast BBC Radio 2, 20 October 2016 (original emphasis); Bruce Springsteen, *Born to Run* (London: Simon and Schuster, 2016), 86–7.

[11] For an excellent in-depth discussion of the phenomenon, see Gael Graham, 'Flaunting the Freak Flag: *Karr v. Schmidt* and the Great Hair Debate in American High Schools, 1965–1975', *The Journal of American History* 91 (2004): 522–43, at 522–3.

[12] Quoted in Graham, 'Flaunting the Freak Flag', 533.

[13] Quoted in Wayne Hampton, *Guerrilla Minstrels: John Lennon, Joe Hill, Woody Guthrie, Bob Dylan* (Knoxville: University of Tennessee Press, 1986), 16.

[14] Ibid., 18.

[15] Quoted in ibid., 18.

[16] Keith Carradine, interviewed in *Hair: Let the Sun Shine In*, documentary by Pola Rapaport and Wolfgang Held, DVD (2007).

[17] Dick Hebdige, *Subculture: The Meaning of Style* (London: Routledge, 1979; repr. 2003), esp. 93–6, 100.

[18] 'After a While Short Hair Begins to Grow on You'.

[19] Jann Wenner, *Lennon Remembers: The Rolling Stone Interviews* (Harmondsworth: Penguin, 1973; first pub. 1970), 11–12.

[20] *Chicago Daily Tribune*, 28 July 1922, 1; *New York Tribune*, 28 July 1922, 3.

[21] Reports on other US cases include: 'She Bobbed Hair, Didn't Like Results, And Killed Herself', *The Atlanta Constitution*, 11 September 1922, 3; 'Worry Over Bobbed Hair Leads Girl to Drown Herself', *NYT*, 11 September 1922, 3; 'Girl's Bobbed Hair Causes Grief That Results in Suicide', *The Washington Post*, 11 September 1922, 1; 'Grief Over Bobbed Hair Leads Girl to Try Suicide: Spent Many Hours Bemoaning Shorn Tresses', *The Atlanta Constitution*, 31 May 1924, 1; 'Bobs Hair, Kills Herself', *NYT*, 1 June 1924, 22. Britain: 'Worried After Having Her Hair Bobbed: Preston Girl's Suicide', *The Manchester Guardian*, 7 February 1925, 12. Vienna case: 'Bobbed Hair Leads to Suicide', *NYT*, 9 November 1926, 7. Jane Walker: 'Suicide After Smack: Father and A Daughter's Bobbed Hair', *The Manchester Guardian*, 13 March 1926, 18.

[22] 'Hair Bob Causes Tragedy: Polish Mother Tries Suicide When Daughter Disobeys Her', *NYT*, 3 May 1927, 18; 'Suicide for Bobbed Hair: Ohio Man Takes Poison When Wife Has Tresses Cut', *NYT*, 24 April 1924, 21; 'Bobbed Hair Leads Sacristan to Hang Himself in Belfrey', *The Atlanta Constitution*, 7 June 1927, 6.

[23] Ruth Hornbaker: 'Would-Be Flapper Commits Suicide', *NYT*, 4 June 1923, 7. Annabelle Lewis: 'Hair Bobbing Delayed, Girl of 15 Ends Life', *NYT*, 7 September 1926, 3.

[24] 'Worried After Having Her Hair Bobbed', *The Manchester Guardian*, 7 February 1925, 12.

[25] For an excellent short introduction to the bob and its social context, Caroline Cox, *Good Hair Days: A History of British Hairstyling* (London: Quartet Books, 1999), 35–57. Also valuable, Steven Zdatny, 'The Boyish Look and the Liberated Woman: The Politics and Aesthetics of Women's Hairstyles', *Fashion Theory* 1 (1997): 367–97.

[26] Gwen Raverat, *Period Piece: A Victorian Childhood* (1952; repr. Bath: Clear Press, 2003), 193, 219.

[27] On early origins: Cox, *Good Hair Days*, 38–42. Also Mary Louise Roberts, 'Samson and Delilah Revisited: The Politics of Women's Fashion in 1920s France', *The American Historical Review* 98 (1993): 659 and note.

[28] Cox, *Good Hair Days*, 52, cf. *EH*, 65.

[29] Raverat, *Period Piece*, 261; Violet, Lady Hardy, *As It Was* (London: Christopher Johnson, 1958), 79.

[30] Lady Cynthia Asquith, *Diaries 1915–1918* (London: Hutchinson, 1968), 75, 214, 292.

[31] 'Crinolines to Return', *DM*, 18 November 1918, 2.

[32] 'Bobbing Banned in Business', *The Times*, 15 August 1921, 8.

[33] *EH*, 65.

[34] On concerns about the bob's relationship to falling birth rates in France, Roberts, 'Samson and Delilah'.

[35] Adrian Maxwell, 'On Giving Up One's Seat in Trains', *DM*, 15 August 1924, 5.

[36] Beatrice Heron-Maxwell, 'A New Type of Girl For Next Year', *DM*, 27 October 1922, 7.

[37] For what follows, see Laura Doan, *Fashioning Sapphism: The Origins of a Modern Lesbian Culture* (New York: Columbia UP, 2001), Chapter 4, (pp. 5–125). My thanks to Suzie Steinbach for this reference.

[38] Gilbert A. Foan (ed.), *The Art and Craft of Hairdressing* (London: Isaac Pitman, 1931), 140.

[39] On Cooney: Andrew Matson and Stephen Duncombe, *The Bobbed Haired Bandit: A True Story of Crime and Celebratory in 1920s New York* (New York: NYU Press, 2006). Examples of news reports on other women: 'Bobbed Hair Bandit is Held in $10,000 Bail', *The Washington Post*, 1 November 1923, 2; 'Bobbed-Hair Bandit Taken in Philadelphia', *NYT*, 29 February 1924, 3; 'Bobbed-Hair Bandit Robs Bride Alone', *The Washington Post*, 7 April 1924, 1; 'Bobbed-Hair Bandit Caught in Buffalo', *NYT*, 12 May 1924, 19; 'Moscow's Girl Bandit Gets 13-Year Term', *NYT*, 29 May 1924, 8; 'Driver Turns Tables on Bobbed Hair Bandit', *The Washington Post*, 2 September 1924, 1; 'Turkey's Bobbed-Hair Bandit', *NYT*, 31 July 1926, 2; 'London Girl Bandit Stirs Scotland Yard', *NYT*, 4 September 1926, 4.

[40] Quoted in Matson and Duncombe, *Bobbed Hair Bandit*, 291.

[41] 'Women Increasing In Crime, He Says. Bobbed Hair and Short Skirts Not Responsible, However, Justice Tells Jury', *NYT*, 15 December 1926, 20.

[42] E.g. 'Back to Bobbed Hair', *DM*, 21 February 1923, 9 (Ancient Egypt and Bolshevist Moscow); 'Vogue of Bobbed Hair', *NYT*, 27 June 1920, 71 (revolutionary Russia and Greenwich Village); 'Bobbed Virtue', *DM*, 30 August 1923, 5 (Chelsea type).

[43] 'Fair Tresses Are Bobbed', *The Washington Post*, 26 March 1916, p. ES14.

[44] Mary S. Lovell, *The Mitford Girls: The Biography of an Extraordinary Family* (London: Little, Brown, 2001; Abacus, 2002), 77, 73.

[45] E.g. 'Wife's Bobbed Hair', *DM*, 15 September 1923, 6.

[46] '"Bobbing Ban" Wives Now Need Permit To Have Hair Cut', *DM*, 19 March 1923, 2. 'Bobbed Hair As Marriage Bar?', *DM*, 20 November 1922, 2.

[47] Salvation army: 'Bobbed Virtue', *DM*, 30 August 1923, 5; 1 September 1923, 5; 4 September 1923, 5. Romford nurses: 'How Might Women Retaliate' (cartoon) and 'Bobbed Hair and Gravity', both in *DM*, 15 November 1924, 5; 'Bobbing Ban', *Chelmsford Chronicle*, 21 November 1924, 2.

[48] 'Bans Bobbed-Hair Nurses', *The Washington Post*, 30 August 1922, 3.

[49] '"Giddy" Teachers Taboo', *NYT*, 23 February 1922, 5.

[50] 'Bobbed Hair Girls Barred By Marshall Field & Co.', *New York Tribune*, 10 August 1921, 18; similarly 'South Draws Hair Line' *NYT*, 9 July 1921, 8. For neutral employers: 'Bobbed Heads Barred? Not So, Employers Say', *Chicago Daily Tribune*, 11 August 1921, 3.

[51] 'Cut Away Tresses: Permission to Bob Means That There Will Not Be a Teashop Girl with Long Hair', *DM*, 17 October 1924, 9; 'Gladys Up-To-Date', *DM*, 31 December 1924, 6.

[52] Louise Edwards, *Women Warriors and Wartime Spies of China* (Cambridge: Cambridge UP, 2016), 87. Also, Lung-kee Sun, 'The Politics of Hair and the Issue of the Bob in Modern China', *Fashion Theory: The Journal of Dress, Body and Culture* 1 (1997): 353–65.

[53] 'Winifred Black Writes About Bobbed Hair and Divorce', *The Washington Post*, 2 June 1922, 26. 'Fair Tresses are "Bobbed"', *The Washington Post*, p. ES14.

[54] Quoted in Cox, *Good Hair Days*, 44.

[55] Foan, 143–4.

[56] Foan, 131.

[57] *EH*, 66.

[58] Compare the census returns for 1921 and 1931, which show the numbers rising from 43,133 to 81,919 (though note this also includes manicurists and chiropodists). See 1921 Census, Table 2: Occupations of Males aged 12 and Years and Over (Census of England and Wales, 1921, Occupations tables BPP 1924 n/a [n/a] 34); 1921 Census, Table 4: Occupations of Females Aged 12 Years and Over (Census of England and Wales, 1921, Occupations tables BPP 1924 n/a [n/a] 105); 1931 Census, Table XLVIII: Occupations of Males and Females Aged 14 and Over (Census of England and Wales, 1931, General report BPP 1950 [n/a] 116). My thanks to Andrew Dunnett for his invaluable help with these statistics. A similar situation pertained in France. In 1896 there were 48,000 people working as hairdressers; in 1926, 62,000; and by 1936, more than 125,000: Steven Zdatny (ed.), *Hairstyles and Fashion: A Hairdresser's History of Paris, 1910–1920* (Oxford: Berg, 1999), 26–7.

[59] In 1921, women accounted for 5,843 of the 43,133 total; in 1931, 33,636 of 82,919: see the census references in n. 58 above. Also on increasing female participation, Zdatny, *Hairstyles and Fashion*, 27; Cox, *Good Hair Days*, 71–5.

[60] 'Hair and Beauty Industry Statistics', National Hairdressers' Federation, http://www.nhf.info /about-the-nhf/hair-and-beauty-industry-statistics/, accessed 18 December 2016. https://www.nhf .info/advice-and-resources/hair-and-beauty -industry-statistics/ (and the percentage is still 88%).

List of illustrations

Figure 0.1. Hair: a part of being human. Photo: B. Blue/Getty Images.

Figure 0.2. François Hollande meeting with apprentice hairdressers. Photo: FRED TANNEAU/AFP/Getty Images.

Figure 0.3. English manual of palmistry, 1648. Wellcome Library, MS. 8727. Photo: Courtesy of the Wellcome Library, London.

Figure 0.4. Circulation leaflet for Prof. Thomas Moore, c.1870. Wellcome Library, EPH557:5. Photo: Courtesy of the Wellcome Library, London.

Figure 0.5. Advertisement for Princes Dye, no date (eighteenth century). Wellcome Library, EPH160B. Photo: Courtesy of the Wellcome Library, London.

Figure 0.6. Ginger Pride Walk, Edinburgh, 2013. Photo: Scott Campbell/Getty Images.

Figure 0.7. Jean Harlow, 1933. Photo: Imagno/Getty Images.

Figure 0.8. Margarita Cansino. Photo: Wikimedia Commons.

Figure 0.9. Rita Hayworth, 1947. Photo: Silver Screen Collection/Getty Images.

Figure 0.10. Barbie, in a hair outfit, 2009. Photo: FRANCOIS GUILLOT/AFP/Getty Images.

Figure 0.11. Hair jewellery, no date (nineteenth century). Wellcome Library, A642442, A642443, A642143. Photo: Courtesy of the Wellcome Library, London.

Figure 0.12. Commemorative old brooch with a reversed crystal intaglio and locket compartment containing hair. British Museum, 1978,1002.201. Photo: © The Trustees of the British Museum.

Figure 0.13. A lock of George III's hair. Wellcome Library, Science Museum A1315. Photo: Courtesy of the Wellcome Library, London.

Figure 0.14. Ebay auction of Britney Spears's hair. Photo: Bruno Vincent/Getty Images.

Figure 0.15. Cap made of human hair, c.1850. Brooklyn Museum Costume Collection at the Metropolitan Museum of Art, 2009.300.1647. Photo: Courtesy of the Metropolitan Museum of Art, New York.

Figure 0.16. 'Perruquier Barbier, Perruques', from Diderot's *Encyclopédie* (1762), vol. 8, Plate VII. Photo: Courtesy of the Wellcome Library, London.

Figure 0.17. Louis Marie Lanté after Georges Jacques Gatine, engraving, no date (early nineteenth century). Wellcome Library, ICV No 20269. Photo: Courtesy of the Wellcome Library, London.

Figure 0.18. 'To Hair Merchants and Hair-Dressers', newspaper advertisement, 1777. Wellcome Library, EPH160B. Photo: Courtesy of the Wellcome Library, London.

Figure 0.19. Michlet, coloured lithograph, from *Le Bon Ton*, April 1865. Wellcome Library, ICV No 20282L. Photo: Courtesy of the Wellcome Library, London.

Figure 0.20a and b. Hair tidies, c.1900, cotton. Nidderdale Museum, 2841 and 3831. Photos: Author, by kind permission of the Nidderdale Museum, Pateley Bridge.

Figure 0.21. Hindu woman having her head shaved. Photo: Allison Joyce/Getty Images.

Figure 1.1. Catherine Maria Fanshawe, after an unknown artist, *Lady Ann Fanshawe*, late eighteenth/early nineteenth century, etching. National Portrait Gallery. Photo: Courtesy of the National Portrait Gallery, London.

Figure 1.2. Ann Fanshawe's receipt book. Wellcome Library, MS.7113/29. Photo: Courtesy of the Wellcome Library, London.

Figure 1.3. Advertisement for macassar oil, no date (nineteenth century). Wellcome Library, EPH160B. Photo: Courtesy of the Wellcome Library, London.

Figure 1.4. Labels for bear's grease, no date (nineteenth century?). Photo: Courtesy of the Wellcome Library, London.

Figure 1.5. Advertisement for Buckingham's Dye, c.1870–c.1900. Boston Public Library. Photo: Digital Commonwealth: Massachusetts Collections Online.

Figure 1.6. *Prince Pückler-Muskau*, engraving from *Deutsches Taschenbuch uf das Jahr 1837* (1837). Photo: Wikimedia Commons.

Figure 1.7. *Elizabeth Vernon, Countess of Southampton*, c.1600, oil on panel. Private collection Duke of Buccleuch and Queensberry. Photo: Wikimedia Commons.

Figure 1.8. Advertisement for Brylcreem, from *Picture Post* (22 May 1954), vol. 63, no. 8, p. 52. Photo: Picture Post/Hulton Archive/Getty Images.

Figure 1.9. Advertisement for Edwards' Harlene, c.1890s. Wellcome Library, EPH154:20. Photo: Courtesy of the Wellcome Library, London.

Figure 1.10. Advertisement for Dr Scott's Electric Hair Brush, 1880s. Wellcome Library, EPH160A. Photo: Courtesy of the Wellcome Library, London.

Figure 1.11. Trade card, J. Marsh, no date (nineteenth century). Wellcome Library, EPH154. Photo: Courtesy of the Wellcome Library, London.

Figure 1.12. An early permanent-wave machine, 1928. Photo: Henry Miller New Picture Service/Archive Photos/Getty Images.

Figure 1.13. Gerard ter Borch, *A Mother Combing the Hair of her Child (Hunting for Lice)*, c.1652–3, oil on panel. Photo: © Mauritshuis, The Hague. Photography: Margareta Svensson.

Figure 1.14. Male human head louse. Photo: Gilles San Martin/Wikimedia Commons.

Figure 1.15. Early shampoo labels, no date. Wellcome Library, EPH157. Photo: Courtesy of the Wellcome Library, London.

Figure 1.16. Advertisement for Petroleum Hair Tonic, no date (early twentieth century). Wellcome Library: EPH154. Photo: Courtesy of the Wellcome Library, London.

Figure 1.17. Advertising leaflet for Edwards' Cremex Shampoo Powder, no date (late nineteenth century). Wellcome Library, EPH154. Photo: Courtesy of the Wellcome Library, London.

Figure 1.18. 'St. Giles and Bloomsbury public baths and washhouses', engraving from *The Builder* (1854), vol. 11, issue 473. Wellcome Library. Photo: Courtesy of the Wellcome Library, London.

Figure 2.1. Lithograph by Jäckel, no date. Wellcome Library, ICV 20148. Photo: Courtesy of the Wellcome Library, London.

Figure 2.2. Trade card, Hawkin's Hair Cutter, no date (early nineteenth century). Wellcome Library, EPH160B. Photo: Courtesy of the Wellcome Library, London.

Figure 2.3. Advertisement for Mr Paintie, ladies' hairdresser, 1778. Wellcome Library, EPH160B. Photo: Courtesy of the Wellcome Library, London.

Figure 2.4. Coloured engraving, no date (early nineteenth century). Wellcome Library, ICV 20046L. Photo: Courtesy of the Wellcome Library, London.

Figure 2.5. R. Bénard after J.R. Lucotte, engraving, 1762. Wellcome Library, ICV 20006. Photo: Courtesy of the Wellcome Library, London.

Figure 2.6. F. Barnard, engraving, 1875. Wellcome Library, ICV 20079. Photo: Courtesy of the Wellcome Library, London.

Figure 2.7. Bernard the Mans Barber, Oxford. Photo: Author.

Figure 2.8. *The Village Barber*, 1778, etching, published by Matthew Darly. Library of Congress, PC 1 - 5517 (A size) [P&P]. Photo: Courtesy of the Library of Congress, Washington, DC.

Figure 2.9. *La Belle Estvuiste*, no date (second half of the seventeenth century). Wellcome Library, ICV 20124. Photo: Courtesy of the Wellcome Library, London. An all but identical image from which this appears to be derived can be found in Jacques Lagniet, *Recueil des plus illustres proverbes divisés en trois livres: le premier contient les proverbes moraux, le second les proverbes joyeux et plaisans, le troisiesme représente la vie des gueux en proverbes ; mis en lumière par Jacques Lagniet . . . [La Vie de Tiel Wlespiegle . . . en proverbes instructifs et divertissans.]* (Paris, 1663): digitized by the Bibliothèque Nationale de France at http://gallica.bnf.fr/ark:/12148/btv1b86267983/f285.image

Figure 2.10. 'Woman Barber Shaves Inmates of a Lincolnshire Workhouse', from the *Daily Mirror*, 22 September 1911, p. 11. Photo: Mirrorpix.

Figure 2.11. Richard Newton, *Sketches in a Shaving Shop*, 1791, coloured etching, published by W. Holland. Wellcome Library, ICV 41273. Photo: Courtesy of the Wellcome Library, London.

Figure 2.12. HIV/AIDS awareness poster in a barbershop in Hyderabad, India. Photo: NOAH SEELAM/AFP/Getty Images.

Figure 2.13. A traditional wet shave with an open razor. Photo: Christopher Furlong/Getty Images.

Figure 2.14. Vidal Sassoon cutting Mary Quant's hair, 1960s. Photo: Ronald Dumont/Getty Images.

Figure 2.15. Sweeney Todd and victim. Photo: © Hulton-Deutsch Collection/CORBIS/Corbis via Getty Images.

Figure 2.16. Lady Cynthia Asquith, by Bassano Ltd, 1912, whole-plate glass negative. National Portrait Gallery, x30857. Photo: © National Portrait Gallery, London.

Figure 2.17. Gossiping at the salon, New York, 1949. Photo: Ivan Dmitri/Michael Ochs Archives/Getty Images.

Figure 2.18. *Intelligence on the Change of the Ministry*, c.1782, etching and engraving, printed and sold for Bowles and Carver. Lewis Walpole Library, 782.05.20.02.2++. Photo: Courtesy of the Lewis Walpole Library, Yale University.

Figure 2.19. *The Barber Politician*, c.1771, etching. Lewis Walpole Library, 771.00.00.61+. Photo: Courtesy of the Lewis Walpole Library, Yale University.

Figure 2.20. *A Hint to [the] Husbands, or, The Dresser, properly Dressed*, 1777, mezzotint with etching, printed for R. Sayer and J. Bennett. Lewis Walpole Library, 777.08.14.01. Courtesy of the Lewis Walpole Library, Yale University.

Figure 2.21. Henry William Bunbury, *Monsieur le Frizeur*, 1771, etching and engraving, published by Matthew Darly. Lewis Walpole Library, Bunbury 771.05.21.01.1. Photo: Courtesy of the Lewis Walpole Library, Yale University.

Figure 2.22. Raymond Bessone, 1954. Photo: Keystone-France/Gamma-Keystone via Getty Images.

Figure 3.1. Hair at Auschwitz. Photo: Chris Jackson/Getty Images.

Figure 3.2. Marine giving a haircut, 2009. Photo: Wikimedia Commons.

Figure 3.3. Young woman receiving chemotherapy. Photo: Kevin Laubacher/Getty Images.

Figure 3.4. John Hayls, *Samuel Pepys*, 1666, oil on canvas. National Portrait Gallery, 211. Photo: Wikimedia Commons.

Figure 3.5. Charles Jervas (studio of), *Jonathan Swift*, 1709–10, oil on canvas. National Portrait Gallery, 4407. Photo: Wikimedia Commons.

Figure 3.6. A set of razors, 1801–1900. Wellcome Library, Science Museum A620159. Photo: Courtesy of the Wellcome Library, London.

Figure 3.7. Straight razor, shaving bowl and badger brush. Photo: MurrayProductions/Getty Images.

Figure 3.8. Waxing a man's hairy back. Photo: Oktay Ortakcioglu/Getty Images.

Figure 3.9. Advertisement for the Gillette safety razor, c.1910. Photo: Popperfoto/Getty Images.

Figure 3.10. Newspaper advertisement for the Mulcuto safety razor, from the *Daily Mirror*, 11 June 1908, p. 15. Photo: Mirrorpix.

Figure 3.11. 'Those Safety Razor Blades', cartoon from the *Daily Mirror*, 12 June 1929, p. 7. Photo: Mirrorpix.

Figure 3.12. Couple with an electric shaver, 1950s. Photo: George Marks/Retrofile/Getty Images.

Figure 3.13. Newspaper advertisement for Trent's Depilatory, no date (late eighteenth/early nineteenth century). Wellcome Library EPH160B. Photo: Courtesy of the Wellcome Library, London.

Figure 3.14. John Singer Sargent, *Madame X (Madame Pierre Gautreau)*, 1883–4, oil on canvas. Metropolitan Museum of Art, Arthur Hoppock Hearn Fund, 16.53. Photo: Courtesy of the Metropolitan Museum of Art, New York.

Figure 3.15. Newspaper advertisement for Decoltene liquid hair remover, from the *Daily Mirror*, 12 November 1919, p. 11. Photo: Mirrorpix.

Figure 3.16. Four women on the beach at Aldeburgh, Suffolk, c.1927. Photo: Fox Photos/Getty Images.

Figure 3.17. Marie Helvin modelling swimwear, c.1980. Photo: Tery O'Neill/Getty Images.

Figure 3.18. Woman shaving her pubic hair. Photo: Michael Heim/EyeEm/Getty Images.

Figure 3.19. Hairs on a wax strip. Photo: Image Source/Getty Images.

Figure 4.1. Juan Pantoja de la Cruz, *The Somerset House Conference*, 1604, oil on canvas. National Maritime Museum, Greenwich, London. Photo: Wikimedia Commons.

Figure 4.2. Anthony van Dyck, *Prince Charles Louis, Elector Palatine*, 1637, oil on canvas. The Museum of Fine Arts, Houston. Photo: Wikimedia Commons.

Figure 4.3. Anthony van Dyck, *Prince Charles Louis, Elector Palatine*, 1641, oil on canvas. Private Collection. Photo: Wikimedia Commons.

Figure 4.3. Christoph Le Blon, after a 1641 portrait by Anthony van Dyck, *Prince Charles Louis, Elector Palatine*, 1652, engraving. Photo: Wikimedia Commons.

Figure 4.4. Daniel Mytens, *Charles I*, 1629, oil on canvas. Metropolitan Museum of Art, Gift of George A. Hearn, 06.1289. Photo: Courtesy of the Metropolitan Museum of Art, New York.

Figure 4.5. Daniel Mytens (after), *Charles I as Prince of Wales*, c.1623, oil on canvas. Photo: Wikimedia Commons.

Figure 4.6. Anonymous (Dutch), *'t Moordadigh Trevrtoneel* (*The Murderous Tragedy*), cropped, 1649, engraving. Wolfenbüttel, Herzog August Bibliothek, Graph. Res. D: 39. Photo: © Herzog August Bibliothek Wolfenbüttel.

Figure 4.7. Anonymous (German), *Newer Kram Laden* (New Haberdashery), 1641, etching and engraving. British Museum, 1872,0113.587. Photo: © The Trustees of the British Museum.

Figure 4.8. Joseph Palmer's tombstone, Evergreen Cemetery, Leominster, Massachusetts. Photo: Courtesy of Bill Bourbeau, https://www.findagrave.com/cgi-bin/fg.cgi?page=gr&GRid=44843658

Figure 4.9. Ary Scheffer, *Charles Dickens*, 1855, oil on canvas. National Portrait Gallery. Photo: adoc-photos/Corbis via Getty Images.

Figure 4.10. Captain Dames of the Royal Artillery, in camp during the Crimean War, 1855. Photo: Roger Fenton/Library of Congress/Corbis/VCG via Getty Images.

Figure 4.11. 'The Moustache Movement', cartoon from *Punch* (21 January 1854), vol. 26, p. 30. Photo: Courtesy of the J.B. Morrell Library, University of York.

Figure 4.12. 'The Beard and Moustache Movement', cartoon from *Punch* (5 November 1853), vol. 25, p. 188. Photo: Courtesy of the J.B. Morrell Library, University of York.

Figure 4.13. 'Rather a Knowing Thing in Nets', cartoon from *Punch* (7 January 1860), vol. 38, p. 6. Photo: Courtesy of the J.B. Morrell Library, University of York.

Figure 4.14. Label for Pomade Hongroise, no date (late nineteenth century?). Wellcome Library, EPH157. Photo: Courtesy of the Wellcome Library, London.

Figure 4.15. Moustache trainer (German), no date (pre-1918), celluloid, cotton and leather. Australian War Memorial, RELAWM00701. Photo: Australian War Memorial, Canberra.

Figure 4.16. Moustache cup, no date (late nineteenth century?). Photo: Courtesy of Parkwood National Historic Site, Ontario.

Figure 4.17. 'Germ Theory of Putrefaction', from *Collected Papers of Joseph, Baron Lister* (1909), vol. 1, Plate XI. Wellcome Library, Slide 6492. Photo: Courtesy of the Wellcome Library, London.

Figure 4.18. D.H. Lawrence, c.1929. Photo: Photo12/UIG via Getty Images.

Figure 4.19. Sir William Orpen, *Augustus John*, 1900, oil on canvas. National Portrait Gallery, 4252. Photo: National Portrait Gallery, London.

Figure 4.20. 'The Guests We Never Ask Again – No. 2', cartoon from the *Daily Mirror*, 18 November 1913, p. 9. Photo: Mirrorpix.

Figure 4.21. Eric Gill, c.1925. Photo: Howard Coster/Hulton Archive/Getty Images.

Figure 4.22. 'Soldier Beckoning', poster, 1915, Parliamentary Recruiting Committee, London. Photo: Galerie Bilderwelt/Getty Images.

Figure 4.23. Ronald Colman, 1927. Photo: John Springer Collection/CORBIS/Corbis via Getty Images.

Figure 4.24. Thomas Phillips, *Portrait of Lord Byron in Albanian Dress*, 1813, oil on canvas. Government Art Collection, British Embassy, Athens. Photo: Wikimedia Commons.

Figure 4.25. George Cole, 1954. Photo: Popperfoto/Getty Images.

Figure 4.26. Fidel Castro and Che Guevara, 1959. Photo: Universal History Archive/UIG via Getty Images.

Figure 4.27. Hipster. Photo: Pexels, Creative Commons.

Figure 4.28. St Wilgefortis. Photo: Frankipank/Wikimedia Commons.

Figure 4.29. Poster of Julia Pastrana, no date (nineteenth century), coloured woodcut and text. Wellcome Library, Iconographic Collection 38980i. Photo: Courtesy of the Wellcome Library, London.

Figure 4.30. Jusepe de Ribera, *Magdalena Ventura with her Husband and Son*, 1631, oil on canvas. Museo Nacional del Prado, Madrid. Photo: Wikimedia Commons. Translation of inscription adapted from W. Michael G. Tunbridge, 'La Mujer Barbuda by Ribera, 1631: A Gender Bender', *QJM: An International Journal of Medicine* 104.8 (2011).

Figure 4.31. 'Barnum and Bailey's Show. A Curious Collection of Freaks', poster, no date (nineteenth century). Wellcome Library. Photo: Courtesy of the Wellcome Library, London.

Figure 4.32. 'Madame Delait en promenade avec son chien' (Madame Delait Walking with Her Dog), postcard, no date (c.1910?). Wellcome Library, EPH499:68. Photo: Courtesy of the Wellcome Library, London.

Figure 4.33. Jennifer Miller, c.2000. Photo: Andrew Lichtenstein/Sygma via Getty Images.

Figure 4.34. Conchita Wurst, 2014. Photo: Ragnar Singsaas/WireImage/Getty Images.

Figure 5.1. John de Critz (attributed), *Henry Wriothesley, 3rd Earl of Southampton*, c.1590–c.1593, oil on panel. Hatchlands Park, Surrey (National Trust). Photo: Wikimedia Commons.

Figure 5.2. Wenceslaus Hollar, *William Prynne*, no date (mid-seventeenth century), etching. Photo: Wikimedia Commons.

Figure 5.3. Title-page image from *A Dialogue, or, Rather a Parley betweene Prince Ruperts Dogge whose name is Puddle and Tobies Dog whose name is Pepper* (London, 1643). Photo: Universal History Archive/Getty Images.

Figure 5.4. Gerrit van Honthorst, *Prince Rupert of the Rhine*, 1642, Lower Saxony State Museum, Landesmuseum Hanover. Photo: Wikimedia Commons.

Figure 5.5. 'Colonel Sir John Hutchinson 1615–1664 and his Son', from J.R. Green, *Short History Of The English People* (London, 1893). It is based on an engraving by James Neagle from 1806, which in turn is based on a contemporary portrait by Robert

Walker. Photo: Universal History Archive/UIG via Getty Images.

Figure 5.6. Wenceslaus Hollar, *Archbishop Laud*, no date (mid-seventeenth century). Photo: Wikimedia Commons.

Figure 5.7. Isaac Cruikshank, *The Knowing Crops*, 1791, etching. Lewis Walpole Library, 794.05.12.55. Photo: Courtesy of the Lewis Walpole Library, Yale University.

Figure 5.8. James Caldwell, *The Englishman in Paris*, 1770, engraving. Lewis Walpole Library, 770.05.10.01+. Photo: Courtesy of the Lewis Walpole Library, Yale University.

Figure 5.9. Villain?, *Un Perruquier*, coloured lithograph, 1780. Wellcome Library, ICV 20153. Photo: Courtesy of the Wellcome Library, London.

Figure 5.10. Isaac Cruikshank, *Favorite Guinea Pigs Going to Market*, 1795, etching, hand coloured. Yale Center for British Art, B1981.25.1221. Photo: Courtesy of the Yale Center for British Art, Paul Mellon Collection.

Figure 5.11. Richard Newton, *Crops Going to Quod*, 1791, etching, hand coloured. Yale Center for British Art, B1981.25.1816. Photo: Courtesy of the Yale Center for British Art.

Figure 5.12. James Gillray, *The Blood of the Murdered Crying for Vengeance*, 1793, etching, hand coloured. Lewis Walpole Library, 793.02.16.01. Photo: Courtesy of the Lewis Walpole Library, Yale University.

Figure 5.13. Isaac Cruikshank, *Whims of the Moment or the Bedford Level!!*, 1795, etching, hand coloured. Yale Center for British Art, B1981.25.1350. Photo: Courtesy of the Yale Center for British Art, Paul Mellon Collection.

Figure 5.14. 'Algernon Sidney', illustration from Samuel Rawson Gardiner, *Oliver Cromwell* (1899),

based on seventeenth-century original. Photo: The Print Collector/Print Collector/Getty Images.

Fig. 5.15. John Russell, *Robert Shurlock*, 1801, pastel on paper, laid down on canvas. Metropolitan Museum of Art, Gift of Alan R. Shurlock, 67.131. Photo: Courtesy of the Metropolitan Museum of Art, New York.

Fig. 5.16. John Russell, *Mrs Robert (Henrietta) Shurlock*, 1801, pastel on paper, laid down on canvas. Metropolitan Museum of Art, Gift of Geoffrey Shurlock, 67.132. Photo: Courtesy of the Metropolitan Museum of Art, New York.

Fig 5.17. Karl Anton Hick, *The House of Commons 1793–94*, 1793–5, oil on canvas. National Portrait Gallery, 745. Photo: Wikimedia Commons.

Figure 6.1. The Beatles, 1963. Photo: Val Wilmer/Redferns/Getty Images.

Figure 6.2. 'James Byrne, 14, covers his hair-trim as he leaves school with his mother', the *Daily Mirror*, 5 June 1964, p. 3. Photo: Mirrorpix.

Figure 6.3. Young women with long straight hair, 1967. Photo: Fotos International/Archive Photos/Getty Images.

Figure 6.4. Hippie and armed guard, 1969. Photo: Robert Altman/Michael Ochs Archives/Getty Images.

Figure 6.5. Hippie at a love-in, 1967. Photo: Bettmann/Getty Images.

Figure 6.6. John Lennon and Yoko Ono, 1969. Photo: Bentley Archive/Popperfoto/Getty Images.

Figure 6.7. Punks on a London street, c.1970. Photo: Erica Echnenberg/Redferns/Getty Images.

Figure 6.8. Fashion plate from *Journal de Dames et des Modes*, 1913. Rijksmuseum, Purchased with the support of the F.G. Waller-Fonds, RP-P-2009-1751. Photo: Courtesy of the Rijksmuseum, Amsterdam.

Figure 6.9. Camille Clifford, c.1905. Photo: Hulton Archive/Getty Images.

Figure 6.10. Camille Clifford, 1916. National Portrait Gallery, x22156. Photo: © National Portrait Gallery, London.

Figure 6.11. Amelia Earhart, 1927. Photo: Bettmann/Getty Images.

Figure 6.12. Fashion plate, 1922. Metropolitan Museum of Art, Costume Institute Fashion Plates, Gift of Woodman Thompson, Plate 050. Photo: Courtesy of the Metropolitan Museum of Art, New York.

Figure 6.13. Radclyffe Hall and Una Trowbridge, 1927. Photo: Fox Photos/Getty Images.

Figure 6.14. Front page of the *New York Daily News*, 22 April 1924. Photo: New York Daily News Archive/Getty Images.

Figure 6.15. 'How Women Might Retaliate', cartoon from the *Daily Mirror*, 15 November 1924, p. 5. Photo: Mirrorpix.

Figure 6.16. Waitresses at a Lyons tea shop, early twentieth century. Photo: Jewish Chronicle/Heritage Images/Getty Images.

Figure 6.17. Waitresses at a Lyons tea shop, 1926. Photo: H.F. Davis/Getty Images.

Figure 6.18. Louise Brooks, 1920s. Photo: John Springer Collection/CORBIS/Corbis via Getty Images.

Figure 6.19. Woman having her hair bobbed at a barber's, c.1920. Photo: PhotoQuest/Getty Images.

Figure 7.1a and b. The author, permed c.1985 and bobbed c.1969.

Abbreviations

DM	*Daily Mirror*
EH	Victoria Sherrow, *Encyclopedia of Hair: A Cultural History* (Westport: Greenwood Press, 2006)
Foan	Gilbert Foan (ed.), *The Art and Craft of Hairdressing: A Standard and Complete Guide to the Technique of Modern Hairdressing, Manicure, Massage and Beauty Culture* (London: Sir Isaac Pitman, 1931)
MOA	Mass Observation Archive
NYT	*New York Times*
ODNB	*Oxford Dictionary of National Biography*, online edition
OED	*Oxford English Dictionary*, online edition
Pepys	*The Diary of Samuel Pepys*, ed. Robert Latham and William Matthews, 11 vols (London: G. Bell, 1970–83)
SP 14	National Archives, State Papers Domestic, James I
SP 29	National Archives, State Papers Domestic, Charles II
SP 34	National Archives, State Papers Domestic, Anne
Stevens Cox	James Stevens Cox, *An Illustrated Dictionary of Hairdressing and Wigmaking* (London: Batsford, rev. edn 1984)
UP	University Press
Vidal	Vidal Sassoon, *Vidal: The Autobiography* (London: Macmillan, 2010)

The diaries of James Woodforde have been published by the Parson Woodforde Society (with no place of publication). Those cited in the text are abbreviated as follows:

Woodforde IV	*The Ansford Diary of James Woodforde, Vol. 4: 1769–1771*, ed. R.L. Winstanley (1986)
Woodforde VI	*The Oxford and Somerset Diary of James Woodforde 1774–1775*, ed. R.L. Winstanley (1989)
Woodforde X	*The Diary of James Woodforde, Volume 10 1782–1784*, ed. R.L. Winstanley (1998)
Woodforde XI	*The Diary of James Woodforde, Volume 11 1785–1787*, ed. R.L. Winstanley and Peter Jameson (1999)
Woodforde XIII	*The Diary of James Woodforde, Volume 13 1791–1793*, ed. Peter Jameson (2003)
Woodforde XIV	*The Diary of James Woodforde, Volume 14 1794–1795*, ed. Peter Jameson (2004)

Bibliography of works cited

Manuscripts

London, The National Archives, SP 14/107

London, The National Archives, SP 29/101

London, The National Archives, SP 34/12

London, Wellcome Library, Boyle Family, MS.1340

London, Wellcome Library, Bridget Hyde, MS.2990

London, Wellcome Library, Caleb Lowdham, MS.7073

London, Wellcome Library, Elizabeth Okeover (and others), MS.3712

London, Wellcome Library, English Recipe Book, 17th–18th century, MS.7721

London, Wellcome Library, English Recipe Book, MS.7391

London, Wellcome Library, Lady Ann Fanshawe, MS.7113

London, Wellcome Library, Med. Ephemera EPH154, Hair care ephemera, Box 1

London, Wellcome Library, Med. Ephemera EPH160B, Hair care ephemera, Box 9

London, Wellcome Library, Corbyn & Co., chemists and druggists, London, Manufacturing recipe books, 1748–1851, MS.5446–5450

Northampton, MA, Smith College, Rare Book Room Cage, MS 134, Kenelm Digby, *Letter Book 1633–1635*

Websites and databases

17th and 18th Century Burney Collection Newspapers, http://gale.cengage.co.uk/

19th Century British Newspapers, http://gale .cengage.co.uk/

19th Century British Pamphlets (JSTOR), http:// www.jstor.org

19th Century UK Periodicals Series 1: New Readerships, http://gale.cengage.co.uk/

American Historical Newspapers (ProQuest), http://search.proquest.com

BBC News, http://www.bbc.co.uk/news

Daily Mirror Digital Archive, 1903 to present (UKpressonline), http://www.ukpressonline.co.uk

Early English Books Online (EEBO), http://eebo .chadwyck.com

Eighteenth Century Collections Online, http:// gale.cengage.co.uk/

The Gentleman's Journal, http://www.the gentlemansjournal.com/

Ginger Parrot, http://gingerparrot.co.uk

The Guardian, https://www.theguardian.com

Habia: Hair and Beauty Industry Authority, http:// www.habia.org/

Health and Safety Executive UK Government, 'Hairdressing', http://www.hse.gov.uk/hairdressing/

John Steed's Flat, http://www.johnsteedsflat.com /index.html

Justice for Magdalenes, https://www.magdalene laundries.com/

London, The National Archives, http://www .nationalarchives.gov.uk/

Mail Online, http://www.dailymail.co.uk/

Mass Observation Online, http://www.mas sobservation.amdigital.co.uk

MeasuringWorth, https://www.measuringworth .com/ukcompare/

Mintel Academic, http://academic.mintel.com/

National Hairdressers' Federation, http://www.nhf .info/home/

Oxford Dictionary of National Biography, http:// www.oxforddnb.com

Oxford English Dictionary, http://www.oed.com

John Johnson Collection, An Archive of Printed Ephemera, http://johnjohnson.chadwyck.co.uk

Performing the Queen's Men, http://the queensmen.mcmaster.ca/index.htm

The Scotsman, http://www.scotsman.com

The Spectator Archive, http://archive.spectator .co.uk/

State Papers Online, 1509–1714, http://gale .cengage.co.uk/

Time, http://time.com/

The Times Digital Archive, 1785 onwards, http:// gale.cengage.co.uk/

U.K. Parliamentary Papers, http://parlipapers .proquest.com

Wellcome Library, digital collections: recipe books, http://wellcomelibrary.org/collections/digital -collections/recipe-books/

Newspapers and periodicals

Athenian Gazette or Casuistical Mercury

The Atlanta Constitution

British Medical Journal

Chelmsford Chronicle

Chicago Daily Tribune

Cincinnati Daily Gazette

Daily Advertiser

Daily Courant

Daily Mirror

Daily News

Daily Post

Devon and Exeter Daily Gazette

The Englishman's Magazine

Evening Mail

The Evening News

Evening Telegraph and Star and Sheffield Daily Times

General Advertiser (1744)

The Gentleman's Journal

The Guardian

The Hairdressers' Journal, devoted to the interests of the profession

Hull Daily Mail

The Lady's Monthly Museum

The Leeds Mercury

London Chronicle or Universal Evening Post

London Gazette

The Manchester Guardian

Metro

Morning Chronicle

Morning Herald and Daily Advertiser

New Statesman

New York Times

New York Tribune

The Norfolk Chronicle: or, the Norwich Gazette

Oracle and Public Advertiser

The Penny Satirist

The Philadelphia Inquirer

Reads Weekly Journal or British Gazetteer

San Francisco Bulletin

St. James's Evening Post

The Scotsman

The Sheffield and Rotherham Independent

The Spectator

Star

Time

The Times

The Washington Post

Weekly Journal or British Gazetteer

Whitehall Evening Post or London Intelligencer

The Young Folk's Budget

Printed primary sources

Andry de Bois-Regard, Nicolas. Orthopædia: Or the Art of Correcting and Preventing Deformities in Children. 2 vols. London, 1743.

Anon. Crosby's royal fortune-telling almanack; or, Ladies universal pocket-book, for the year 1796. London, [1795].

Anon. The English Fortune-Teller. London, 1670–9.

Anon. To her Brown Beard. [London], 1670–96.

Anon. In Holborn over against Fetter-lane, at the sign of the last, liveth a physition. London, 1680.

Anon. A new ballad of an amorous coachman. [London], 1690.

Anon, See, heer, malignants foolerie retorted on them properly The Sound-Head, Round-Head, Rattle-Head well plac'd, where best is merited. [London],1642.

Anon, A short, compendious, and true description of the round-heads and the long-heads shag-polls briefly declared. London, 1642.

Aronson, Kristan J., Geoffrey R. Howe, Maureen Carpenter and Martha E. Fair. 'Surveillance of Potential Associations between Occupations and Causes of Death in Canada, 1965–91'. Occupational and Environmental Medicine 56 (1999): 265–9.

Aspinall-Oglander, Cecil. Admiral's Widow: Being the Life and Letters of the Hon. Mrs. Edward Boscawen from 1761 to 1805. London: Hogarth Press, 1942.

Asquith, Lady Cynthia. Diaries 1915–1918. London: Hutchinson, 1968.

B.[ulwer], J.[ohn]. Anthropometamorphosis: man transform'd: or the artificiall changling. London, 1653.

Baker, J.L., et al. 'Barbershops as Venues to Assess and Intervene in HIV/STI Risk among Young, Heterosexual African American Men'. American Journal of Men's Health 6 (2012): 368–82.

Banister, John. An antidotarie chyrurgicall containing great varietie and choice medicines. London, 1589.

Barbarossa [Alexander Ross]. A Slap at the Barbers. London, [c.1825].

Beasley, Henry. The Druggist's General Receipt Book. London: John Churchill, 1850.

Beaton, Cecil. The Glass of Fashion. London: Weidenfeld and Nicolson, 1954.

Beeton, Isabella. The Book of Household Management. 1861. Facsimile reprint. London: Jonathan Cape, 1977.

Bonsor, Sacha. 'A Tender Touch'. Harper's Bazaar (October 2013): 127.

Bremmer, L. Paul. My Year in Iraq. New York: Simon and Schuster, 2006.

Brontë, Charlotte. Jane Eyre. 1847. Reprinted. London: Penguin, 2012.

Brown, John. Plain Words on Health Addressed to Working People. [n.p.], 1882.

Burney, Frances. The Court Journals and Letters of Frances Burney, vol. 1. Edited by Peter Sabor. Oxford: Clarendon Press, 2011.

Campbell, R. The London tradesman. Being a compendious view of all the trades. London, 1747.

Chamberlain, John. The Letters of John Chamberlain. Edited by Norman Egbert McClure. 2 vols. Philadelphia: American Philosophical Society, 1939.

Chambers, Amelia. The ladies best companion; or A Golden Treasure for the Fair Sex. London, [1775?].

Christie, Agatha. The Man in the Brown Suit. 1924. Reprinted in Agatha Christie: 1920s Omnibus. London: HarperCollins, 2006.

Clifford, Anne. The Diaries of Lady Anne Clifford, edited by D.J.H. Clifford. Stroud: Alan Sutton, 1990.

Cobbett's Parliamentary History of England [Cobbett's Parliamentary Debates]. 36 vols. London: Printed by T.C. Hansard, for Longman et al., 1806–20.

Coke, Lady Mary. The Letters and Journals of Lady Mary Coke. 1889–96. Edited by J.A. Home. 4 vols. Reprinted. Bath: Kingsmead Reprints, 1970.

Copland, Robert. *The shepardes kalender*. London, 1570.

Crouch, Humphrey. *My Bird is a Round-head*. London, 1642.

Cumberland, Richard. *The Memoirs of Richard Cumberland*. Edited by Richard Dircks. 2 vols in 1. New York: AMS Press, 2002.

Darwin, Charles. *Descent of Man, and Selection in Relation to Sex, Part Two*, in *The Works of Charles Darwin*. Edited by Paul Barrett and R.B. Freeman. Vol. 22. London: William Pickering, 1989.

Emlinger Roberts, Rebecca. 'Hair Rules'. *The Massachusetts Review* 44 (2003/2004): 714–15.

Entry 3 / Level 1 VRQ in Hairdressing and Beauty Therapy, The City & Guilds Textbook. London: City & Guilds, 2012.

Erondell, Pierre. *The French garden: for English ladyes and gentlewomen to walke in*. London, 1605.

Evelyn, John. *The Diary of John Evelyn*. Edited by E.S. de Beer. 6 vols. Oxford: Oxford UP, 1955.

Fanshawe, Lady Ann. *The Memoirs of Anne, Lady Halkett and Ann, Lady Fanshawe*. Edited by John Loftis. Oxford: Oxford UP, 1979.

The First Book of Fashion: The Books of Clothes of Matthäus and Veit Konrad Schwarz of Augsburg. Edited by Ulinka Rublack and Maria Hayward. London: Bloomsbury, 2015.

Frampton, Mary. *The Journal of Mary Frampton*. Edited by Harriot Georgiana Mundy. London: S. Low, Marston, Searle and Rivington, 1885.

Franklin, Benjamin. *Benjamin Franklin's Autobiography*. Edited by J.A. Leo Lemay and P.M. Zall. New York: Norton, 1986.

Fraser, M., et al. 'Barbers as Lay Health Advocates: Developing a Prostate Cancer Curriculum'. *Journal of the National Medical Association* 101 (2009): 690–7.

Freeling, Arthur (ed.). *Gracefulness: Being a Few Words Upon Form and Features*. London: Routledge, [1845].

Gaskell, Elizabeth. *North and South*. 1855. Reprinted. London: Penguin, 2012.

Gill, Eric. *Clothes: An Essay Upon the Nature and Significance of the Natural and Artificial Integuments Worn by Men and Women*. London: Jonathan Cape, 1931.

Gipps, George. *A Sermon preached (before God, and from him) to the Honourable House of Commons*. London, 1644.

Gowing, Thomas S. *The Philosophy of Beards*. 1854. Reprinted. London: British Library, 2014.

Green, Martin, and Leo Palladino. *Professional Hairdressing: The Official Guide to Level 3*. 4th edn. London: Thomson, 2004.

Gregory the Great. *Dialogues*.

Gronow, R.H. *Captain Gronow's Recollections and Anecdotes of the Camp, the Court, and the Clubs, At the Close of the last War with France*. London: Smith, Elder and Co., 1864.

Guillemeau, Jacque. *Child-birth or, The happy deliuerie of vvomen*. London, 1612.

H.M. *Why Shave? or Beards v. Barbery*. London, [n.d., c.1888].

Hale, Cynthia M., and Jacqueline A. Polder. *ABCs of Safe and Healthy Child Care: A Handbook for Child Care Providers*. US Public Health Service, 1996.

Hall, Madame Constance. *How I Cured my Superfluous Hair*. London, [1910?].

Hardy, Lady Violet. *As It Was*. London: Christopher Johnson, 1958.

Harrold, Edmund. *The Diary of Edmund Harrold, Wigmaker of Manchester 1712–15*. Edited by Craig Horner. Aldershot: Ashgate, 2008.

Hart, John. *An address to the public, on the subject of the starch and hair-powder manufactures*. London, [1795].

Hays, Mary. *Appeal to the Men of Great Britain in Behalf of Women*. London, 1798.

Hutchinson Almond, Hely. *The Difficulty of Health Reformers*. [n.p], 1884.

Hutchinson, Lucy. *Memoirs of the Life of Colonel Hutchinson*. Edited by N.H. Keeble. London: Dent, 1995.

Jeamson, Thomas. *Artificiall embellishments, or Arts best directions how to preserve beauty or procure it*. Oxford, 1665.

Jenyns, Soame. *The Works of Soame Jenyns, Esq.*, 4 vols. London, 1790.

Jones, David K. 'Promoting Cancer Prevention through Beauty Salons and Barbershops'. *North Carolina Medical Journal* 69 (2008): 339–40.

La Fountaine, *A brief collection of many rare secrets*. [n.p.], 1650.

Lawrence, D.H. *The Collected Letters of D. H. Lawrence*. Edited by Harry T. Moore. 2 vols. London: Heinemann, 1962.

Levens, Peter. *A right profitable booke for all disseases Called The pathway to health*. London, 1582.

Lockes, Shaun. *Cutting Confidential: True Confessions and Trade Secrets of a Celebrity Hairdresser*. London: Orion, 2007.

MacDonald, John. *Memoirs of an Eighteenth-Century Footman: John MacDonald's Travels (1745–1779)*. Edited by John Beresford. London: Routledge, 1927.

Mayhew, Henry, and John Binny. *The Criminal Prisons of London and Scenes of Prison Life*. 1862. Reprinted. London: Frank Cass and Co., 1971.

Modern Etiquette in Public and Private. London: Frederick Warne and Co., [c.1887].

Moore, William. *The art of hair-dressing*. Bath, [1780].

Pafford, J.H.P. *John Clavell 1601–43: Highwayman, Author, Lawyer, Doctor. With a Reprint of his Poem 'A Recantation of an Ill Led Life, 1634*. Oxford: Leopard Press, 1993.

Papendiek, Charlotte. *Court and Private Life in the Time of Queen Charlotte: Being the Journals of Mrs Papendiek, Assistant Keeper of the Wardrobe and Reader to Her Majesty*. Edited by Mrs Vernon Delves Broughton. 2 vols. London: Richard Bentley and Son, 1887.

The Parliamentary register; or, history of the proceedings and debates of the House of Commons. 45 vols. London: printed for J. Almon and J. Debrett, 1781–96.

Partridge, John. *The widowes treasure plentifully furnished with sundry precious and approoued secretes in phisicke and chirurgery for the health and pleasure of mankind*. London, 1586.

Pepys, Samuel. *The Diary of Samuel Pepys*. Edited by Robert Latham and William Matthews. 11 vols. London: G. Bell, 1970–83.

Pharmaceutical Formulas: A Book of Useful Recipes for the Drug Trade. Annotated by Peter MacEwan. 3rd edn. London: The Chemist and Druggist, September 1898.

Pharmaceutical Formulas: A Book of Useful Recipes for the Drug Trade. Annotated by Peter MacEwan. 4th edn. London: The Chemist and Druggist, October 1899.

Pharmaceutical Formulas: A Book of Useful Recipes for the Drug Trade. Annotated by Peter MacEwan. 5th edn. London: The Chemist and Druggist, February 1902.

Pharmaceutical Formulas: Being 'The Chemist and Druggist's' Book of Useful Recipes for the Drug Trade. By Peter MacEwen. 7th edn. London: The Chemist and Druggist, 1908.

Pharmaceutical Formulas: Being 'The Chemist and Druggist's Book of Useful Recipes for the Drug Trade. By Peter MacEwen. 8th edn. London: The Chemist and Druggist, 1911.

Pharmaceutical Formulas: Being 'The Chemist and Druggist's Book of Useful Recipes for the Drug Trade. By Peter MacEwen. 9th edn rev. and enl. London: The Chemist and Druggist, 1914.

Pharmaceutical Formulas: Being 'The Chemist and Druggist' Book of Selected Formulas from the British, United States and other Pharmacopoeias. By S.W. Woolley and G.P. Forrester. 2 vols. 10th edn entirely rev. London: The Chemist and Druggist, 1934.

Pharmaceutical Formulas Volume II: (P. F. vol. II) Formulas. 11th edn. London: The Chemist and Druggist, 1956.

Plat, Sir Hugh. *Delightes for ladies to adorn their persons.* London, 1608.

Platter, Felix. *Platerus golden practice of physick fully and plainly disovering.* London, 1664.

Pope, Alexander. 'The Rape of the Lock', in *The Restoration and the Eighteenth Century,* The Oxford Anthology of Literature, edited by Martin Price, 321–44. Oxford: Oxford University Press, 1973.

Prynne, William. *The vnlouelinesse, of loue-lockes.* London, 1628.

Pückler-Muskau, Hermann, Fürst von. *Pückler's Progress: The Adventures of Prince Pückler-Muskau in England, Wales and Ireland as Told in Letters to his Former Wife, 1826–9.* Translated by Flora Brennan. London: Collins, 1987.

Raverat, Gwen. *Period Piece: A Victorian Childhood.* 1952. Reprinted. Bath: Clear Press, 2003.

Releford, B.J., et al. 'Cardiovascular Disease Control through Barbershops: Design of Nationwide Outreach Program'. *Journal of the National Medical Association* 102 (2010): 336–45.

Ritchie, David. *A Treatise on the Hair.* London, 1770.

Ross, Alexander. *A treatise on bear's grease.* London, 1795.

Sassoon, Vidal. *Vidal: The Autobiography.* London: Macmillan, 2010.

Sayers, Dorothy. *Have His Carcase.* 1932. Reprinted. London: New English Library, 1986.

Sennert, Daniel. *The Art of chirurgery explained in six parts.* London, 1663.

Shakespeare, William. *A Midsummer Night's Dream.*

Sitwell, Georgiana. *The Dew, It Lyes on the Wood.* In *Two Generations,* edited by Osbert Sitwell. London: Macmillan, 1940.

Smith, J.T. *Ancient Topography of London.* London: John Thomas Smith, 1815.

The soundheads description of the roundhead. Or The roundhead exactly anatomized in his integralls and excrementalls. London, 1642.

Springsteen, Bruce. *Born to Run.* London: Simon and Schuster, 2016.

Squire, Balmanno. *Superfluous Hair and the Means of Removing It.* London: J.A. Churchill, 1893.

Steele, Elizabeth. *Memoirs of Sophia Baddeley.* 6 vols. London, 1787.

Stuart Royal Proclamations, vol. II *Royal Proclamations of King Charles I 1625–1646.* Edited by James Larkin. Oxford: Clarendon Press, 1983.

Stuart, Lady Arbella. *The Letters of Lady Arbella Stuart.* Edited by Sara Jayne Steen. New York: Oxford UP, 1994.

Stubbes, Philip. *The second part of the anatomie of abuses conteining the display of corruptions.* London, 1583.

Swift, Jonathan. *The Correspondence of Jonathan Swift,* edited by H. Williams. 5 vols. Oxford: Clarendon Press, 1963.

Swift, Jonathan. *Journal to Stella,* edited by H. Williams. 2 vols. Oxford: Blackwell, 1974.

T. J. *A Medicine for the Times. Or an antidote against Faction.* London, 1641.

Taylor, John. *Superbiae flagellum, or, The vvhip of pride.* London, 1621.

Taylor, John. *The Devil turn'd Round-head.* [London], 1642.

Theoharris, Athan (ed.). *From the Secret Files of J. Edgar Hoover.* Chicago: I.R. Dee, 1991.

Theologos. *Shaving: A Breach of the Sabbath.* London, 1860.

Thomson, Elizabeth, and David Gutman (eds). *The Lennon Companion: Twenty-Five Years of Comment.* Houndmills and London: Macmillan Press, 1987.

Titmus, Keryl. *Level 2 NVQ Diploma in Hairdressing,* The City & Guilds Textbook. London: City & Guilds, 2011.

Torriano, Giovanni. *The second alphabet consisting of proverbial phrases.* London, 1662.

Valeriano, Pierio. *A treatise vvriten by Iohan Valerian a greatte clerke of Italie, which is intitled in latin Pro sacerdotum barbis translated in to Englysshe.* [London, 1533].

Walpole, Horace. *Selected Letters.* 1926. Edited by William Hadley. Reprinted, London: Dent, 1948.

Wenner, Jann. *Lennon Remembers: The Rolling Stone Interviews.* 1970. Harmondsworth: Penguin, 1973.

[W.M.], *The Queens closet opened incomparable secrets in physic, chyrurgery, preserving, and candying &c.* London, 1655.

Woodforde, James. *The Ansford Diary of James Woodforde, Vol. 4: 1769–1771.* Edited by R.L. Winstanley. [n.p.]: Parson Woodforde Society, 1986.

Woodforde, James. *The Diary of James Woodforde, Volume 10 1782–1784.* Edited by R.L. Winstanley. [n.p.]: Parson Woodforde Society, 1998.

Woodforde, James. *The Diary of James Woodforde, Volume 11 1785–1787.* Edited by R.L. Winstanley and Peter Jameson. [n.p.]: Parson Woodforde Society. 1999.

Woodforde, James. *The Diary of James Woodforde, Volume 13 1791–1793.* Edited by Peter Jameson. [n.p.]: Parson Woodforde Society, 2003.

Woodforde, James. *The Diary of James Woodforde, Volume 14 1794–1795.* Edited by Peter Jameson. [n.p.]: Parson Woodforde Society, 2004.

Woodforde, James. *The Oxford and Somerset Diary of James Woodforde 1774–1775.* Edited by R.L. Winstanley. [n.p.]: Parson Woodforde Society, 1989.

Woodforde, James. *Woodforde at Oxford 1759–1776,* edited by W.N. Hargreaves-Mawdsley, Oxford Historical Society, n.s. 21 (1969).

Woolley, Hannah. *The Accomplish'd lady's delight.* London, 1675.

Wraxall, Sir N. William. *Historical Memoirs of my own Time.* 1815. Reprinted. London: Kegan Paul, Trench, Trubner and Co., 1904.

Wrecker, John Jacob. *Cosmeticks, or, the beautifying part of physic.* London, 1660.

Wright Proctor, Richard. *The Barber's Shop.* Manchester and London, 1883.

Zdatny, Steven (ed.). *Hairstyles and Fashion: A Hairdresser's History of Paris.* Oxford: Berg, 1999.

Printed secondary sources

Adam, Rachel. *Sideshow USA: Freaks and the American Cultural Imagination.* Chicago: University of Chicago Press, 2001.

Amann, Elizabeth. *Dandyism in the Age of Revolution: The Art of the Cut.* Chicago and London: University of Chicago Press, 2015.

Andrews, William. *At the Sign of the Barber's Pole: Studies in Hirsute History.* 1904. Reprinted. [n.p.]: Dodo Press, [n.d.].

Archer, John E. *Social Unrest and Popular Protest in England 1780–1840.* Cambridge: Cambridge UP, 2000.

Arnold, Janet. *Queen Elizabeth's Wardrobe Unlock'd.* Leeds: Maney, 1988.

Aspin, Richard. 'Who Was Elizabeth Okeover?'. *Medical History* 44 (2000): 531–40.

Baker, Paul. *Polari: The Lost Language of Gay Men.* London: Routledge, 2002.

Baron, Steve, and Kim Harris. 'Case Study 1: Joe & Co, Hairdressing'. In *Services Marketing: Texts and Cases,* by Steve Baron and Kim Harris, 206–211. 2nd edn. Basingstoke: Palgrave, 2003.

Barrell, John. *The Spirit of Despotism: Invasions of Privacy in the 1790s.* Oxford: Oxford UP, 2006.

Beard, Mary. *It's a Don's Life.* London: Profile Books, 2009.

Beaujot, Ariel. *Victorian Fashion Accessories.* London: Berg, 2012.

Beetles, Andrea C., and Lloyd C. Harris. 'The Role of Intimacy in Service Relationships: An Exploration'. *Journal of Services Marketing* 24 (2010): 347–58.

Biddle-Perry, Geraldine, and Sarah Cheang (eds). *Hair: Styling, Culture and Fashion.* Oxford: Berg, 2008.

Bogdan, Robert. *Freak Show: Presenting Human Oddities for Amusement and Profit.* Chicago: University of Chicago Press, 1988.

Boroughs, Michael, Guy Cafri, and J. Kevin Thompson. 'Male Body Depilation: Prevalence and Associated Features of Body Hair Removal'. *Sex Roles* 52 (2005): 637–44.

Bove, Liliana L., and Lester W. Johnson. 'Does "True" Personal or Service Loyalty Last? A Longitudinal Study'. *Journal of Services Marketing* 23 (2009): 187–94.

Brown, Jonathan, and Richard L. Kagan. 'The Duke of Alcalá: His Collection and Its Evolution'. *The Art Bulletin* 69 (1987): 231–55.

Cavallo, Sandra. *Artisans of the Body in Early Modern Italy: Identities, Families and Masculinities.* Manchester: Manchester UP, 2007.

Chemers, Michael M. *Staging Stigma: A Critical Examination of the American Freak Show.* New York: Palgrave Macmillan, 2008.

Clarke, Bob. *From Grub Street to Fleet Street: An Illustrated History of English Newspapers to 1899.* Aldershot: Ashgate, 2004.

Cole, Shaun. 'Hair and Male (Homo) Sexuality: "Up Top and Down Below"'. In *Hair: Styling, Culture and Fashion,* edited by Geraldine Biddle-Perry and Sarah Cheang, 81–95. Oxford: Berg, 2008.

Cooper, Wendy. *Hair: Sex Society Symbolism.* London: Aldus Books, 1971.

Corson, Richard. *Fashions in Hair: The First Five Thousand Years.* London: Peter Owen, 1971.

Cox, Caroline. *Good Hair Days: A History of British Hairstyling.* London: Quartet Books, 1999.

Cunnington, C. Willett, and Phillis Cunnington. *Handbook of English Costume in the Nineteenth Century.* 3rd edn. London: Faber, 1970.

Davis, Fred. *Fashion, Culture, and Identity.* Chicago and London: University of Chicago Press, 1992.

Dawson, Mark S. 'First Impressions: Newspaper Advertisements and Early Modern English Body Imaging'. *Journal of British Studies* 50 (2011): 277–306.

De Groot, Jerome. *Royalist Identities.* Houndmills: Palgrave Macmillan, 2004.

Doan, Laura. *Fashioning Sapphism: The Origins of a Modern Lesbian Culture.* New York: Columbia UP, 2001.

Draper, R.P. (ed.). *D. H. Lawrence: The Critical Heritage.* London: Routledge and Kegan Paul, 1970.

Durbah, Nadja. *Spectacle of Deformity: Freak Shows and Modern British Culture.* Berkeley: University of California Press, 2010.

Durbin, Gail. *Wig, Hairdressing and Shaving Bygones.* Oxford: Shire, 1984.

Eales, Jacqueline. *Puritans and Roundheads: The Harleys of Brampton Bryan and the Outbreak of the English Civil War.* Cambridge: Cambridge UP, 1990.

Edwards, Eiluned. 'Hair, Devotion and Trade in India'. In *Hair: Styling, Culture and Fashion,* edited by Geraldine Biddle-Perry and Sarah Cheang, 149–66. Oxford: Berg, 2008.

Edwards, Louise. *Women Warriors and Wartime Spies of China.* Cambridge: Cambridge UP, 2016.

Evenden, Doreen. 'Gender Difference in the Licensing and Practice of Female and Male Surgeons in Early Modern England'. *Medical History* 42 (1998): 194–216.

Falaky, Fayçal. 'From Barber to Coiffeur: Art and Economic Liberalisation in Eighteenth-Century France'. *Journal for Eighteenth-Century Studies* 36 (2013): 35–48.

Fisher, Will. *Materializing Gender in Early Modern English Literature and Culture.* Cambridge: Cambridge UP, 2006.

Foan, Gilbert (ed.). *The Art and Craft of Hairdressing: A Standard and Complete Guide to the Technique of Modern Hairdressing, Manicure, Massage and Beauty Culture.* London: Sir Isaac Pitman, 1931.

Fornaciai, Valentina. *'Toilette', Perfumes and Make-up at the Medici Court: Pharmaceutical Recipe Books, Florentine Collections and the Medici Milieu Uncovered.* Livorno: Sillabe, 2007.

Friesen, Ilse E. *The Female Crucifix: Images of St. Wilgefortis Since the Middle Ages.* Waterloo, ON: Wilfrid Laurier UP, 2001.

Gere, Charlotte, and Judy Rudge. *Jewellery in the Age of Queen Victoria A Mirror to the World.* London: British Museum Press, 2010.

Gieben-Gamal, Emma. 'Feminine Spaces, Modern Experiences: The Design and Display Strategies of British Hairdressing Salons in the 1920s and 1930s'. In *Interior Design and Identity,* edited by Susie McKellar and Penny Sparke, 133–54. Manchester: Manchester UP, 2004.

Graham, Gael. 'Flaunting the Freak Flag: *Karr v. Schmidt* and the Great Hair Debate in American High Schools, 1965–1975'. *The Journal of American History* 91 (2004): 522–43.

Guéguen, Nicolas. 'Hair Color and Courtship: Blond Women Received More Courtship Solicitations and Redhead Men Received More Refusals'. *Psychological Studies* 57 (2012): 369–75.

Hall, Stuart. 'The Hippies: An American "Moment"', Occasional Paper, Sub and Popular Culture Series: SP No. 16. Centre for Cultural Studies, University of Birmingham, 1968.

Hampton, Wayne. *Guerrilla Minstrels: John Lennon, Joe Hill, Woody Guthrie, Bob Dylan.* Knoxville: University of Tennessee Press, 1986.

Hawksley, Lucinda. *Moustaches, Whiskers and Beards.* London: National Portrait Gallery, 2014.

Hebdige, Dick. *Subculture: The Meaning of Style*. 1979. Reprinted. London: Routledge, 2003.

Herzog, Don. 'The Trouble with Hairdressers'. *Representations* 53 (1996): 21–43.

Hill, Christopher, and Edmund Dell (eds). *The Good Old Cause: The English Revolution of 1640–1660*. Revised edn. London: Frank Cass, 1969.

Holbrook, Stuart. 'The Beard of Joseph Palmer'. *The American Scholar* 13, no. 4 (1944): 451–8.

Holm, Christine. 'Sentimental Cuts: Eighteenth-Century Mourning Jewelry with Hair'. *Eighteenth-Century Studies* 38 (2004): 139–43.

Holroyd, Michael. *Augustus John: The New Biography*. London: Vintage, 1997.

Hunt, Tristam. *The The English Civil War at First Hand*. London: Weidenfeld and Nicolson, 2002.

Huxley, Gervas. *Endymion Porter: The Life of a Courtier 1587–1649*. London: Chatto and Windus, 1959.

Immergut, Matthew. 'Manscaping: The Tangle of Nature, Culture, and Male Body Hair'. In *The Body Reader*, edited by Lisa Jean Moore and Mary Kosut, 287–304. New York and London: New York UP, 2010.

Johnston, Mark Albert. 'Bearded Women in Early Modern England'. *Studies in English Literature 1500–1900* 47 (2007): 1–28.

Jones, Geoffrey. 'Blonde and Blue-eyed? Globalizing Beauty, c.1945–c.1980'. *Economic History Review* 61 (2008): 125–54.

Larson, Jessica. 'Usurping Masculinity: The Gender Dynamics of the coiffure à la Titus in Revolutionary France'. BA dissertation, University of Michigan, 2013.

Leach, E.R. 'Magical Hair'. *The Journal of the Royal Anthropological Institute of Great Britain and Ireland* 88, pt 2 (1958): 147–64.

Lesnik-Oberstein, Karin (ed.), *The Last Taboo: Women and Body Hair*. Manchester: Manchester UP, 2006.

Lethbridge, Lucy. *Servants: A Downstairs View of Twentieth-Century Britain*. London: Bloomsbury, 2013.

Lovell, Mary S. *The Mitford Girls: The Biography of an Extraordinary Family*. 2001. Reprinted. London: Abacus, 2002.

Mabey, Richard. *Flora Britannica*. London: Sinclair-Stevenson, 1996.

Mack, Robert L. *The Wonderful and Surprising History of Sweeney Todd*. London: Continuum, 2007.

Maguire, Laurie. 'Petruccio and the Barber's Shop'. *Studies in Bibliography* 51 (1998): 117–26.

Mahawatte, Royce. 'Hair and Fashioned Femininity in Two Nineteenth-Century Novels'. In *Hair: Styling, Culture and Fashion*, edited by Geraldine Biddle-Perry and Sarah Cheang, 193–203. Oxford: Berg, 2008.

Mansfield, Howard. *The Same Axe, Twice: Restoration and Renewal in a Throwaway Age*. Hanover, NH: UP of New England, 2000.

March, Rosemary. 'The Page Affair: Lady Caroline Lamb's Literary Cross-Dressing', available at http://www.sjsu.edu/faculty/douglass/caro/PageAffair .pdf

Matson, Andrew, and Stephen Duncombe. *The Bobbed Haired Bandit: A True Story of Crime and Celebratory in 1920s New York*. New York: NYU Press, 2006.

Melling, Joan. *Big Bad Wolves: Masculinity in the American Film*. New York: Pantheon Books, 1977.

Moller, Herbert. 'The Accelerated Development of Youth: Beard Growth as a Biological Marker'. *Comparative Studies in Society and History* 29 (1987): 748–62.

Muddiman, J.G. *Trial of King Charles the First*. Edinburgh and London: W. Hodge and Company, 1928.

Murray, I. 'The London Barbers'. In *The Company of Barbers and Surgeons*, edited by Ian Burn, 73–86. London: Ferrand Press, 2000.

Nickell, Joe. *Secrets of the Sideshows*. Lexington: University of Kentucky Press, 2005.

Nicolson, Virginia. *Among the Bohemians: Experiments in Living 1900–1939*. London: Penguin, 2003.

Nightlinger, Elizabeth. 'The Female *Imitatio Christi* and Medieval Popular Religion: The Case of St Wilgefortis'. In *Representations of the Feminine in the Middle Ages*, edited by Bonnie Wheeler, 291–328. Dallas: Academia, 1993.

October, Dene. 'The Big Shave: Modernity and Fashions in Men's Facial Hair'. In *Hair: Styling, Culture and Fashion*, edited by Geraldine Biddle-Perry and Sarah Cheang, 67–78. Oxford: Berg, 2008.

Ofek, Galia. *Representations of Hair in Victorian Literature and Culture*. Farnham: Ashgate, 2009.

Oldstone-Moore, Christopher. 'Moustaches and Masculine Codes in Early Twentieth-Century America'. *Journal of Social History* 45 (2011): 47–60.

Oldstone-Moore, Christopher. *Of Beards and Men: The Revealing History of Facial Hair*. Chicago: University of Chicago Press, 2016.

Oldstone-More, Christopher. 'The Beard Movement in Victorian Britain'. *Victorian Studies* 48 (2005): 7–34.

Orgel, Stephen and Roy Strong (eds). *Inigo Jones: The Theatre of the Stuart Court*. 2 vols. [London]: Sotheby Parke Bernet, 1973.

Pearl, Sharrona. *About Faces: Physiognomy in Nineteenth-Century Britain*. Cambridge, MA: Harvard University Press, 2010.

Pelling, Margaret. 'Appearance and Reality: Barber-surgeons, the Body and Disease'. In *London 1500–1700: The Making of a Metropolis*, edited by A.L. Beier and Roger Finlay, 82–110. London: Longman, 1986.

Pelling, Margaret. *The Common Lot: Sickness, Medical Occupations and the Urban Poor in Early Modern England*. London: Longman, 1998.

Pergament, Deborah. 'It's Not Just Hair: Historical and Cultural Considerations for an Emerging Technology'. *Chicago-Kent Law Review* (75): 48–52.

Peterkin, Allan. *One Thousand Beards: A Cultural History of Facial Hair*. Vancouver: Arsenal Pulp Press, 2001.

Phillips, Clare. *Jewelry: From Antiquity to the Present*. London: Thames and Hudson, 1996.

Pickering, Paul. 'Class Without Words: Symbolic Communication in the Chartist Movement'. *Past and Present* 112 (1986): 144–62.

Pierce, Helen. *Unseemly Pictures: Graphic Satire and Politics in Early Modern England*. New Haven and London: Yale UP for the Paul Mellon Centre for Studies in British Art, 2008.

Piper, David. *The English Face*, edited by Malcom Roger. Revised edn. London: National Portrait Gallery, 1992.

Pitman, Joanna. *On Blondes. From Aphrodite to Madonna: Why Blondes Have More Fun*. London: Bloomsbury, 2003.

Pointon, Marcia. *Brilliant Effects: A Cultural History of Gem Stones and Jewellery*. New Haven and London: published for The Paul Mellon Centre for Studies in British Art by Yale UP, 2009.

Rahm, Virginia L. 'Human Hair Ornaments'. *Minnesota History* 44 (1974): 70–4.

Reynolds, Reginald. *Beards: An Omnium Gatherum*. London: George Allen and Unwin, 1950.

Ribeiro, Aileen. *Facing Beauty: Painted Women and Cosmetic Art*. New Haven and London: Yale UP, 2011.

Ribeiro, Aileen. *Fashion in the French Revolution*. London: Batsford, 1988.

Roberts, Mary Louise. 'Samson and Delilah Revisited: The Politics of Women's Fashion in 1920s France'. *The American Historical Review* 98 (1993): 657–84.

Robertson, Geoffrey. 'Who Killed the King?'. *History Today* 56, no. 11 (2006).

Rycroft, Eleanor. 'Facial Hair and the Performance of Adult Masculinity on the Early Modern English Stage'. In *Locating the Queen's Men, 1583–1603: Material Practices and Conditions of Playing*, edited by Helen Ostovich, Holder Schott Syme and Andrew Griffin, 217–28. Aldershot: Ashgate, 2009.

Schulenburg, Jane Tibbetts. *Forgetful of their Sex: Female Sanctity and Society ca. 500–1100*. Chicago: University of Chicago Press, 1998.

Sherrow, Victoria. *Encyclopedia of Hair: A Cultural History*. Westport: Greenwood Press, 2006.

Sheumaker, Helen. '"This Lock You See": Nineteenth-Century Hair Work as the Commodified Self'. *Fashion Theory: The Journal of Dress, Body and Culture* 1 (1997): 421–45.

Sinclair, Rodney. 'Fortnightly Review: Male Pattern Androgenetic Alopecia'. *British Medical Journal* 317, no. 7162 (26 September 1998): 865–9.

Skoski, Joseph R. 'Public Baths and Washhouses in Victorian Britain, 1842–1914'. Ph.D. thesis, Indiana University, Bloomington, 2000.

Smit, Christopher R. 'A Collaborative Aesthetic: Levinas's Idea of Responsibility and the Photographs of Charles Eisenmann and the Late Nineteenth-Century Freak-Performer'. In *Victorian Freaks: The Social Context of Freakery in Britain*, edited by Marlene Tromp, 238–311. Columbus: Ohio State UP, 2008.

Smith, Virginia. *Clean: A History of Personal Hygiene and Purity*. Oxford: Oxford UP, 2007.

Spufford, Margaret. *The Great Reclothing of Rural England: Petty Chapmen and their Wares in the Seventeenth Century*. London: Hambledon Press, 1984.

Stevens Cox, James. *An Illustrated Dictionary of Hairdressing and Wigmaking*. Rev. edn. London: Batsford, 1984.

Sullivan, Eric, and Andrew Wear. 'Materiality, Nature and the Body'. In *The Routledge Handbook of Material Culture in Early Modern Europe*, edited by Catherine Richardson, Tara Hamling and David R.M. Gaimster, 141–57. London: Routledge, 2017.

Sun, Lung-kee. 'The Politics of Hair and the Issue of the Bob in Modern China'. *Fashion Theory: The Journal of Dress, Body and Culture* 1 (1997): 353–65.

Swami, Viren, and Seishin Barrett. 'British Men's Hair Color Preferences: An Assessment of Courtship Solicitation and Stimulus Ratings'. *Scandinavian Journal of Psychology* 52, no. 6 (2011): 595–600.

Synnott, Anthony. 'Hair: Shame and Glory'. In *The Body Social: Symbolism, Self and Society*, by Anthony Synnott, 103–27. London: Routledge, 1993.

Szreter, Simon, and Kate Fisher. *Sex before the Sexual Revolution: Intimate Life in England 1918–1963*. Cambridge: Cambridge UP, 2010.

Taavitsainen, Irma. '*Characters* and English Almanac Literature: Genre Development and Intertextuality'. In *Literature and the New Interdisciplinarity: Poetics, Linguistics, History*, edited by Roger D. Sell and Peter Verdonk, 163–78. Amsterdam and Atlanta: Rodopi, 1994.

Tarlo, Emma. *Entanglement: The Secret Lives of Hair*. London: Oneworld Publications, 2016.

Toerien, Merran. 'Hair Removal and the Construction of Gender: A Multi-Method Approach'. Ph.D. thesis, University of York, 2004.

Trainor, Sean. 'Fair Bosom/Black Beard: Facial Hair, Gender Determination, and the Strange Career of Madame Clofullia, "Bearded Lady"'. *Early American Studies* 12 (2014): 548–75.

Tunbridge, W. Michael G. 'La Mujer Barbuda by Ribera, 1631: A Gender Bender'. *QJM: An International Journal of Medicine* 104 (2011): 733–6.

Velasco, Sherry. 'Women with Beards in Early Modern Spain'. In *The Last Taboo: Women and Body Hair*, edited by Karin Lesnik-Oberstein, 181–90. Manchester: Manchester UP, 2006.

Velody, Rachel. 'Hair-"Dressing" in Desperate Housewives: Narration, Characterization and the Pleasures of Reading Hair'. In *Hair: Styling, Culture and Fashion*, edited by Geraldine Biddle-Perry and Sarah Cheang, 215–27. Oxford: Berg, 2008.

Vigarello, George. *Concepts of Cleanliness: Changing Attitudes in France since the Middle Ages*. Cambridge: Cambridge UP, 1988.

Vincent, Susan. 'Beards and Curls: Hair at the Court of Charles I'. In *(Un)dressing Rubens: Fashion and Painting in Seventeenth-Century Antwerp*, edited by Abigail Newman and Lieneke Nijkamp. New York: Harvey Miller, forthcoming.

Vincent, Susan. 'Men's Hair: Managing Appearances in the Long Eighteenth Century'. In *Gender and Material Culture in Britain Since 1600*, edited by Hannah Grieg, Jane Hamlett and Leonie Hannan, 49–67. London: Palgrave, 2016.

Vincent, Susan. *The Anatomy of Fashion: Dressing the Body from the Renaissance to Today*. Oxford: Berg, 2003.

Waugh, Norah. *The Cut of Men's Clothes, 1600–1900*. 1964. Reprinted. Abingdon: Routledge, 2015.

Wedgwood, C.V. *The Trial of Charles I*. London: Collins, 1964.

Weitz, Rose. *Rapunzel's Daughters: What Women's Hair Tell Us About Women's Lives*. New York: Farrar, Strauss and Giroux, 2004.

White, Carolyn L. *American Artifacts of Personal Adornment 1680–1820: A Guide to Identification and Interpretation*. Lanham, MD: Altamira Press, 2005.

Wiesner-Hanks, Merry. *The Marvelous Hairy Girls: The Gonzales Sisters and their Worlds*. New Haven: Yale UP, 2009.

Willen, Diane. 'Guildswomen in the City of York, 1560–1700'. *The Historian* 43 (1984): 204–28.

Williams, Tamsyn. '"Magnetic Figures": Polemical Prints of the English Revolution'. In *Renaissance Bodies: The Human Figure in English Culture, c. 1540–1660*, edited by Lucy Gent and Nigel Llewellyn, 88–94. London: Reaktion, 1990.

Withey, Alun. 'Shaving and Masculinity in Eighteenth-Century Britain'. *Journal for Eighteenth-Century Studies* 36 (2013): 225–43.

Wright, Lawrence. *Clean and Decent: The Fascinating History of the Bathroom and the Water Closet*. London: Routledge and Kegan Paul, 1960.

Zdatny, Steven. 'The Boyish Look and the Liberated Woman: The Politics and Aesthetics of Women's Hairstyles'. *Fashion Theory* 1 (1997): 367–97.

Index

Bobs, beards, blondes and beyond, *Hair* takes us on a lavishly illustrated journey into the world of this remarkable substance and our complicated and fascinating relationship with it.

Taking the key things we do to it in turn, this book captures its importance in the past and into the present: to individuals and society, for health and hygiene, in social and political challenge, in creating ideals of masculinity and womanliness, in being a vehicle for gossip, secrets and sex.

Using art, film, personal diaries, newspapers, texts and images, Susan Vincent unearths the stories we have told about hair and why they are important. From ginger jibes in the 17th century to bobbed-hair suicides in the 1920s, from hippies to Roundheads, from bearded women to smooth metrosexuals, *Hair* shows the significance of the stuff we nurture, remove, style and tend. You will never take it for granted again.

Susan J. Vincent is Research Fellow at the Centre for Renaissance and Early Modern Studies (CREMS) at the University of York, UK.

"This richly illustrated book reveals the power and importance of hair, from the 16th century to the present day. Amazing, amusing and erudite, Susan Vincent brings historical hair practices into lively dialogue with the hair on our heads today."

Sarah Cheang, Royal College of Art, London, UK

"Meticulously documenting hair as an object, a commodity, a gift, a fond memory of a person and, sometimes, an animal, Vincent covers 500 years of European hair history in clever chapter titles: from hair care, to those who care for hair, those who are hairy, and those who are hairless. Well written and strategically illustrated, her account is thoroughly absorbing."

Joanne B. Eicher, Editor in Chief, *Encyclopedia of World Dress and Fashion*

"*Hair* is 'extraordinary stuff' are the closing words of this informative and witty examination of its history in developed societies. The text is complemented by 150 images providing readers with a well-illustrated primer on hair in its myriad forms."

Valerie Cumming, author of *Understanding Fashion History* and Editor, *Costume: The Journal of the Costume Society*

Cover image: *Pot Pou...*
(1864-1920), Priva...

ISBN13: 978 — 0 — 85785 — 171 — 8
ISBN10: 0 — 85785 — 171 — 3